Nikkei Baseball

Nikkei Baseball

*Japanese American Players from
Immigration and Internment
to the Major Leagues*

SAMUEL O. REGALADO

UNIVERSITY OF ILLINOIS PRESS

Urbana, Chicago, and Springfield

Manufactured in the United States of America
1 2 3 4 5 C P 5 4 3 2 1
∞ This book is printed on acid-free paper.

Library of Congress Cataloging-in-Publication Data
Regalado, Samuel O. (Samuel Octavio), 1953–
Nikkei baseball : Japanese American players from
immigration and internment to the major leagues /
Samuel O. Regalado.
p. cm.
Includes bibliographical references and index.
ISBN 978-0-252-03735-1 (hardcover : alk. paper)—
ISBN 978-0-252-07883-5 (pbk. : alk. paper)—
ISBN 978-0-252-09453-8 (e-book)
 1. Japanese American baseball players—Biography.
 2. Discrimination in sports—United States—History.
 3. Baseball—United State—History. I. Title.
GV865.A1R378   2013
796.3570922—dc23   2012013875
[B]

To My Dad

Contents

Acknowledgments

The roots of this book have their origins in my upbringing. Raised in the Los Angeles suburbs, I grew up in an ethnically mixed neighborhood. The Shundo family was among those on my block, and our families got to know each other through my friendship with their eldest son, Mike, with whom I went to school. In the course of time, I learned that Mike's father, when a young man, played competitive baseball. Given my passion for the game, I was naturally curious about his days on the diamond. As such, I shared this interest with my parents, who politely informed me that Mr. Shundo's playing career was cut short when "they took them away." Unsure at the time of that statement's meaning, years later I learned the awful truth.

As I grew older, their saga came to me in bits and pieces. But not until one of my college professors assigned me Roger Daniels's book *Concentration Camps: USA* (1971) did I learn the fate of the Shundos and the Nikkei community during the Second World War. As a college senior, I authored a seminar paper on the topic, but I did little else on it after I entered graduate school. While earning my scholarly stripes, my research interests led back to baseball, and my reputation grew through my publications on the Latino experience in the national pastime. The precursor to this work came with the publication of my first monograph, *Viva Baseball!: Latin Major Leaguers and their Special Hunger* (1998). But my appetite for Japanese American history never abandoned me. I remained committed to telling their story, one that I found wrought with injustice and laced with courage. Drawn in part by my personal affinity for the Nikkei, the story of Mr. Shundo's short-lived baseball career struck me as a good point of inspiration.

Though I had lost touch with his family years earlier, I reasoned that there must have been others like him, whose own stories were seemingly lost underneath an avalanche of scholarly works on Japanese Americans, most of which did everything but include the Nikkei love for the national pastime. So, by the early 1990s, as I continued my work on the Latin baseball experience, I adopted a dual research identity and wrote essays on the Nikkei athletic endeavors. Doing so brought into focus the depth and expansive interest in which they engaged in sport, particularly the national pastime. In time, I became convinced that not only was participation in baseball their most popular athletic activity, but one that helped shape their American identity.

My first foray into Nikkei sports came in 1990 when I decided to investigate the athletic interests in the Yamato Colony, a small and historic community just south of my university in Turlock, California. The data I accumulated came to fruition in the form of a 1992 essay that appeared in the *Journal of Sport History*. From there, the story of Nikkei baseball took on a life of its own. My work led to a 1994 fellowship with the Smithsonian Institution, which gave me access to important government documentation throughout Washington, D.C. Other research opportunities and articles followed and, as a result, through the years I accumulated an extensive supporting cast for this project. California State University, Stanislaus, helped at different stages with funding that came from Affirmative Action and Research, Creativity, and Action grants. As mentioned earlier, a Smithsonian Institution Faculty Fellowship afforded me the opportunity to spend time at the Library of Congress and National Archives. Along the way, the following institutions and their personnel, with patience and good cheer, provided me tremendous help: the Japanese Historical Society in San Francisco; the Japanese American National Museum; the Nikkei Legacy Center in Portland, Oregon; the Nisei Baseball Research Project in Fresno, California; and the White River Valley Museum in Auburn, Washington. Archivists and their assistants also helped me tap into the archives of Arizona State University Special Collections; California State University, Fresno Special Collections; California State University, Stanislaus Special Collections; Sacramento State University Special Collections; University of California, Berkeley Bancroft Library; University of California Los Angeles; University of the Pacific; University of Utah Special Collections; University of Washington Libraries Special Collections; and University of Wisconsin, La Crosse. I also owe gratitude to the Oakland Athletics and Toronto Blue Jays for giving me access to Kurt Suzuki and Don Wakamatsu.

Finally, the following sites provided me with the digital images found in this book: the National Baseball Hall of Fame Library, Cooperstown, New York; the Nisei Baseball Research Project; the Oakland Athletics; the Japanese American Archival Collection, Department of Special Collections and University Archives at the Library, California State University, Sacramento ; the Seattle Mariners; University of Washington Libraries, Special Collections.

I also wish to recognize the following people, without whose help this manuscript could not have been completed: former students Jodi Netherwood, now Dr. Steely, and Sonja Has-Ellison helped with transcripts. Alexandra Vicknair, my student assistant, patiently and with competence helped me with the burdensome task of attaining permissions for the digital images. Sheryl Okuye Sauter, at the outset of this study, introduced me to those in her Merced (Calif.) County community, some of whose interviews appear in this book and others that added invaluable insight. Patricia Kay Wolf, my good friend in Washington State, collected newspapers for me and made contacts with Nikkei in Seattle's King County. Gary Otake, an early advocate of Nisei baseball and coordinator of the "Diamonds in the Rough" exhibit, and Rosalind Tonai of the Japanese National Historical Society in San Francisco, are two people whom I owe a debt of gratitude. So, too, do I thank Brian Niija in Hawaii. My colleagues in the Department of History at CSU Stanislaus, Bret Carroll, Phil Garone, Katherine Royer, Marjorie Sanchez-Walker, and Shuo Wang, who reviewed my early drafts on chapter 1, and Richard Weikart, and our administrative assistant Cathy Lanzon, all deserve recognition for their support. Bret Carroll, in particular, patiently listened and gave me important feedback on my observations. My dear friends Nancy Taniguchi, a longtime colleague of mine, and her husband Robert Taniguchi, former president of the Merced Chapter of the Japanese American Citizens League and former JACL regional governor, helped me with information, contacts, and, many times, treated me to their warm hospitality and Bob's skills as a chef. I also thank Dorothy Zeisler-Vralsted, who so often arranged for me to speak at her respective institutes and, in doing so, helped me polish my perspectives and share my insights with colleagues and students. My friend Pat Kearns receives my gratitude for his embrace of this book. Also, my cousin Larry Sepulveda, who encouraged me to become a history major in college. And I also recognize Roger Daniels, whose groundbreaking book *Concentration Camps: USA* opened my eyes, and whose encouragement through the years helped make this book possible. I am also indebted to Kerry Yo Nakagawa, who deserves credit for drawing national attention to the story of the Nisei players through his own book, movies, and, along with Gary Otake, work on the "Diamonds in the Rough" exhibit.

In the North American Society for Sport History, I have been the benefactor of good advice from such scholars as Dick Crepeau, Mark Dyreson, Sarah Fields, Gerry Gems, Larry Gerlach, and Steve Gietschier. To be sure, the Nisei players, many of whose stories are in the book and names in the bibliography, were so very kind and patient. Mr. George Azumano and Dr. Homer Yatsui provided important observations. They, and their peers, treated me with tremendous hospitality and shared with me their vast knowledge.

I am also indebted to Willis G. "Bill" Regier, director of the University of Illinois Press. His friendship and support of my work through the years, along with his professionalism, left for me little doubt about where I believed this book should be published. As well, the staff at UI Press was patient, respectful, and thorough in the production phase of *Nikkei Baseball*.

On a personal level, my sisters, Sus, whose keen eye was helpful on the photos, and Bonnie, and my late mother, Eva, were consistent with their interest in this project. My father, Salvador, was especially helpful with his support of this work, and his encouraging words were instrumental in keeping the flame alive on this story.

Finally, to those families whose friends and relatives participated in Nikkei baseball and are no longer here, I am thankful for your willingness to talk to me about them in a candid manner. Indeed, it is because of their trials and tribulations, and their grace and courage on and off the baseball diamond, that I have come to appreciate a deeper meaning of what it is to be an American.

Nikkei Baseball

1

Baseball in Nikkei America

Japanese American baseball served a
meaningful socio-economic role and
entertainment lifestyle for this closely knit
ethnic group on the wrong side of the tracks.
—Fred Oshima, *Nichibei Shimbun*[1]

One by one they filed into the outfield of San Francisco's Candlestick Park. Some
trotted, while others walked. Still others required assistance. And, apart from
their friends and relatives in the seats, fans in attendance recognized none of
the elderly men who were part of this pregame ceremony. Most had come to
see Hideo Nomo, the then–Los Angeles Dodgers pitching sensation from Japan,
who was scheduled to throw that day against the hometown Giants. But, the
Nomo appearance notwithstanding, July 20, 1996, belonged to the men who
stood in the center field grass wearing flannel pinstriped jerseys that bore the
inscription "Nisei" across their chests. Though to the casual observer the uniform
name portrayed that of a single team, in reality, if the clock could turn back, the
uniform inscriptions would have more accurately read "Asahis," "Yamatos," and
"Nippons," among several other names. Nearby, their families and old friends
beamed while Kerry Yo Nakagawa, the event organizer whose own uncles had
at one time competed against Babe Ruth and Lou Gehrig, announced the players' names over the stadium's public address system that echoed throughout the
windswept park. "Kelly Matsumura, George Omachi, Shig Tokumoto" were
among those whose names boomed in the cavernous stadium.

The ceremony held that day honored Japanese Americans from the *Nisei* (second-generation) era. Along with an entourage of some three thousand supporters, forty-nine players came together to share old friendships and memories and,
for the moment, recapture the spirit that had embodied the game as they played

First Major League tribute to Nisei baseball. July 20, 1996, at Candlestick Park, San Francisco. (Courtesy of the Nisei Baseball Research Project)

it during the period of the 1930s and while incarcerated in the 1940s.[2] Within the next two years, the Dodgers organization and the Oakland Athletics held similar events. Other testimonials also appeared. In 1997, the California legislature, whose predecessors were anything but kind to the Nisei during their prime years, voted unanimously in support of a resolution to permanently honor them with an exhibit in the National Baseball Hall of Fame.[3] By February 1998, a temporary exhibit of artifacts from their baseball history made it into Cooperstown.[4]

◆ ◆ ◆

The bestowal of honors was ironic in that most mainstream baseball follow-ers knew little or next to nothing about the game that the ethnic Japanese in America, the *Nikkei*, once played. And these fans were not alone. In their works, scholars of the Japanese people in America, at best, only included passing ref-erences about the Nikkei affinity to baseball. And the same held true of those whose own expertise was, in fact, sports history. By the late 1990s, filmmak-ers, authors, and historians who had chronicled baseball's past through their books, movies, and academic symposiums gave emphasis to blacks, Latinos, and women. In the meantime, apart from the efforts of some Japanese Americans themselves, the history of Nikkei baseball went untouched. Ironically, even in its heyday in the early twentieth century, compared with the attention other ethnic-based leagues and ballplayers of color received, Nikkei baseball remained in the shadows. Rarely did any mainstream newspapers include even the box scores of games played in the Nikkei communities. And in an era of racial discrimination, Japanese American players ranked below blacks and Latinos, who, at the very least, established a presence in professional baseball.

Japanese American baseball, by contrast, was completely an amateur game. As such, its renown during their most prominent decades of competition was limited. Their invisibility, in fact, was such that when Japanese American players entered incarceration during the Second World War, some camp administrators were surprised to learn that the Nikkei understood and played baseball. Thus, from past generations to the present, only a handful of observers appreciated their contributions to the game, let alone knew that baseball had been part of the Nikkei community since 1903, when the first all-Japanese club formed in San Francisco.

Not surprisingly, from 1903 through 1941, mainstream Americans, even in the West, dealt very little with the Japanese in their midst. And those that did often held preconceived notions about Asians in general as a result of the nineteenth-century "yellow peril" crusades that were then aimed at the Chinese. As such, the negative connotations toward "Orientals" led to a slew of policies that state and local leaders mandated to deter opportunities for the newcomers from Japan. To be sure, the Japanese faced mounting perceptions during the 1920s and 1930s that were based more on stereotypes than built on truth. Their darkest days, of course, came after the December 7, 1941, bombing of Pearl Harbor. Wearing the face of the enemy, as many Americans believed, not only led to the then-popular and callous characterization that a "Jap was a Jap," but to their imprisonment into American concentration camps.

In reality, since the late nineteenth century the Nikkei were a small but vibrant group who, like so many other immigrants, had adopted America as their home. They peacefully raised their offspring and practiced time-honored American virtues of hard work and perseverance. And, of their activities, baseball, the most popular sport in their respective communities, was as familiar to them as it was to those outside their enclaves. The game, in fact, helped to shape their American identity, and the Nikkei used it to build global and cultural bridges on several fronts. The action on the field of play and its meaning to them beyond the foul lines factored into their daily routines in large urban centers and in distant rural communities. In short, baseball was unequivocally a part of the chemistry that supplied the heartbeat of their world.

In their history, Japanese Americans who played the game did so with zeal and passion in conditions that were often Spartan. Pickup trucks served as team buses and, in some locales, gravel pits were molded into makeshift fields. But the field of play and competition was only part of the story. Regional tournaments sparked patriotic fervor. And games even offered opportunities for potential courtship. Additionally, these men of Japanese descent and their supporters captured the true spirit of baseball's pastoral roots and helped to strengthen relationships in their regional communities. Sandlot games were magnets for neighborhood and ethnic cohesion. Traveling squads exchanged information about relatives and friends. And the games ignited a form of boosterism akin to that of American baseball's nineteenth-century past.

The significance of the game to the Nikkei increased after the February 19, 1942, announcement of Executive Order 9066, a policy that led to their incarceration. Unjustly interned, the competitive Japanese turned to baseball and other sports as a means to temper their dreary circumstances. Almost immediately, assembly center newsletters trumpeted a call for athletes; players enthusiastically responded. Schedules were arranged and requests for equipment routinely appeared in camp directors' administrative offices. And the same held true after Japanese Americans were relocated into each of the ten internment camps around the country. Residents transformed firebreaks into "stadiums" and built backstops from chicken wire, and the games themselves became the focal point for a people whose circumstances appeared, at times, to be intolerable and bleak. Without baseball, said one former internee, the camps "would have been maddening."[5]

◆ ◆ ◆

Of course, baseball could not have been the important factor it was during internment had it not been strongly anchored in the world of the Nikkei to begin with. Throughout the history of their people in the United States, the national pastime resonated strongly among the Japanese from the time that its sojourners, the *Issei*, came to America to that of the *Yonsei*, the fourth generation. And, much more than a recreational activity, the game commanded respect as it grew to become part of their heritage. Baseball, as they organized and played it, also crossed geographical and generation boundaries. Rooted in the land of their forefathers, the Nikkei resurrected it in the American communities where they landed. "Their baseball" was metropolitan and rural and employed as a means to network with kin in other regions. Teams not only competed in many of the West Coast's largest cities, but they also crisscrossed the agricultural regions of California's inland valleys as well as the snow-capped peaks of the Cascades to take on opponents. These clubs galvanized communities and fostered relationships with others like themselves across the West. "A championship year," claimed writer David Mas Masumoto, ". . . solidified a sense of community."[6]

Baseball, many hoped, would help to demonstrate their "Americanism" to the mainstream. While their *Meiji* forefathers viewed the game as a symbol of global competition against, among others, the Americans, the Nikkei saw it as game to help better define themselves simply as "Americans." Thus, not surprisingly, the Japanese American press in all locales always found room in their columns to relate American values and principles with the national pastime and to hammer home the point that they were one and the same. To that end, the press promoted and sponsored Fourth of July tournaments throughout their world and demonstrated their Americanism with patriotic gestures and good, competitive baseball.

Japanese American baseball, on the North American continent, was most active and in its largest scale on America's West Coast. Seattle, San Francisco, and Los Angeles all housed the largest population of Japanese Americans. And cities like Sacramento, Stockton, Portland, and Fresno, too, had sizable Nikkei enclaves. In between these larger municipalities, dozens of smaller communities like Walnut Grove, Guadelupe, Monterey, Livingston, Hood River, Salem, and Wapato, among so many others, proudly displayed their own teams. Of course, rivalries grew from their regional identities and provided incentive for many in the small communities to better their urban opponents on the field of play. Often dubbed "yokels" by their haughty urbanite brethren, the rural Japanese generously pooled their assets so that they could travel to larger cities to teach their citified opponents a lesson. Baseball was just as important to the Japanese in Hawaii, as well. Indeed, the roots of the game predated that of the game's Nikkei origins on the mainland and developed at a faster pace.

◆ ◆ ◆

Nikkei baseball on the mainland was largely a segregated game. Though a number of early clubs did "cross over" and compete against non-Japanese teams, given the anti-Asian sentiments of the early twentieth century, they only did so because there was then not enough of their own kind to form exclusive leagues. However, as their numbers increased, by the mid-1920s more and more leagues made up entirely of Nikkei players started to appear. Also, many played the games in ballparks built to house only Nisei players and their entourage. Japanese American baseball was, to a degree, a microcosm of the dilemma they faced during their overall North American experience. Their attempts to assimilate usually fell under extreme scrutiny or outright defiance from mainstream nativists. As well, federal and state laws were contrived to frustrate the Japanese and encourage them to go "home." Beyond their communities, their economic opportunities were few and far between. Discrimination, thus, was no stranger to the Japanese in America, and their baseball activities were, to an extent, a reflection of their discomfort with the attitudes they experienced beyond their world.

On the other hand, their leagues were a safety net from the outside and allowed them to demonstrate their cultural traits before an audience of their own. And cultural identity was important to them. Team names, such as "Asahi" or "Yamato," were an expression of heritage. However, rarely did the Nisei use such names when they played in municipal city leagues, opting instead for such titles as "Giants," "Dodgers," or other American labels. The teams, thus, were a reflection of the players' upbringing and the community, as a whole. Those who attended Buddhist or Christian churches, operated local Japanese businesses, taught at the *gakueans,* or cultural language schools, all at one time or another frequented or participated in the games. Some ball diamonds were even on church grounds. And group elders, too, were part of the baseball environment. Many who were born in Japan encouraged cultural activities as a means to maintain old folkways and included the American national pastime in their menu. Baseball, in their eyes, bridged the traits of their traditional customs to those of the newer society of which they and their children belonged. In short, they saw in baseball an instrument of the past that held components applicable for the future—a "bridge," of sorts, between cultures and generations. "Baseball," said writer Wayne Maeda of the Issei and Nisei connections with the game, "allowed each generation to interpret the meaning of the sport."[7]

◆ ◆ ◆

Nikkei Baseball is about the game's relationship to the Japanese American community. The focus, therefore, is on why the game was important in the construction of their identity. Their transition from being social outcasts at the outset of their presence in America to a position of respect nearly a century later was a step-by-step process or, to put it another way, taken "one base at a time." And the national pastime had a hand in this process. Its impact in their world was not mutually exclusive from such key historical factors as the Meji modernization policies, American anti-Asian sentiments, and the internment of the Japanese during World War Two, or the postwar transition, economic and educational opportunities in the 1960s, and the rise of the "Asian American" identity. Baseball had a presence and played a role in all of the aforementioned events and, as such, is a window from which one may understand and analyze Japanese history in the United States. Finally, *Nikkei Baseball* largely observes the game as they played it along the Pacific Coast states. In that region Japanese Americans competed in the community's largest geographic scale, and it is where they faced their greatest challenges as a people.

As to the game itself, as seen in the number of leagues that spanned the West, baseball drew the highest level of attention and competition. The game linked generations, and was a mechanism for ethnic solidarity and support and an athletic activity by which Nisei ballplayers could reasonably compete, with some success, against Caucasian clubs. Promoters of baseball saw it as an example of patriotic values. Plus, the Japanese American press featured and marketed the national pastime with zeal.

The Nikkei game on the West Coast also provided more documentation from which scholars of sport and popular culture could best probe the impact of the national pastime. As opposed to the professional game, Japanese Americans did not play for profit. They voluntarily spent their Sundays on the ball diamonds, and aficionados freely surrendered their sometimes-meager funds in support of the baseball competition. Even incarceration during the Second World War did not deter the passion they held for the game, and they continued to play it behind barbed wire. The Nikkei players were also among the first to practice globalism. Long before professionals from the United States engaged in baseball exchanges with their Japanese counterparts, Issei like Frank Fukuda organized goodwill baseball trips that date back to the 1920s. And, well in advance of the time when Japanese players like Ichiro Suzuki of the Seattle Mariners stepped into the batter's box of Major League games, Japanese Americans players like Kenichi Zenimura and Johnny Nakagawa competed against players from both sides of the Pacific. One Nisei, Wally Yonamine, who played professional baseball in Japan, even made it into that nation's baseball hall of fame. But rarely was any of this touted outside their circles. In step with the modesty that came with their cultural conditioning, Nikkei players rarely bragged about their kudos as ballplayers to those outside their enclaves. And not until the mid- to late nineties did their accounts find an audience to take them seriously. However, as players like Lenn Sakata, Don Wakamatsu, and Kurt Suzuki, among others, appeared on Major League rosters by the end of the twentieth and into the twenty-first century, the Nikkei visibility in baseball increased. Of course, the great success of Japanese nationals like Hideo Nomo, Ichiro Suzuki, and Hideki Matsui accelerated attention to all players with Asian features. As such, while the public identified them as a whole, it also clouded the fact that a core of these players carried with them a heritage that had a distinct American background and whose forefathers played the national pastime for a community with a past grounded in courage, tenacity, and tears.

Nikkei Baseball is not a history that covers all components of the Nikkei world. Their communities varied and people did not always respond to problems as a united front. As such, their history is a complicated one and has triggered the publication of several books that explore their past through the lens of law, race, and ethnicity. And, of course, a good deal more research and stories center on the incarceration during the Second World War. The Hawaii Nikkei baseball story only touched upon in this work merits greater scholarly attention in its own separate study. Indeed, a number of the most significant Japanese American baseball stars emerged from the islands. Furthermore, it needs to be said that not every Japanese American followed or played baseball. Many played other sports or engaged themselves in activities such as the crafts and arts. Nisei women, too, were heavily involved in recreation, and their story is one that deserves to be told. There were those among the Nikkei who consumed themselves in their studies and went on to positions of leadership in academics and politics. Still others simply concentrated on making a living and little else. But research findings make it clear that baseball was much more than simply a frivolous activity. As such, the attentive historian is obliged to ask: what did it mean to Japanese Americans as a factor in the shaping of their history and how does it reveal more about their past?

This account of their baseball history, therefore, uncovers a unique and rewarding feature of the American past, and one that profiles a people who turned to the national pastime for respite during their darkest moments. "Japanese American baseball served a meaningful socio-economic role and entertainment lifestyle for this closely knit ethnic group on the wrong side of the tracks," summarized the *Nichibei Shimbun* writer Fred Oshima, who covered the San Francisco Bay area Nisei sport scene.[8] The story of the Nikkei love for baseball also is one that transcends United States history and includes Japan's own past, from which leaders in a late-nineteenth-century era called the Meiji observed, with great intrigue, a new game in their midst.

2

The New Bushido

... [baseball] symbolized the "new bushido"
spirit of the age.
—Donald Roden[1]

This great victory is more than a victory for our
school, it is a victory for the Japanese people.
—Student sentiment after beating a U.S. team[2]

Baseball's arrival in Japan was most timely. By the 1870s, Japanese boys held bats in their hands and tossed about baseballs. Less than a decade later, in some prefectures competitive games graced the environment. Yet, none of this could have occurred had there not been a dramatic change in their country only a few years earlier. With the fall of the Tokugawa Bakafu in 1867, in part as a result of the Western powers who had forced upon the Japanese the infamous "unequal treaties," leaders in Japan recognized a watershed moment in their national history and many felt that to offset further threats, they needed to better understand the world beyond their own.[3] This was not an easy chore. For all of those entrusted to lay a blueprint for the future, their own upbringing was built upon hallowed traditions that were cemented in an isolated existence. As such, they opted to forge a future not solely for the purpose of incorporating the trappings of modernization, but "change [was] carried out in the name of old values."[4] Still, while those old values provided a principled core in the construction of reforms, they also represented a romanticized past. Understandably there lay doubt that the order of the samurai could coexist in an era of obvious change. Therefore, to challenge the very powers that had helped trigger the downfall of the Tokugawa regime, pragmatism needed to win the day. And among the cadre who took a hard look at the future, there were pragmatists who recognized that any restoration had to include a transformation of the nation's economic protocols as it related to the world; a world that fell upon them. For those who adopted this position, it seemed inconceivable that their country could survive and develop into a power in the modern age unless its facelift included elements of the West. After all, how might the Japanese people be able to climb out from under the thumb of their rivals unless they better understood the ways of their oppressors? To that end, the leaders of the new regime, the Meiji, embarked upon a series of programs to deal with the problems at hand. "Although they lacked a clear blueprint for the future," wrote Kenneth Pyle, "the new Meiji leaders had many revolutionary attributes; experimental, open to the world, prepared to try new institutions and test new values, they were intent on reordering Japanese society and government."[5]

With the adoption of new ideological approaches, the leadership laid the groundwork for a modern constitutional system of government and industrialization. They also laid the welcome mat at the feet of incoming "Western" ideas and culture. And Fukuzawa Yukichi and Okubo Toshimichi had much to do with that. Among the most influential men in the new regime, they were enthusiastic about the prospects of reform for their country. Burdened with the millstone of the archaic Tokugawa era, the new Meiji leaders sought the advancement of progressive ideas. At the same time, in deference to their heritage, reformers like Fukuzawa and Okubo recognized the balancing act that needed to include the preservation of their nation's traditions and practices, which gave Japan its identity.

Born in 1835, Fukuzawa, an educator and author, visited San Francisco in 1860 as part of a diplomatic delegation. Intrigued not so much with Western technology as he was with social custom, the descendant of a samurai order wrote extensively about his observations. The trip had clearly increased his motivation to ". . . open this 'closed' country of ours and bring it wholly into the light of Western civilization. For only then may Japan become strong in both the arts of war and peace."[6] By the 1880s, he stood among the leaders who campaigned for an overhaul of Japanese culture.[7]

Okubo Toshimichi trumpeted Fukuzawa's platform for change. Eleven years after Fukuzawa's trip to San Francisco, Okubo, a government leader, also visited the West in an effort to temper the effects of the unequal treaties. While in England, Okubo became impressed by British industrial advancements. He noted "the excellence of the English transportation network with its railways and canals reaching into remote areas with its well-kept carriage roads and bridges."[8] Like

Fukuzawa, Okubo returned to Japan convinced of his country's need to refashion its industrial and social milieu.

To that end, Okubo took it upon himself to serve as an example of change. He "Westernized" his attire, hair, furniture, and mannerisms. Indeed, Okubo's actions came to symbolize Japan's model for change. To compete and, inevitably, temper Western industrial and military hegemony, the Japanese believed in the need to adopt their traits. This strategy also opened the door for cultural expansion. From the level of the elite and intellectual to that of the agricultural commoner, Western fashions and ideas flooded into the daily lives of the Japanese. And it was in this environment that American baseball found yet another home.

◆ ◆ ◆

In an era of neocolonial ventures, baseball stood as one of America's top export items. Formulated into a distinct game by the mid-1840s, deemed a professional spectator sport by the 1870s, and crowned the country's "national pastime" by the 1880s, Americans came to view baseball as the "watchword of democracy." As the Civil War diminished as a topic of attention for many Americans, so too did the cadre of war heroes evaporate. Baseball and the personalities that came from it were primed to fill this vacuum. Proponents proudly advocated its American virtues. And the popularity of some players was often akin to that of national heroes. Adrian "Cap" Anson of Chicago White Stockings fame (and who is also infamous for having led the movement to ban black players from professional baseball) and his teammate, the beloved Michael "King" Kelly, captivated the attention of baseball aficionados during that era.

Baseball's popularity expanded as the new technologies of that time made it possible to report the news more quickly. As newspapers, journals, and dailies sparred with each other for subscribers, stories concerning sports captivated readers. Richard Kyle Fox, for example, well recognized that reports on the "Great John L. (Sullivan)" boxing great were of great financial value to his *National Police Gazette*. Joseph Pulitzer and William Randolph Hearst also realized the gold mine in sports reporting and eventually came to devote entire sections of their dailies to the games that interested their readers. But it was Henry Chadwick, an English-born resident of Brooklyn, through his columns for the *Brooklyn Eagle* and *New York Clipper,* who touted the game to an ever-increasing and very interested audience. His contributions both as a writer and initiator of baseball statistics rightfully earned him the title "Father of Baseball."[9]

America's national pastime also had practical value to industrialists. In a period when strained relationships between management and employees were common, manufacturers often sponsored work-related baseball clubs for their "congruency" value. Seen by some as a replication of the workplace, companies hoped the teams might foster not only good morale among the employees but, more important, greater productivity.[10] And, of course, it was a plus that by promoting baseball, companies were practicing true "Americanism" with an activity that was "modern."

Americans were not shy about promoting "their game." Like religious zealots, baseball advocates saw the game as yet another means of expanding American principles—and its accompanying market—throughout the world. Indeed, this philosophy was much in step with the long-held belief that historian Edward M. Burns described an "American example [that] would fire the imaginations of foreign peoples and stir their countries from sluggishness and from enslavement to outworn habits and institutions."[11] In the neocolonial era of the late nineteenth century, this seemed like an opportune time for the self-proclaimed national pastime to "follow the flag around the world."[12] Albert Spalding was both the first and most prominent American to take this course of action. Spalding viewed "himself and his ballplayers as missionaries," reported Peter Levine. ". . . A. G. hoped to spread American manliness and virtue by introducing baseball to the world in dramatic style."[13] As a former player, cofounder of the National League, and, by 1882, a thirty-two-year-old owner of the Chicago White Stockings and a sporting goods magnate, Spalding took both his club and goods on a worldwide junket in 1888 and 1889 to promote the game and expand his profits.[14] Though he converted few to the game, others took it to such outposts as Latin America and Hawaii. And some even carried the game into Japan.

◆ ◆ ◆

Baseball landed in Japan equipped with all of the proper ingredients—patriotism, industrial productivity, and modernization—to support the reform mentality of the Meiji leaders.[15] American promoters of baseball tirelessly reminded potential converts of the game's democratic values. Most important, here was a Western activity that seemingly posed no threat to Japanese tradition. Many of Japan's leaders, in spite of any revitalization sentiments, did not, as earlier noted, seek to alienate their ties to heritage. On the contrary, their sense of Japanese distinctiveness was strong and exhibited no cracks. They remained devoted to their emperor. The continuation of Shinto was never in doubt. And leaders' passion and loyalty to the state harkened back to the remnants of the late Tokugawa period, when a sense of national consciousness evolved into a national passion.

Into this world stepped Horace Wilson, an educator from Maine who, following his service in the Civil War, migrated westward and landed in San Francisco. In 1871, Wilson was part of a delegation hired by the Japanese government to participate in that nation's education reform programs. In an effort to incorporate a physical education program, the American expatriate sometime in the next year introduced baseball, a sport of which he was an aficionado, to his students.[16] As such, those on both sides of the Pacific see Wilson as the individual most responsible for having introduced the game to the Japanese.[17] Still, there were others to whom credit might be attributed.

To be sure, to portray the Japanese themselves as merely the recipients of ideas is an unfair characterization. Indeed, those of the Meiji era were very much proactive. Without even knowing Horace Wilson, Hiraoka Hiroshi adopted baseball. A supervisor in the Meiji Ministry of Engineering, in 1871 Hiroshi visited the United States to observe and advance his skills in railroad technology, an industry then exploding in the Western country. In his six years there, the Japanese engineer witnessed the baseball euphoria. Here before him, he surely thought, was a modern sport in a modernized society that was clearly in step with the reform mentality of Japan. Upon the completion of his studies, the young scientist, who was also an accomplished painter and musician, returned to Japan armed not only with the new techniques of his trade but with baseball equipment. In 1878, seven years after Wilson had introduced the game as a recreational pastime for schoolchildren, Hiroshi created the Shimbashi Athletic Club, Japan's first organized baseball team, made up, unsurprisingly, of railroad officials.[18]

As its popularity grew in Japan, baseball characterized many elements of the social Darwinist thinking of the late nineteenth century. Adopted as a theory to justify success in America, the Darwinian philosophies of the West seemed well-suited for the competitive Japanese. "Meiji Japan was moving from an aristocratic, militant social structure toward a democratic, industrialized society," claimed Kenneth Pyle.[19] Seen by resident foreigners of the 1870s and 1880s as "essentially a feeble" people, Japan, within a few short years, wore a different cloak. "Japan the exotic," wrote historian Akira Iriye, became "Japan the competitor."[20] And baseball's role was not unimportant for, along with its competitive methodology, according to Donald Roden, the game "seemed to emphasize precisely those values that were celebrated in the civic rituals of state: harmony, perseverance, and self-restraint."[21]

Finally, as Hiroshi discovered while in the United States, baseball was modern. And this—modernity—lay at the heart of the progressive-minded Japanese plan for their country. The game's Western origins, its speed, and the very fact that the biggest manufacturing country in the world promoted it greatly attracted the Japanese of the Meiji period. But to be deemed simply "civilized" was, of course, not enough. All of the "manifestations of change," wrote historian W. G. Beasley, ". . . were parts of a whole that embodied universal, not just Western values; to excel in them was to be civilized."[22] In an era when the Japanese middle- and upper-class urbanites donned Western dress, ate foreign foods, and embraced Western architecture, baseball, a game touted by its creators as a potentially global sport, proved a natural fit.

Competitive sports in Japan, of course, existed prior to baseball's appearance. Sumo, for instance, was part of Japanese tradition preceding even the Tokugawa period. And kendo and judo, whose appearance as competitive sports evolved during the era of the Meiji, were distinctly Japanese.[23] However, as in many other societies, organized sport was the bastion of the privileged, a symbol of status. Still, while these sports engendered the virtues of courage and honor, they did little to advance the national interest. "Judo and kendo were too solitary to engender the kind of public excitement required of a 'national game.'"[24] Instead, educators and administrators promoted athletic clubs as a means of engendering intercollegiate competition and school spirit. Baseball's concept of "team play" was not insignificant to a country where a cohesive national spirit was essential. "Winning was an inherently collectivist enterprise, inherently engendering solidarity," wrote Ronald Story in his interpretation of America's nineteenth-century hunger for baseball. The Japanese adopted a similar approach when the game reached their region.[25] Games deemed "simple fun" were set aside for ". . . Western team sports characterized by formal organization, rigorous training, strict rules, and the presence of officials at all matches."[26] In that vein, baseball stepped into the Japanese recreational spotlight. And as had already happened in the Caribbean and the United States, the Japanese, by the late 1880s, stood at the dawn of a phenomenon known as baseball fever. By then, many Americans were spending more time in Japan.

◆ ◆ ◆

The 1854 Kanagawa Treaty of Friendship between Japan and the United States not only opened the door for trade relations but also guaranteed the safety of American sailors. It also allowed for a U.S. consul to set up operations in Shimoda. As a result, many diplomats, businessmen, Christian missionaries, and educators began spending considerable time in Japan. In the 1880s alone, American Protestant churches boasted a membership that had grown from four thousand in 1882 to twenty-five thousand six years later.[27] Moreover, others, like the Young Men's Christian Association, driven by the spirit of the "Muscular Christianity" phase of that era, salivated at the thought of more recruits. ". . . [N]ow's the time and now's the hour for a critical epoch-making movement among the students and young men," Luther Wishard, a YMCA emissary in Japan, strongly argued in encouragement of mass Association sites in the land of the rising sun.[28] But even before the YMCA influence took hold in Japan, other visitors already were hard at work in that region, like the baseball pioneer, Horace Wilson. Educators like Wilson were firmly convinced that local boys might easily adopt the trappings and virtues of baseball. As such, it fueled educators' drive to teach their Japanese students about America's national pastime.[29] Despite this enthusiasm, baseball did not take immediate hold in the country. In fact, games were played sporadically and "generally regarded throughout the 1880s as a novelty to be played along with the capture-the-flag on university field days."[30]

Still, Japan's youth of the 1870s and 1880s were eager for change. Tokutomi Iichiro was instrumental in that quest. As Fukuzawa Yukichi and Okubu Tochimichi had done earlier, Tokutomi, a popular figure in Japan who went by "Tokutomi Soho," his pen name, trumpeted the call for progress. His books, such as *Youth of the New Japan* (1885) and *The Future of Japan,* were a stimulant for a generation of young Japanese in search of a new identity for their country.[31] Tokutomi, born in 1863, not only touted the advantages of Westernization but also impressed upon his youthful readers that modernization, as opposed to the "feudalistic" status quo of elders, was their destiny. "Your great foe," he wrote, "may well be the old people whom you have always loved and respected. . . . They are relics of yesterday's world; you are the masters of the future."[32]

Much like the global youth movements of the 1960s, Tokutomi's call to reject traditional values was in keeping with his counterparts in America and, interestingly, baseball symbolized this rebellion. Baseball in the United States, claimed Ronald Story, "was not only a counterpart to 19th century revivalism and temperance, it was a precursor to 20th century movies and rock and roll."[33] A visionary in his day, Tokutomi saw potential for similar movements in Japan. The Japanese intellect, Kenneth Pyle pointed out, "argued that there was a common pattern of social development in the world whose outlines were already clear in many Western countries, and that this pattern was beginning to emerge in Japan."[34]

Japan's fervor with Western ideas served as an important foundation for proponents of baseball to expand interest in the game. As a result, by the 1880s, it appeared with greater regularity in preparatory schools at the university level. First Higher School (Ichiko) was the first to produce a prominent baseball program. Between the mid-1890s and 1910, the elite preparatory school had few rivals. But it was one of their rivals, Waseda University, that spearheaded Japanese baseball on the international level.

Isoo Abe coached the Waseda club during its most successful years. Though at one point in his life he had studied in the United States, ironically he first witnessed a baseball contest while on a visit to London. "Extremely impressed with [the game's] sportsmanship and fair play," Abe returned to Japan, secured a coaching position, and promised his club that if they could achieve a perfect season he would reward them with a trip to America.[35] In 1904, Abe's club responded to his challenge. And, true to his word, the coach won government permission and secured the financial sponsorship needed to compete overseas.[36]

Winning government support for this venture was not likely a difficult task for the coach. The Japanese continually sought ideas from outside their realm. As early as 1872, in their quest "to gain acceptance into the comity of Western nations," Ito Hirobumi, during a visit to Sacramento, California, declared that Japan must look to the West, "whose modern civilizations is now our guide."[37] And by 1904, the movement toward what Okuma Shigenobu, an early Meiji leader, sought—that Japan should "attain an equal footing with other powers"—seemed well on its way to success.[38] The formula had been a combination of Western influences and Japanese initiative. Hence, the baseball exchanges offered the opportunity to learn more, particularly from a powerful competitor like the United States. "The communication system," claimed Ryoichi Shibazaki in his master's thesis, "was not fully developed at that time, so the Japanese people had to rely on actual contact with the foreign countries. Baseball helped to facilitate this international contact."[39]

In the spring of 1905, Tokyo's Waseda University played baseball in the United States against American colleges. Competing largely against West Coast clubs, which included the University of Washington, the University of Oregon, and Stanford University, in a game that drew two thousand spectators, the Japanese team won only seven games out of the thirty-three played. In an attempt to cast a positive light on their plight, the *Seattle Post-Intelligencer* concluded that "the Japanese players were especially strong in their fielding, and if they could bat as well, they would make any of the collegiate teams of this country hustle to beat them."[40]

In Japan, proponents of baseball and Western philosophies triumphed heavily over the naysayers, like Inoue Tetsujiro, who remained ambivalent to the Japanese competitive ability when the Ichiko students from Tokyo took on the largely American team from the Yokohama Athletic Club in a series of games beginning in the spring of 1896.[41] In the first of these contests, the supposedly inferior Ichiko students defeated the shocked Americans by a score of 29-4. Ichiko went on to win several more games, including one by the score of 32-9, which reverberated across the land.[42] The Japanese had not only proved their worthiness as baseball players, but also further illuminated the larger goal of Japan's ability to survive and compete in a more global fashion.

Japanese baseball teams continued for several years to play against American collegiate and semiprofessional squads in annual exchanges. By the 1930s, Major League players also spent time on Japanese baseball fields as the game developed into that country's national pastime. By then, however, games against former Japanese residents who had migrated to the Hawaiian Islands and the mainland United States also appeared on the schedule.

◆ ◆ ◆

John Tyler will never go down as one of the most electrifying figures in the history of the U.S. presidency. But in December 1842 Tyler, after having bestowed formal recognition to Hawaiian King Kamehameha III's government, took a page from his predecessor James Monroe and issued an edict, the so-called Tyler Doctrine, that set the stage for America's expansion into the Pacific and beyond. The doctrine not only blanketed those Pacific Islands—known then as the Sandwich Islands—within America's sphere of influence, but, effectively, invited United States business interests to move into the region. That the Tyler administration sought to prevent "undue control over the existing Government, or any exclusive privileges or preferences in matters of commerce" other than by the United States served as a greater inducement for American commercial interests to stake their claim in the Pacific.[43]

During the remaining years of the nineteenth century, Hawaii's importance to the United States' overall interests greatly increased. Commerce, in particular, spearheaded the American attraction there. From the period of the U.S. Civil War to 1900, "King Sugar" and the pineapple industry rapidly grew to the point that Hawaii lacked the necessary manpower to satisfy company demands. As a result, plantation barons brought in Chinese laborers for help. From 1877 through 1890, the number of Chinese workers grew at what some on the islands believed to be an alarming rate. Furthermore, Gavan Daws pointed out, "Not all of the [contract workers] went home when their contracts expired, and a good many of those who stayed came to the towns when their stint on the plantations was over."[44] Fearful that their kingdom might be overrun with Chinese settlers, in 1886 Hawaiian officials negotiated an immigration treaty with Japan that opened the door for Japanese contract laborers to work in the islands' sugarcane and pineapple fields.[45] By 1896, 24,407 Japanese—nearly one-fourth of the kingdom's population—were living in Hawaii.[46]

Many of these migrants were those who had left Japan as a result of the Meiji modernization programs. Because large-scale industrialization was expensive, the Meiji government raised land taxes to finance its aims. Consequently, this constituted a hardship on the country's farmers, and as many as 300,000 lost their properties. "The future in Japan seemed bleak for these financially distressed farmers, and thousands of them were seized by an emigration *netsu*—a 'fever' to migrate to the Hawaiian Islands and the United States," stated Ronald Takaki.[47] Hence, contract labor in Hawaii "offered them a chance to succeed."

To the Japanese, Hawaii was as much a frontier as was the Far West to U.S. citizens on the North American continent. Along with the trauma that came with leaving the homeland, life on the Hawaiian plantation was hard. Migrants had little time to enjoy the trappings of what contemporary tourists experience on their vacations. Plus, the Issei population, as it was at the outset of their migration to North America, was largely a male society. Most important, contrary to the American version of a frontier that epitomized freedom and independence, the Japanese frontier, said Hilary Conroy, "was one controlled by other men."[48]

Not all who made up those numbers were contract laborers. Various skilled workers, such as teachers, physicians, journalists, students, and priests, among others, who paid their own passages, also made up a portion of the ever-increasing Japanese community there.[49] Hence, by the last decade of the nineteenth century, the Issei—first-generation Japanese—presence in Hawaii was distinct. And within the next ten years, the foundations for a society in growth were established—Japanese-language newspapers, a Buddhist temple and Christian churches, and Japanese-language schools for settlers' offspring.[50] They also played baseball.

◆ ◆ ◆

The origins and development of the game stemmed from those who came to the islands from both the East and the West. From the United States, travelers emboldened in the spirit of commercial and religious expansion saw Hawaii as being on the periphery of Manifest Destiny. As such, business magnates, educators, and missionaries looked to stake their claims on both the resources and souls of the indigenous. And from the western rim of the Pacific, Chinese and Japanese leaders struck deals with the Hawaiian kingdom and entrepreneurs to provide employment for their migrating citizenry. Hence, in one manner or another, baseball was the benefactor of this increased attention to the Pacific.

Alexander Cartwright was among the mid-nineteenth-century sojourners who arrived at the islands in the late 1840s. Credited with having brought baseball into its "modern" era a few years earlier, he no doubt had a hand in transplanting the game in Hawaii. As happened in the Caribbean, baseball gained popularity with all segments of the population. Perhaps in an effort to appease the Americans on their national day of independence, natives played the first recorded game against the "foreigners" on July 4, 1866, and defeated them 2–1.[51]

The 1866 game occurred at the dawn of baseball's emergence as the "national pastime" in the United States. Ten years later, the professional National League was founded and, during the same period, universities across the land created baseball programs. Albert Spalding, whose global tour took him into Europe and Africa, also visited Hawaii in his travels and praised natives who were, in his estimation, "developing skill at the pastime."[52] The Muscular Christianity movement also advanced the game's popularity both on the mainland and into the Pacific. In an effort to advance the relationship between God and athletics, American proponents of Muscular Christianity surged as its aficionados also incorporated nationalism into their positions. The Young Men's Christian Association was the movement's chief protagonist in this regard. Founded in England in 1840 as a means to keep discipline and piety among the nation's youth, the YMCA's popularity reached American shores in 1866 and within a few years landed in several U.S cities. Americans Protestants, of course, saw their mission as one geographically greater than the mainland United States. Some even adopted the phrase "The evangelization of the world in this generation" as their motto.[53] Mindful of the popularity of competitive sports, the YMCA was often the catalyst in this mission. The organization, said Clifford Putney, "labored overseas as in

America to show why healthy bodies were loved by God."[54] The efforts of the YMCA and other proponents of Muscular Christianity helped create a foundation for organized sport from which baseball could land and develop.

By the 1890s, Hawaiian amateur baseball was in play in the form of the Hawaii Baseball League. At this stage, native Hawaiians made up the lion's share of players in the league.[55] However, in a short time both Chinese and Japanese Hawaiians also infiltrated the island's baseball circles. By the early twentieth century, a team that identified itself as the "All Chinese" club emerged as the most notable of those who carried Asian ancestral origins. But by then the Japanese, too, had actively engaged in the game.

◆ ◆ ◆

The Japanese who resided in Hawaii were relative latecomers when it came to the development of their baseball interests. Reverend Takie Okumura, a Christian minister who boarded Japanese youth, apparently saw value in the popular game's "Americanizing" influence. In 1899 he formed a ball club from his residents, and called them the Excelsiors.[56] Ever concerned about the anti-Japanese feelings on the islands, Okumura saw an immediate need to assimilate the Issei into American culture. But Okumura's interpretation of assimilation did not necessarily equate to the total abandonment of Japanese culture. To the reverend, cultural identity remained key to the family unit and, in 1896, he founded the first of what came to be hundreds of Issei-built Japanese-language schools. "Just so long as Japanese blood flows in their veins," he claimed, "[our youth] should grasp the real spirit of Bushido, Americanize it, and carry it along with them."[57] To the point, Okumura touted a philosophy of "conciliation."[58] And to that end, he undertook several island tours to preach his cause.[59] Reverend Okumura, in 1902, also founded the Japanese community's first YMCA.[60] Clearly, his influence on Japanese American sport was instrumental. But, though Okumura's Excelsiors represented the first Japanese ball club on the islands, it certainly was not the last.

Within the next few years, some thirty to forty Japanese ball clubs, generally made up of teens, began to sprinkle the Hawaiian landscape. But not all of the clubs came together driven by a goal to "Americanize." Because it was not uncommon in that era for even young boys to frequent saloons, Japanese parents viewed sport as a noble alternative to potential debauchery. "Very likely," claims Joel Franks, "these early Hawai'ian nines, as well as many pioneering Asian Pacific teams formed on the mainland, were organized less out of a desire to encourage assimilation through baseball than to keep young men out of gambling and opium halls."[61]

The Asahi team was the most prominent of these. In 1908, five years into their existence, Steere G. Noda, then only eighteen and founder of the club, took his players into the newly formed Americans of Japanese Ancestry (AJA) league.[62] As Nisei—second-generation—ballplayers later did during their years of play, the Asahis and other teams in the division competed largely against Japanese squads. The club even gathered enough in the way of donations to fund a trip to Japan, where they played a series of games in Yokohama. As the team and their skills matured, the Asahis eventually left the AJA and, in 1925, competed in the all-ethnic Hawaii Baseball League.[63]

During one of the earliest stages of what is referred to today as "Pacific Rim" relations, in the first decade of the twentieth century, two of the world's most baseball-obsessed nations—the United States and Japan—began regular visits to the islands to compete against one another and against Hawaii-based clubs. University teams, such as Stanford, Ohio State, and the University of Washington, among others from the United States, and Waseda and Keio universities from Japan, all played on Hawaiian diamonds and helped fuel baseball interest in that region still further.[64]

Baseball also found its way into the sugarcane fields. There, the Hawaiian Sugar Planters' Association, as a means to curb disenchantment among its workers, encouraged plantation owners to ". . . encourage this sport, which every nationality of laborers is keen for, prizes could be offered to winning teams."[65] This was not unimportant. From 1900 to 1910, relations between management and labor were tenuous, at best. In 1900 alone there were twenty Hawaiian strikes. Moreover, "blood unions"—workers whose bonds were based on ethnicity— further exacerbated the turmoil.[66] Hence, any means to curb tensions were welcomed. And baseball appeared to be the common denominator to bring about a semblance of peace. On some plantations, according to one enthusiastic owner, this proved a winning formula. "Every Sunday we have baseball games between the Filipino laborers and our young Japanese and Portuguese boys in which our timekeepers and some of our overseers join."[67] Ironically, and no doubt much to the chagrin of plantation owners, the games were also recruitment grounds for the fledgling unions, particularly in the sugar industry. Michael M. Okihiro, who chronicled the game's past in Hawaii, observed that Hideo "Major" Okada, a star pitcher in the late 1920s and 1930s who also labored in the sugarcane fields, "enlisted several of his closest friends, mostly people with whom he had played baseball, and this figured prominently in the early stages of the unionization of the sugar industry."[68]

◆ ◆ ◆

By 1910, baseball was a well-established sport in both Japan and Hawaii. In Japan, the Meiji modernization programs were instrumental backdrops, which helped to fuel baseball's growth. Had the country kept its doors closed to outside influence, baseball could not have caught hold in the land of the rising sun. But baseball did catch on in Japan in an era when a new sense of purpose captivated the country's global agenda. Modernization and nationhood were among the foremost goals. But the tenacious Japanese also saw the sport as yet another window by which they might learn more about their Western competitors. To that end, baseball exchanges between Japan and the United States took on a role that transcended the field of play. The game, in the wake of the unequal treaties, also helped to create a national spirit for the Japanese. In that manner, Meiji leaders voiced no objections to the implementation of an adopted game within their younger generation.

Baseball's entry into Hawaii, too, held important meaning. Given its geographical locale, it served as an obvious bridge between the culture of the East and that of the West. It also served as the first forum by which several nationalities competed against one another. In the Hawaiian frontier, between 1900 and 1910, nationals from the United States, the Philippines, Portugal, China, and Japan all formed teams and leagues. College teams from Japan and the United States also sought Hawaiian ball diamonds to compete against both the natives and each other. Indeed, by 1910, the manner of play in baseball was brisk and active in the middle of the Pacific.

Of course, as Japan basked in its late-nineteenth-century reforms and cultural advancements, along with its increased industrial and military prowess, not everyone prospered under the new order. For many in the southern prefectures, the region's most agricultural area, the rise of the Meiji meant declining fortunes for those who toiled in the fields. Making ends meet and living by one's wits was a way of life. Hisa Wakamatsu's father, she recalled, not only toiled on his small rice farm, but in the evening he and his family walked to eight different villages and "repaired night-soil containers at people's homes," along with broken wooden clogs.[69] As a result of burdensome tax codes and other agricultural reforms, beginning in 1885 and lasting through 1907, many Japanese laborers left the country for financial stability on what they believed to be only a temporary basis, or *dekasegi*.[70] The highest number of emigrants came from those prefectures that, understandably, had the least to offer. In Hiroshima, for instance, on average, family-owned farm acreage amounted to a paltry 2.7, which was "insufficient to support a family at that time," Linda Tamura noted. As such, "the prefecture in Japan with the smallest amount of farmland per person, it issued the highest number of passports in Japan between 1899 and 1903."[71] Of course, the sense of adventure, for some, also contributed to the exodus. Fukuzawa Yukichi, a journalist and educator, encouraged this phase of the migration. Profiling America, for instance, in glowing terms, his reports captivated the fancy of many a young man, a number of whom were of former samurai families.[72] In all, between 1885 and 1907, approximately 155,000 Japanese left their nation and traveled eastward.[73] Though some thirty thousand emigrants took on contract labor positions in Hawaii, others looked past the Pacific Islands in the hope of finding some semblance of fortune in North America. And some of them even played baseball.

3

Transplanted Cherries

Transplanted cherry, set in alien soil . . .
Who brought you, and when?
Rooted now, your pale flowers,
Grace the American spring.

—Yoneko Noji[1]

. . . the little fellows are wonderful fielders,
fast, and good base runners.

—assessment of Issei baseball team,
Seattle Post-Intelligencer, May 23, 1910[2]

To be sure, the arrival of Issei travelers from Japan was a slow process. Moreover, contrary to the nativist "yellow peril" theory, the Japanese who came to the continental United States largely hoped to return to their homeland. Those who arrived with intentions to remain were, in fact, a minority among the migrants. By 1890, census agents for the United States counted 2,039 on the mainland, with the majority having settled on the West Coast.[3] During the next twenty years, others trekked across the vast Pacific. Among these first-generation pioneers, forever known as Issei, came Chiura Obata, Frank Fukuda, and Kenichi Zenimura. At the outset of the twentieth century, these, along with other young men, traveled to the United States with optimism on their minds and baseball in their hearts.

But all of their optimism could not overshadow the depths of resentment Asians faced upon their arrival to North America. "The western United States in general and California in particular had learned to despise Orientals before this Japanese migration began," stated historian Roger Daniels.[4] Indeed, the anti-Asian feelings had festered some fifty years prior to the appearance of the Japanese. Since 1849, when Chinese migrants, drawn to California during the gold rush, came to seek their fortunes, resistance to their presence was apparent.

As early as 1852, California Governor John Bigler announced, "Measures must be adopted to check this tide of Asiatic immigration."[5] Ten years later, Leland Stanford, while governor of California, also trumpeted the call to repress the Chinese, who he considered a "degraded" people.[6] By the mid-1870s, economically depressed conditions stimulated further harassment and outright violence against the Chinese. Among the most horrifying accounts occurred in Los Angeles, where, in 1871, an urban anti-Chinese riot led to the brutal murders of twenty-one. But the Los Angeles incident was not an isolated one. Even in the far reaches of Idaho, the Chinese encountered criminal assault. Between 1866 and 1867, a little more than one hundred died at the hands of mobs.[7] Throughout this difficult period, local and state mandates were quickly adopted to curb Asian influence.[8] Ironically, in 1869, a year that saw the completion of the United States' first transcontinental railroad—an achievement attained with considerable Chinese labor—mainstream nativists, thanks to the writings of Henry George, adopted the "yellow peril" slogan as symbolic of their concerns that an Asian invasion of the West was imminent.[9] By 1882, the rising western paranoia over the perceived "yellow peril" culminated with the passage of the infamous Chinese Exclusion Act.

Both economic and racial elements stood at the core of the anti-Chinese sentiment. The California white working class, many led by Denis Kearney and his Workingman's Party—were threatened by the incoming Chinese, who competed for jobs. Hence, "The Chinese Must Go!" declarations in California comfortably augmented the "Yellow Peril" theme rampant across the West. Indeed, by the mid-1880s, changing demographics also contributed to a racially driven xenophobic atmosphere. Historian Ronald Takaki notes that California's white population, which made up 99 percent of the state in 1850, decreased to 87 percent by 1880. He surmised that whites "felt the need to protect their white society and saw the entry of Chinese women and families as a threat to racial homogeneity and their view of America as a 'white man's country.'"[10] Thus, on the eve of significant Japanese migration into the United States, the phrase "yellow peril" was already part of the western lexicon.

◆ ◆ ◆

Though a sprinkle of Japanese first appeared on the United States mainland in the mid-nineteenth century, the initial wave took place in the 1890s. By 1900, 24,057 had moved into America, 10,008 in California alone.[11] Driven to cross the Pacific largely for economic reasons, like others who ventured to America in the nineteenth century, Issei sojourners used their ideals to fuel their journey. "America was the first choice of places to go for almost everybody in Japan at that time," recalled Riichi Satow, a farmer who came with the early migrants. "We thought lots of jobs were available and the wages were double. . . . Our minds were filled with such dreams."[12] While California received the lion's share of Japanese, another eight thousand landed in Oregon and Washington.[13] "The intersections were clogged with crowded trolleys going in all directions and horsedrawn carriages threading their way between them. My eyes were dazzled," recalled one newcomer from Japan as he wandered for the first time through downtown Seattle in 1903.[14] The majority settled into the Seattle and Portland metropolitan areas, while others moved inland to such outposts as the Yakima region in Washington and the Hood River valley in Oregon.

As Issei communities grew throughout the West, so too did there emerge civic organizations designed to look out for the interests of the newcomers. The Greater Japanese Association was among the earliest of these agencies. Chinda Sutemi, the Japanese consul housed in San Francisco, in 1891 created the agency "to increase friendly intercourse among Japanese residents, to promote mutual aid in times of need, and to safeguard the Japanese national image."[15] For all of its noble appearances, however, the Japanese associations, which eventually established offices largely in the western metropolitan areas, leaned far more heavily on protecting Japan's image in America than they did to work as a "mutual aid" resource for their immigrating brethren. ". . . [T]he associations were, in fact, semiofficial organs of the imperial government," historian Roger Daniels points out.[16] "The special relationship between the associations and the Japanese government meant that leadership in the Japanese community devolved upon individuals who were far from independent."[17] Japan's noble destiny, after all, and its quest to end the unequal treaties could not, in the eyes of its leaders, be tainted with disrespectful behavior toward its citizens abroad.

While the Issei settled into their new environs, journalists among them began to take root. The importance of the Japanese American dailies cannot be understated. Probably more than any other agency, institution, church, or social and recreational activity, this element of Japanese society in America was the magnet that tied the community together both locally and regionally. These newspapers were the forums for reporting, networking, marketing, and counseling for its subscribers. Issei, in particular, leaned on their newspapers for information. "Because only a minimum of first-generation Japanese read the American newspapers, the Japanese newspapers are significant," said sociologist S. Frank

Miyamoto in 1939 regarding Seattle's early Japanese community. "Here, then, is an important organ for the formation of public opinion which has an almost uncontested supremacy."[18] Indeed, by the time Miyamoto published his findings, the Japanese American press had become a paramount player in the development of activities within their respective communities.

The first Japanese American newspaper, the *Shinonome Zasshi,* initially published in 1886, appeared San Francisco. But the *Nichibei Shimbun,* which Kyutaro Abiko launched in 1899 and was also based in San Francisco, was the first paper of significance. The future publisher arrived at the then-growing California town in 1885 packing but a single dollar in his pocket. Enterprising from the start, Abiko took on all kinds of jobs, attended some classes at the nearby University of California in Berkeley, and, after having developed businesses in the restaurant and laundry industries, founded the daily.

Core to Abiko's beliefs was his goal of establishing a permanent Japanese community in the United States. In an effort to reach this end and, at the same time, advance a positive reputation for his people, the publisher pressed his countrymen to "abandon their life-style of bunkhouses and gambling houses and try to live respectfully, worthy of acceptance in American society."[19] The establishment of farming communities in the central California towns of Livingston and Cortez, approximately ninety miles east of the San Francisco region, came with his plan. "Kyutaro Abiko's dream," recalled Bill Noda, whose family was among the founding members of the settlement, "was to establish a Christian colony in California for the young immigrants from Japan to take firm roots here in America and not think about making lots of money and go back to Japan."[20] Founded in 1907 and 1919 respectively, these communities served as models for other such settlements throughout the American West.

Abiko's ingenuity was instrumental in the advancement of the Japanese people who settled in the United States. His efforts were equally important in establishing cohesion among the settlers in their quest to survive in their new environs. Without Abiko and other Issei like him, the first-generation Japanese sojourners most likely would have lived a scattered life in the United States, culturally detached from one another and lacking in the resources needed to advance their circumstances in America. But the creation and implementation of civic organizations and newspapers helped build a foundation by which the Japanese could both contribute and possibly assimilate into the American mainstream. Moreover, the early establishment of these communities provided an important springboard for those Issei who came to America already armed with the love of baseball.

◆ ◆ ◆

Chiura Obata entered San Francisco during these formative years of the Japanese in the United States. The future sojourner was born in 1885 in Sendai, a seaport in northwestern Honshu. At age fourteen, the self-proclaimed "rough-neck" ran away from home to find his destiny in Tokyo.[21] There, his interest and propensity in freehand art earned him an apprenticeship. Having adopted a trade name—"Chiura" (a thousand bays)—Obata gained renown as a painter. But the restless artist was dissatisfied with the Japanese capital and yearned for other adventures. "The greater the view, the greater the art, the wider the travel, the broader the knowledge," he told his father as the young Obata prepared, in 1903, to venture eastward to the United States.[22]

Having arrived that same year, the talented painter wandered into what was, for the Japanese, a traumatic climate. "Far from the rapturous accounts of earthly paradise reported in Japan, California offered the most inhospitable environment imaginable for the Japanese immigrant," recounted writer Susan Landauer.[23] At times spat on and assaulted by Caucasians, Obata most likely was "clearly disappointed with the San Francisco he encountered" shortly after his appearance there.[24] But San Francisco, for most young adventurers, was teeming with excitement and carried the potential for economic opportunities. And, to that end, Obata opted to endure the discomforts of the discrimination he encountered.[25]

As the publisher Kyutaro Abiko had done after his arrival, the eighteen-year-old Obata worked as a domestic and studied English. And, to earn extra money, he utilized his skills and drew illustrations for various Japanese-language publications. Once he developed friendships in Japantown, Obata exhibited another passion, which he had apparently acquired in Japan: that for baseball.

Young and full of optimistic energy after only one year in San Francisco, in 1903 Obata brought together other like-minded Issei and formed a baseball team called the Fuji Athletic Club. This organization was the first United States mainland baseball team made up entirely of Japanese players. Though Obata's own playing skills are not entirely known, his ability to draw athletically minded Issei together was pioneering. With apparent enthusiasm, the artistic and ambitious newcomer designed the team uniforms and logos.[26] To be sure, this display of organization, accompanied with impressive uniforms for the players, drew the attention of other like-minded Issei, including many who, like Obata and his teammates, had familiarity with the game.

The Fuji Club. Founded in 1903 in San Francisco. Chiura Obata sits at
the bottom right. (Courtesy of the Nisei Baseball Research Project)

Only a year after the Fuji Club formed, a rival outfit, the KDC, came into
existence. The team, who like many early Issei clubs adopted names that reflected their prefectures, competed against teams of varied ethnic groups.[27] In
an era of outright hostility, however, contests against mainstream whites were
played with caution. "A lot of these white teams didn't take losing very well. As
the game got closer to the end and we were winning, we would start gathering
up our equipment and as soon as the game ended, we would grab our gear and
run," recalled one Nisei of his father's ball-playing experiences.[28]

In 1906, a devastating earthquake struck San Francisco, which, in addition to
a large toll on lives, rendered thousands of people homeless and unemployed.
Though some Japanese had already migrated to other locales, the disaster drove
still more to such spots as Sacramento, San Jose, and various locations in the Bay
Area. Not surprisingly, like it had with the migration across the Pacific, the Issei
baseball fever sustained these moves away from San Francisco. As a result, new

clubs emerged in new locales. San Jose saw its first Issei team in 1910. Farther east, in the Sacramento community of Florin, Issei settlers founded their baseball club in 1912. And in Oakland, the game appeared in the Japanese enclave as early as 1915. In each of these districts, baseball grew to become an important activity.[29]

◆ ◆ ◆

Like Chiura Obata, Frank Tokichi Fukuda too sought adventure in the United States. Born in Shimonoseki in 1889, he made the trek across the Pacific and landed in Seattle in 1906.[30] Fukuda's own baseball roots stemmed from his days at Shimonoseki Commercial School, where he completed his formal education. Upon his arrival in Seattle, Fukuda, like Abiko to the south, advanced his education in a local business school, learned the rudiments of the English language, and started a laundry service. By 1908 and more firmly settled, he joined the Mikados, a club formed only a year earlier.[31]

Baseball had actually taken hold of the tiny Seattle Japanese community prior to Fukuda's appearance. As early as 1904, first-generation immigrants formed the Nippon team, who initially played games against mediocre Caucasian clubs. Baseball interest in that area, however, greatly increased when the Japanese team from Waseda University competed in the Puget Sound area in 1905. The advent of this trip signified two important factors for the Japanese community and baseball: first, it greatly stimulated baseball interest in the Pacific Northwest and, second, led to several more trips, which was imperative for those Issei who wanted to maintain strong ties with the homeland.[32] And, with respect to the latter point, Fukuda eventually played an important role.

Playing second base for the Mikados, one of the most popular teams in that area, Fukuda developed ties with other baseball-minded Issei like himself. "The Mikado team dominated the Japanese baseball league the next few years and Fukuda became a premier second baseman in the league," claimed writer Ryochi Shibazaki.[33] In fact, so good were the Mikados that the *Seattle Post-Intelligencer* posted a picture of the club, with the caption "Japanese Baseball Champions of the Northwest," after a 1910 victory over the Columbias of Tacoma, another Issei team.[34] In an assessment of the club's parity with Caucasian teams, the daily was gracious but cautious. "The Japanese team is not the best amateur aggregation in the city, but it can give any of [their opponents] a battle," the paper announced. ". . . [They] have shown that they rank well with the American players. While a little weak in batting, the little fellows are wonderful fielders, fast, and good base runners."[35]

Michio Saito. Mikado baseball team, Seattle, Washington, 1911.
(Courtesy of the University of Washington Libraries
Special Collections, SOC0629)

But Fukuda's eventual role as a motivator for the expansion of Japanese American baseball in the Pacific Northwest overshadowed his significance as a player. An important step in that direction took place when, in 1909, Fukuda founded a young Nisei club that he called the "Cherry" team. Akin to the contemporary Little League level, Fukuda's devotion to the community's youth and the enclaves' future, plus his respect for heritage and personal love for the game, served as fuel for his eventual drive to see their baseball activities blossom within and beyond the Puget Sound area. In 1912, Fukada christened the Cherry team the "Asahi Club" and promoted it as a social organization for young men.[36]

Clubs like the Asahis were common in Issei communities. Though the names carried recreational connotations, these institutions had a much broader appeal.

Selleck, Washington, baseball team. Frank Fukuda is standing third from the left. (Courtesy of the University of Washington Libraries Special Collections, SOC0167)

Most included those Issei who saw themselves as "refined." "The Asahi club," Ryoichi Shibazaki points out, "was not a baseball team in the strict sense. It was an organization consisting of Japanese students and the main purpose was to produce the future leaders of Japanese society in Seattle through various activities like baseball."[37] The clubs also served as an important bridge between the first and second generation. Kenji Kawaguchi, a Seattle Nisei, recalled with passion his early desire for inclusion into one of the clubs: "We wanted to belong. Everybody wanted to be part of the Taiyo Athletic Club. We wanted to be affiliated with the older boys so as to get their support."[38]

Strong on initiative, Fukuda, then a clerk and eventually a vice president in a Seattle Japanese bank, took the Asahi club and expanded its largely social functions to include recreation. Given Fukuda's upbringing in competitive-minded Meiji Japan, it is not surprising that he and others like himself might have seen sport as a key factor to the assimilating process in their new surroundings. And, as had been the case in the San Francisco region, Seattle's Issei, between 1905 and 1910, "were moving toward genuine immigrant status rather than simply transient workers from Japan."[39] Therefore, it seems reasonable to assume that

most, if not all, of Fukuda's Asahi club's goals were designed for long-range results. To that end, he was the primary influence behind several baseball teams
that emerged from that original club.

In 1927, the bank where he was employed went out of business. Soon thereafter, Fukuda left Seattle for a position as principal in a Portland, Oregon, Japanese-
language school. During the next few years, while teaching Japanese off and on
at various language schools in the Portland region, along with a brief stint as an
instructor in Japan, Fukuda, as he had done in Seattle, nurtured the baseball
interests of both Issei and Nisei in northern Oregon.

◆ ◆ ◆

In Portland, according to an 1899 report of the Oregon Editorial Association, a
brief essay incorrectly reported, "the first time the little brown race of the Orient,
the land of the rising sun, appeared at this beautiful basin city on the banks of the
Willamette, was about 14 or 15 years ago."[40] In actuality, the first Japanese to settle
in Portland did so in 1880. Throughout the decade, labor contractors induced
other Japanese to come to the area. By 1900, pockets of Japanese settlements
appeared both on the periphery and in Portland proper. Caucasian residents
watched with apprehension as the community grew, and white impressions
formed. "In the winter the people put on thick wadded kimonos, sit on their feet
and hold their hands over a little charcoal brazier," wrote *The Oregonian*.[41] However, indicative of the daily's limited observation of the city's Japanese residents,
it concluded that "for recreation they go out to the family burying ground to
worship the spirits of their ancestors or to a shrine to see the cherry blossoms."[42]

The recreational appetite of Portland's Issei, of course, was much greater than
The Oregonian had imagined. By extension, the Japanese Association in the Portland area stimulated the athletic interests of those in that region. The Association,
particularly during the first decade of the twentieth century, was the chief liaison
between the Japanese and mainstream populations. But "social enrichment" also
was part of their blueprint for the settlers.[43] To that end, the Association encouraged churches, language schools, and other civic groups to organize activities so
that the Issei might better settle into their new surroundings.

As was the case in Seattle, initially some Issei in northern Oregon came with
designs to integrate with mainstream whites. Masuo Yasui, for instance, an Issei from Okayama, migrated to the United States in 1902. After having traveled
throughout the Northwest, he settled in Portland, where, at eighteen years old,
Yasui got involved in community activities. He never intended to return to Japan

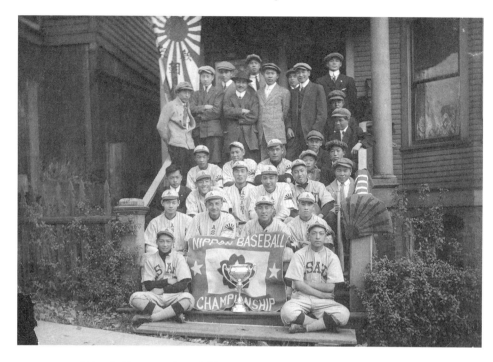

Asahi baseball team at their clubhouse in Seattle, Washington. (Courtesy of the University of Washington Libraries Special Collections, UW23721z)

and in 1908 built a general store at Hood River, some sixty miles east of Portland, where he was instrumental in establishing a Japanese settlement. An acknowledged leader to the northern Oregon Japanese, Masuo envisioned a day when Japanese and Caucasians might coexist as a single society, and "urged his fellow countrymen to spread out and mingle with their white neighbors."[44]

But Yasui's words did not resonate with many of his peers, who simply found assimilation an uncomfortable and intimidating task. For one thing, mainstream Americans in their region and along the West Coast made no secret of their concern and disdain for Japanese residents. Second, the Portland Issei, as with others, were "primarily Japanese speaking," recalled Nisei George Katagiri. "Consequently, it was very difficult for them to assimilate into the local community. And so they had a kind of Japanese community where they depended on each other to make a living or run a business."[45]

Nihonmachi—Portland's "Japantown"—served as a center for Issei organizations and activities."[46] Cultural events, such as the *undokai* (picnic and sport contests) community gatherings, which consisted of a variety of recreational competitions, received enthusiastic attendance. Much the same took place in Hood River, where some three hundred Issei came together annually in Parkland, near the base of Mt. Hood, to eat and participate in light-hearted recreational activities.

During the Issei era, evidence of baseball activities in northern Oregon is sparse. Prior to 1928, when Seattle's *Japanese American Courier* launched its business and surveyed news from both its home base and beyond, coverage of Japanese community affairs in that region fell to the *Oshu Nippo* (*Oregon News*), which started operations in 1909. Sadly, the federal government, on the pretense that the paper was potentially subversive, confiscated the entire business, and records remain lost. Hence, largely through the recollections of their offspring have chroniclers of the Japanese American past come to know Issei baseball in northern Oregon.[47] Moreover, one can deduce that the Nisei enthusiasm when it came to baseball resulted from the prodding of the Issei in that area—a prodding in which Frank Fukuda had played a major role.

Though his most prominent baseball years were behind him, Fukuda in the Portland area, as he would do in his later years in Wapato, Washington, where he died in 1941, continued his work with the Nisei youth and happily coached baseball teams in both areas. In the absence of documented sources, Nisei oral accounts testify to the lasting impressions he made upon them in their youth. "Coach Fukuda taught us how to play baseball and he always said to play hard and give 100% to the team," recalled Homer Yasui. Of all among the early notable baseball pioneers, Fukuda was the only one who taught in the Japanese-language schools. During these early years of the developing Nikkei identity, this was not unimportant. In adopting a dual role of being an advocate for America's national pastime alongside that of his duty to impart Japanese cultural mores upon his Nisei students, Fukuda had positioned himself to help create for the second generation a balance so that they might fulfill their destiny as model U.S. citizens of Japanese ancestry.

◆ ◆ ◆

Along with developments in the north, the Los Angeles area represented yet another major center that attracted Issei settlers. Apart from the accommodating climate, first-generation Japanese found economic opportunities, with respect to business and fishing, in abundance. Evidence of this attraction is seen in the population figures that indicate an increase in the Los Angeles–area Japanese community, which rose from 204 in 1900 to 8,461 in 1910.[48] Between 1910 and 1920, the numbers increased further, as 19,911 Japanese settled in the southern California basin.[49] Los Angeles, by this time, held more than twice the number of Japanese residents found in other West Coast urban centers. Sizable communities in the downtown area, the San Fernando Valley, and near San Pedro harbor quickly developed as the migrating Japanese sought cultural havens for their families.

Though greater Los Angeles, even in the early twentieth century, was vast, Issei settlers managed to stay in touch with one another. "Perhaps the most distinctive characteristic of the Issei generation was the intense level of community organization," claimed Paul R. Spickard.[50] The Japanese Association there had something to do with that. Founded in Los Angeles in 1915, the Association, eight years later, expanded in that area to twenty-three chapters, the largest along the West Coast.[51] But cultural activities, much like those found in Portland and Hood River, also brought the Issei together, even in an area as vast as Los Angeles. *Kenjinkais* played a role in these functions. These kinships had survived the long journey from Japan and provided an important sense of familiarity to the residents in these enclaves. The dialect, cuisine, and other cultural affinities that they practiced not only were a throwback to the old country but of their locales in Japan, as well. From the *ken*, practical functions also emerged. They not only contributed to the employment of their brethren but also "organized recreational activities and gave people a place to belong."[52] Said one woman about importance of *Kenjinkai* gatherings, "You know, we have a store which is run by my family. We are poor, busy, and have many children. We cannot go out like other families. But we have never missed a *Kenjinkai* picnic; it is the only occasion when we can meet many friends and hear about them. Children always make good friends at the picnic. We eat, drink, and chat in our native dialect."[53]

Sporting activities proved an important component in developing cohesion among the Los Angeles–based Issei. Baseball drew the greatest attention from the varied communities. The mild year-round southern California temperatures set the Los Angeles baseball circuit apart from many others along the West Coast. Hence, outdoor sports were a natural draw. Though documented evidence of baseball activities prior to 1926 is sparse, a sufficient number of teams were by then in existence to warrant the creation of an all-Japanese league. That year, the Los Angeles–based *Rafu Shimpo* reported the creation of the Southern California Japanese Baseball League, an organization that included teams from throughout that city's basin.[54]

◆ ◆ ◆

In the meantime, the Issei encountered a new challenge when, in 1924, Congress announced the passage of a stiff new immigration bill that, for the Japanese immigrant, had dire consequences. The Immigration Act (Johnson-Reed Act) of 1924 was, at that time, the most recent of several attempts by U.S. policy makers and their xenophobic lobbyists in the West to curtail and all but end Asian migration to the nation. The anti-Oriental movement of the late nineteenth century, which fueled the Chinese Exclusion Acts of 1882 and brought on the Gentlemen's Agreements of 1907, did little to temper the aggressive and hostile behavior on the part of the mainstream toward Asians. In fact, as seen in the adoption of several state antialien land acts, the movement to rid the West of, in this case, Japanese, grew considerably worse. As a result of and akin to the Chinese plight in the 1880s, and assured of a winning hand when it came to re-election, federal representatives in both houses of Congress pushed forward an immigration bill that increased quotas for European "undesirables" and ended any further immigration from Japan. Riding upon the xenophobic sentiments of the 1920s, President Calvin Coolidge happily signed the discriminatory bill into law. Moreover, in devastating fashion, the new law prevented those born in Japan from attaining United States citizenship.[55]

While depleting the Issei of what little rights they had, the Immigration Act of 1924 also hastened the need to properly train their offspring, the Nisei, to understand and appreciate the trappings of their generation. Issei, like Abiko, determined that the fate of the Japanese in America rested in their hands. For many of the elders, they viewed the harshness of the bill as indicative of the new balance of power that existed in the twentieth century. If the Nikkei and their culture were such an insignificant lot, would such a bill have targeted them? As such, the notion of the "bridge" concept was built upon a belief that in the twentieth century the center of the world shifted from the Atlantic to the Pacific. Some believed that increased familiarity with Asian culture would someday bring a cultural blending of "Oriental and Occidental."

Concerned that the second generation faced a "marginal" identity, Issei leaders anticipated that to curb the so-called "Nisei problem," they needed to engage in some form of social engineering.[56] While the approaches to do so varied, the majority agreed that any program must include as its core principle the values found in Japanese culture, or what many referred to as the *Nippon seishin,* or "Japanese spirit."[57] "The immigrant generation believed the Nisei problem could be solved only by drawing on the spirit of race history instead of by merely losing the influences of the old culture and traditions and merging into white America," observed historian Eiichiro Azuma.[58]

Of course, Issei attempts to mold the Nisei mind, even before 1924, had already met with controversy and resistance. In 1921, California adopted a law that forced all textbooks in the Japanese-language schools, known as *gaukuens*, to adopt those that emphasized only traditional United States history in lieu of anything that spoke to Japanese culture. Furthermore, some determined that attempts to create a balance between the Japanese spirit and an American identity was foolhardy and would lead to the creation of "half-baked Americans who are neither American nor Japanese."[59] Others, however, did not subscribe to that point of view and pointed to the Japanese-language schools as a hindrance in the quest for assimilation. Ultimately, the prevailing position was that of a Japanese identity interwoven with American nationalism. Indeed, when it came to the Nisei education, as Azuma pointed out " [immigrant teachers] usually reduced the essence of the Japanese spirit to a set of moral precepts and behavioral norms that they felt would help their children grow, first and foremost, into good citizen-subjects of the American state."[60] In the quest for this balance, some believed that it had to begin with a firsthand knowledge of Japan itself.

◆ ◆ ◆

Kyutaro Abiko, by then perhaps the most recognizable and respected voice in the San Francisco Bay–area Nikkei community, already had a blueprint in mind to bottle the Japanese spirit for the second generation. As the publisher he had worked to create a stable community for his Japanese compatriots, and his editorials consistently encouraged readers to adopt the United States as a place for permanent settlement. But, as noted earlier, many Caucasian leaders were threatened by the possibility of increased Japanese migration, and their lobbying gained momentum in the state and federal legislative circles, such as with the 1924 immigration bill. As resistance to the Japanese increased, Abiko concluded that much of the xenophobic atmosphere stemmed from ignorance about Asian culture. To offset this trend, the publisher developed an educational plan that he called the *kakehashi,* a strategy that largely involved their second generation, the Nisei. That Abiko actually coined the word *kakehashi* is unclear. But what is clear is his belief in its concept. This "bridge of understanding" was, in his eyes, imperative if the Nikkei was to remain in the United States.[61]

By 1908 Issei sojourners, many of whom had arrived in the mid-1890s and had originally planned to return to Japan, instead redirected their future. With the conclusion of the 1907 Gentlemen's Agreement between Japan and the United States, one that halted continued Japanese labor migration but left open the door for wives and family to migrate, Issei already in the United States either had to remain or face the likelihood of never again returning to America. Many inevitably decided to remain in the country, and largely through the use of proxies married and brought their wives across the Pacific.[62]

As they settled into family life, the Issei recognized the need for their children to assimilate into the mainstream. However, they also wanted their offspring to appreciate Japanese culture and traditions. In a sense, the "ideal" Nisei was one who best understood the virtues of both Japan and the United States and could be the "bridge" between the two cultures. In the eyes of Issei like Abiko, this model was imperative. He viewed the Nisei as an "extension of the Yamato race outside of Japan and believed that the ultimate worth of the Japanese people as a whole would be measured by the success or failure of the Nisei generation in the United States."[63]

One of the first such trips to Japan occurred in the spring of 1924, near the time when Congress moved to approve the Immigration Act of that year. Seattle Issei shopkeepers and other leaders accumulated funds and sent to Japan four scholastically accomplished Nisei girls in what was conceivably the first of several tours under the *kengakudan* concept. Upon their return several weeks later, Issei leaders beamed at the observation shared by Sumire Obazaki, one of the four students: "The trip has brought me very much closer to Japan. [I] realize the great responsibility which rests upon us, the American-born Japanese," she claimed. "In our hands lies the power to bring these two nations into closer relationship and understanding."[64] As demonstrated in the very same town where Obazaki had dwelled, baseball was, by then, already used to achieve the same ends.

◆ ◆ ◆

Frank Fukuda was instrumental in initiating these transnational activities long before the *kakehashi* was put into formal practice. Among Fukuda's greatest achievements were the international games he arranged between his Asahi clubs and their Japanese counterparts. Having adopted the moral position later echoed by Abiko, Coach Fukuda believed that his Nisei players would benefit from trips to Japan so that they might, upon their return to Seattle, be better

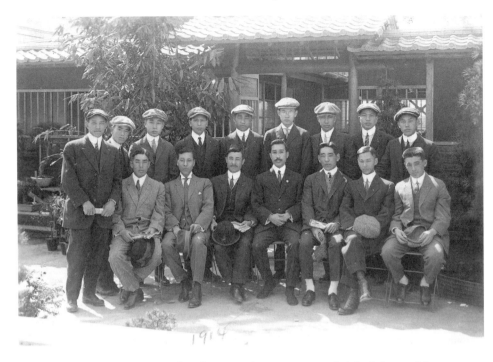

Seattle Asahi players on their first tour of Japan, 1914. Frank Fukuda is seated first from left. (Courtesy of the University of Washington Library Special Collections)

suited for civic leadership.[65] To that end, on three different occasions in 1914, 1918, and 1921, he arranged and led the Seattle Japanese across the Pacific to play ball in the land of his birth.[66] In Japan, games such as these afforded newspapers an opportunity to promote and advance their subscription rates.[67] Mindful of who represented his club, Fukuda took only those players who were highly accomplished students and well mannered. And this was not unimportant. Along with the notion that his players needed to increase their knowledge of all things Japanese, he also understood that Americans of Japanese descent were not seen on par with Japanese nationals. Thus, it was equally as important to present a dignified profile to the Japanese audience as it was for the players to absorb Japanese culture so that they might better inform Americans as to its positive traits.[68] Indeed, by the mid-1920s, this *kakehashi*-like practice also took hold of the practitioners of Nikkei baseball in California, men like Kenichi Zenimura.

◆ ◆ ◆

Though records show his birth in Hiroshima in 1900, not much else is known about Zenimura's family life in Japan, apart from the fact that his father, Masaka-chi, was a farmer and, within a few years after Kenichiro's birth, took the family from Japan and to Hawaii in part to escape conscription.[69] And there, during his formative years and in the sandlots of Oahu, baseball entered his life. In a Hawaiian Nikkei environment where baseball's popularity was on the increase, it did not take long for the newcomer to develop skills that drew attention. Though his parents reportedly sought to discourage him from playing baseball for fear that their small son might get hurt, he continued to engage in games.[70] In 1916, Zenimura joined the Hawaiian Asahi, a club destined to become a legend in the annals of the island's baseball history. Two years later, in a season in which his teammates named him captain of the club, he led Mills High School to the Island High School championship.[71] After high school, Zenimura moved to California and eventually landed in Fresno in 1920, where baseball had already taken hold.

Named by the Spaniards because of its large number of blackened ash trees, the community of Fresno lingered as a small agricultural town in the southern fringe of the state's San Joaquin Valley until the mid-1880s, when the Southern Pacific Railroad included it on its statewide line. With more access to move both people and goods, Fresno, like many of its sister towns along the route, increased in size. By 1900, the town also had in its midst some five thousand Chinese who, in their own quarter, boasted an opera house.[72] Following the establishment of the Yamato Colony to its north in 1907, Japanese migrants began to settle in communities in and around Fresno itself. In such towns like Clovis, Reedley, Del Rey, and others, Issei farmers toiled on the rich California farmland. And for many, the region was a long way from everything. Of Del Rey, one Nikkei farmer said, "Del Rey is about 20 miles south of Fresno, 200 miles from San Francisco or Los Angeles and 100 years from Japan."[73]

Shortly after his own 1920 arrival, Zenimura threw himself into community affairs. In less than a year he started the Fresno Athletic Club (FAC). As was common with most if not all athletic clubs in other Japanese American communities, the FAC drew young people together to socialize. This, of course, was all the more important in the Fresno County area, given that the majority of Japanese there lived on farmland resting on the fringe of the city. Only twenty years old at the time and working as a mechanic and in a restaurant to make ends meet, the gregarious Zenimura used the FAC as a means to observe those athletically inclined and organize a league that eventually featured ten teams.[74] That he could recruit enough players to make up an entire league of five to six

Lou Gehrig and Babe Ruth barnstormed through Fresno, California, on October 29, 1927, and competed with Kenichi Zenimura (in the middle) and Nikkei teammates. (Courtesy of the Nisei Baseball Research Project)

teams in less than a year spoke to the area's appetite for the national pastime. His intentions, however, were not solely intended for Nikkei unity, but also to make an impression upon the mainstream by exhibiting the competitive virtues of his people. Fine-tuning his players, Zenimura regularly scheduled games against barnstorming Mexican American semiprofessional clubs, Negro League teams, and teams from the Pacific Coast League.[75]

By the mid-1920s, San Francisco–based Nikkei newspapers began to print regular baseball updates from Fresno. "Rain or shine, when baseball season comes, it comes and is welcomed with joy by ardent followers of the 'great game.' During the weekend, it seems as if there aren't anything else 'cept' baseball games going on," claimed one reporter.[76] Zenimura's baseball "activism" also brought him in closer touch with Fresno's Caucasian baseball hierarchy and city leaders. He had earned such respect that city fathers invited him to compete in an October 1927 exhibition that featured Babe Ruth and Lou Gehrig, who were then barnstorming the West following their legendary season, one that included Ruth's sixty home runs. Zenimura's appearance, along with three marquee players from his Nikkei league, catapulted the Issei to high status among Nikkei baseball aficionados. However, Fresno Japanese American players had already attained much notice by virtue of their success in the Northern California Japanese Baseball League by the mid-1920s.

For Zenimura, baseball's potential as a component to advance the Nikkei people needed nurturing. To be sure, it is likely that few, if any, of the Fresno Nisei had traveled extensively beyond their California rural community. That those who played ball had an opportunity to compete elsewhere in the state, particularly against urban teams, must had been a thrill in its own right. But following his 1920 arrival in Fresno, the ambitious Zenimura not only organized Nisei baseball there but also worked to establish ties with counterparts in Japan.

Though the distance between Japan and places like Fresno was vast, the logistics in organizing games between them were not always difficult. For one, college and amateur teams in Japan were open to competition against U.S. teams. Professional baseball, by the mid-1920s, had not yet taken hold there. And, because some of the teams had recently played in the states against selected Nikkei clubs and were impressed with their skills, they encouraged international visits. Second, Issei like Zenimura had relatives who were baseball enthusiasts. Thus, arrangements for overnight accommodations, as well as the all-important press coverage, were made much easier. Ultimately for traveling squads, the lion's share of expenses was for steamship tickets.[77]

In 1924, Zenimura, as Fukuda had done in Seattle, handpicked the best players from the entire San Joaquin Valley. In the summer of that year, operating with the *kakehashi* in mind, he took the first California-based Nisei baseball club to play games against the Waseda University team, a squad that played in the United States some years prior. Other teams soon followed. The San Jose Asahis, among the most skilled in California, made the journey a year later. And in 1928, the Stockton Yamatos all-Nisei team ventured across the Pacific.[78] The 1925 San Jose Asahi trip, one in which organizers scheduled an ambitious forty-game itinerary, even caught the attention of the local Caucasian paper, the *San Jose Mercury Herald,* which ran a team photo atop its sports section.[79]

By the mid to late 1920s, Fresno Japanese American baseball, often referred to as "FAC" (Fresno Athletic Club), established itself as high caliber, one by which others gauged their own talent level. Under Zenimura's direction, players and teams from Fresno were lauded by the Japanese American press and routinely measured other clubs as ranking "below" their caliber.[80] Along with their membership in the Northern California League, they took on the most high-profile non-Japanese competitors in games that were well advertised. And, like their counterparts to the south, the Los Angeles Nippons, the FAC traveled to play games in Japan. In a notable 1927 tour, the club concluded a series of games with one against the Philadelphia Royal Giants, a Negro League team that had also barnstormed the country. Moreover, the games also proved beneficial to the baseball organizers in Japan, who were then making attempts to create quality professional baseball programs. Author Kerry Yo Nakagawa concluded, "The Fresno Athletic Club's exploits demonstrated the quality of Japanese American baseball and helped to elevate the play of the game in Japan—a primary purpose of summer barnstorming. Teams such as the FAC and the Philadelphia Royal Giants provided a snapshot of the baseball competence that Nisei and black players shared with their white counterparts at a time when racial divisions created separate but equal leagues in the United States."[81]

The barnstorming Nisei teams took the players into prefectures where they came into direct contact with relatives and people familiar with their ancestors. Outside the ballpark they engaged in discussions primarily with baseball fans, but came to better understand the land and environment of their heritage—a goal of the *kengakudan*. Still, when engaged in a game, Japanese fans did not shy away from reminding the Nisei players of their foreign status, sometimes to the embarrassment of local journalists. In one game where San Jose was playing in Keijo, one writer for the *Keijo Nichinichi* chided his countrymen for their rude behavior. "Keijo fans were not broadminded enough to cheer for their overseas countrymen, guests from afar," he wrote. "Keijo fans betrayed the expectations of San Jose's players who wanted to bring back good expectations of their land and countrymen."[82] Of course back home, by the 1930s, the Nisei prowess in baseball made it abundantly clear to their Japanese brethren that the game's "empire" was strong and continued to expand on both sides of the Pacific. And under no circumstances could any form of the *kengakudan* through baseball have succeeded without the game's further development as an institution on the United States home front.

◆ ◆ ◆

The practice of baseball's *kengakudan* also exposed players traveling from the mainland and Japan to the emergence of Nikkei baseball in the Hawaiian Islands. Since its embryo stage at the outset of the twentieth century, by the 1920s the game was thriving in the Pacific. As the Japanese community distanced itself from its plantation society roots to a more urbanized environment, their numbers expanded to where, by 1920, they made up 43 percent of the overall population.[83] Thus, they found themselves in a position where they could sustain themselves with all-Japanese institutions. The Americans of Japanese Ancestry (AJA) Baseball League was one of them. Following its 1908 inaugural season, the league drew strength directly from their own community, for "there were no other opportunities for young Japanese American men to play baseball outside of the AJA League," observed Karleen C. Chinen.[84] Though the AJA did not have the reputation as strongest of all leagues in Hawaii, it remained a fixture in the Nikkei community through the twentieth century and "provided welcome entertainment for the growing Japanese communities."[85] By 1911, the AJA boasted that it had increased the number of leagues to four in Oahu and Kauai. And by the 1930s, AJA-affiliated teams were located on each of the Hawaiian islands.[86] From these circles, "all-star" squads were selected, and they competed against Japanese and Japanese American clubs barnstorming their way to either end of the Pacific.[87]

Kensho Nushida was among those who had played with one of the traveling squads. A right-handed pitcher from Hilo, Nushida was sixteen when he joined the powerful Asahi club, and in the next few seasons developed a reputation as a star hurler. Nushida pitched for Mills High School in Honolulu, where he was a teammate of Kenichi Zenimura.[88] In 1923 he went to California with a Hawaiian all-star team and decided to move to Stockton. As Nushida played ball with mainland Nikkei clubs, in 1932 the Sacramento Solons of the Pacific Coast League took notice and signed him to a contract. Though he only pitched for half of the season, Nushida nonetheless earned the distinction of being the first Nikkei player to sign a professional contract at a level one step below the Major League.[89]

By the 1920s, the most powerful Nikkei baseball club remained the Asahis. Unlike other teams, they did not play in the Japanese exclusive AJA. Instead, they opted for the stiffer competition found only in those leagues that had teams of mixed ethnic backgrounds. The Hawaiian Baseball League (HBL) was just such an institution, and in that era it featured teams made up exclusively of indigenous, Portuguese, Chinese, and Caucasian players.[90] Having captured league championships in 1925 and 1926, the Asahi teams effectively put Nikkei baseball in Hawaii on the map. Their reputation induced ball clubs from Japan and the United States to schedule games against them, such as the Waseda University team from Japan, the Philadelphia Royal Giants of the Negro Leagues, and several U.S. college teams, including Stanford and Santa Clara universities.[91]

Honolulu Asahis, 1915. Honolulu, Hawaii.
(Courtesy of the Nisei Baseball Research Project)

Players like Nushida, along with AJA and the Asahi ball club, were indicative of the talent found in Hawaiian Nikkei baseball. Through the 1930s, baseball was an important part of the Japanese American identity in the islands. In observation of the AJA, for instance, Samuel Hideo Yamashita concluded, "By 1940, the AJA leagues had more than 50 teams, proof that baseball had taken root in Hawai'i's Japanese community."[92] Second-generation Japanese fans and players, in particular, idolized the legendary Asahi. Said Michael M. Okihiro, "it was the dream of every sandlot Nisei ballplayer to be invited to join the mighty Asahi and play at Honolulu Stadium."[93] As the competition increased both at the amateur and professional level in Hawaiian baseball, teams from both Japan and the United States saw Hawaii not just as a pit stop but as a legitimate forum for high-level baseball. Baseball fever, to be sure, increased with the 1933 appearance of the great Babe Ruth, who played in two exhibition games on a team made up entirely of Hawaiians.[94] Perhaps not too surprisingly, it was from Hawaii that, years later, the first stream of Nikkei big-leaguers emerged.

◆ ◆ ◆

In the meantime, the Japanese population in the contiguous United States grew. Almost entirely concentrated in the Pacific Coast states, between 1920 and 1930, it grew from 111,055 to 138,834, with the most notable increase seen in the native-born population.[95] Theirs was a radical jump: 29,671 to 68,357 during the 1920s.[96] Moreover, they were largely a citified group. Indeed, according to data compiled by Roger Daniels, by 1930, using the 36,866 Japanese living in the Los Angeles County, "almost two-thirds, or 23,321, lived in the city of Los Angeles."[97]

Picture brides were a key component in advancing the Japanese numbers. With a male population so predominant among the young Issei, whites who wished to temper or even end Japanese migration to the West Coast rejoiced at the announcement of the 1907 Gentlemen's Agreement, one that called for an end to further Japanese labor migration to the United States. But, any hope they fancied in seeing the end of an Asian presence on their shores was short-lived. Faced with the prospects of returning to Japan to face unemployment or, worse yet, military service, the majority of Issei decided to stay. Though many Issei migrants made considerably less income relative to Caucasians, compared with their brethren in Japan, their financial circumstances on the American mainland were favorable. Furthermore, Japanese associations found loopholes in the agreement between the United States and Japan that made it permissible for Issei men to marry Japanese women from afar and bring them to North America. These arranged marriages, generally handled by agents in Japan, involved the use of pictures to lend some comfort to the deals. Though imperfect, the system nonetheless led to a migration of young women, "picture brides," who left their country to start new lives in America. But any excitement that came with the adventure was usually replaced with apprehension and fear of what lay ahead. Attired in traditional Japanese kimono and *geta* (wooden clogs), Hisa Waka-matsu, in 1915, stepped onto the dock at Tacoma, Washington, thinking, "all the people had white skin and hair of different colors! I thought I had landed here by mistake!" Though arriving in the United States because of her marriage contract, she nonetheless pondered, "For what purpose did I come here?"[98]

Of course, not every woman from Japan came to American shores as a picture bride. Nor did all of those who migrated overseas declare themselves as such.

But, this much is clear: from 1907 to 1922, birthrates among the Japanese in the United States steadily climbed. In California alone, for instance, in 1907 there were 221 births recorded. In 1922, the number of birth recorded in Issei households rose to 5,066.[99] Indeed, not in any single year during that period did the numbers diminish. And, while they remained tiny relative to the larger mainstream community, the Issei offspring, as they matured, helped to shape Japanese identity in the United States. Perhaps more important, the children of the Issei had rights; they could vote and own land. As the Nikkei community increased both in the cities and rural areas, they came to experience growing pains in how they interpreted their identity in the United States. The first generation was emotionally attached to the old folkways and heritage. The second generation sought to look ahead. Members from both generations had many among them who loved baseball.

4

Baseball Is It!

The Nisei is a new American. Racially of
the Orient, he is true and loyal citizen of
the United States, his native land. Young,
ambitious, hopeful, though at times oppressed,
he seeks to take his place in civic development
and community progress.
—John Maeno, Chair, 1936 Nisei Week festival[1]

. . . we should prompt [our Nisei boys] to take
whatever sports they like. Baseball is it!
—The *Los Angeles Rafu Shimpo,* 1926[2]

Long before the 1930s, baseball's foothold in California had been strong. In 1859,
for instance, a group of San Franciscans, a number of whom had migrated from
the New York area, formed the area's first organized team, called the Eagles
Base Ball Club.[3] Shortly thereafter, others also appeared. The avalanche of clubs
that came with baseball "mania" hit the Bay Area in the immediate post–Civil
War years. Only a year later, Bay Area baseball aficionados, who had already
formed some twenty-five clubs, organized the Pacific Base Ball Convention.[4] As
a means to advance the game's popularity there, they sent an invitation, indeed,
a challenge, to the country's most prolific professional team, the Cincinnati
Red Stockings, to play a series of games in the San Francisco area in the fall of
1869. The Cincinnati club took up the challenge and, much to the dismay of the
locals, easily swept the five games played.[5] But, discouragement aside, interest
in the game rebounded quickly and its popularity spread throughout the state.

By 1900, California baseball was popular enough to prompt various business
owners to sponsor a four-club professional entity called the California League.
At this stage, they fielded teams from Los Angeles, Oakland, Sacramento, and

San Francisco. Sensing the potential for growth and profits, league organizers embarked upon a blueprint for expansion. As such, in 1902 the association abandoned the strictly California profile, added franchises in Portland and Seattle, and christened itself the Pacific Coast League (PCL).[6] For the next several years, the PCL adapted and readapted itself in size. More important, the league advanced the game's prominence in the communities where the teams resided. Few, if any, institutions personified the notion of "American" values as did baseball in the hearts of its aficionados. And, among the growing number of Japanese living in California, the game's popularity and symbolic meaning was not lost.

◆ ◆ ◆

After the turn of the century, no other state in the union held a greater number of Japanese residents than did California. Employment, land, climate, and, to an extent, the California myth of opportunity all were important factors drawing the Issei to the West Coast state. By 1900, of the 24,326 Japanese who lived in the United States, California held 10,151. During the next twenty years, the numbers increased to 73, 912. And in 1930, 97,456 people of Japanese descent lived in California. This represented 70.2 percent of all Japanese in the United States.[7]

Los Angeles and San Francisco were the primary residences for the majority of Japanese. By 1910, 4,518 Issei lived in San Francisco and another 4,238 in Los Angeles.[8] At these points of entry, such institutions as the Japanese Association, Japanese ethnic newspapers, and other civic organizations began operations. As these establishments became rooted in the state's larger urban centers, other Japanese traveled farther inland. By 1910, Sacramento, with 1,437, became their largest community away from the coast. During these years, the Issei migrated to other smaller communities, such as Walnut Grove, Livingston, and Fresno. Though not on par with the size of the Nikkei enclaves found in the larger cities, the Japanese in these tiny townships also eventually developed institutions via their churches and farming cooperatives.

◆ ◆ ◆

As the second-generation Nisei came of age, their world tugged at them from two ends: their Japanese heritage and American nationality. "It's a wonder we weren't all schizos," recalled one Nisei woman. "Our parents were always telling us to be 'good Japanese.' Then they'd turn right around and tell us to be 'good Americans.'"[9] Gaukueans (Japanese-language schools) were among the institutions employed by the Issei to help maintain the Japanese culture among their children. Community activities, such as theater and literature readings, provided another method to keep the Japanese elders and their offspring close to one another.[10] But athletics, above all, was the enclave's most popular activity.

Initially, athletic programs centered on maintaining traditional Japanese sports such as sumo wrestling and kendo. Issei parents, in this manner, could teach the principles of Japanese heritage to the Nisei. Not surprisingly, community leaders sponsored these activities in their respective regions. American sports captured Nisei interests. To that end, basketball, volleyball, softball, and football activities drew many recruits among males and females. Buddhist and Christian churches, Gaukuens, and Japanese YMCA and YWCAs all sponsored leagues and teams, while the ever-expanding Japanese dailies touted the competition.[11] Baseball most often took center stage.

◆ ◆ ◆

By 1935, as with other regions in the West, baseball euphoria took hold of Nisei in the San Francisco region and beyond. In Monterey to the south, the Minatos of that fishing village spearheaded the eight-team California Coast Counties Athletic Association. In the San Joaquin and Stanislaus regions, the Livingston Dodgers and Stockton Yamatos led a cast of several clubs in the Central California League, while, to their north, the Florin Athletic Club, near Sacramento, dominated their Nisei counterparts in their Rural League. And, in those towns near San Francisco Bay, the Asahis of San Jose, Oakland Merritts, and Alameda Kono routinely competed for honors in the Northern California Japanese Baseball League (NCJBL). Remarkably, by the Nisei era, many of the aforementioned clubs had a history. Issei formed the San Jose Asahis in 1917. By the mid-1930s, Japanese American baseball was already a tradition.[12]

But its "golden age" came during the Nisei period. And there stood several reasons for its development. First, by the mid-1930s, the Japanese American community had increased in numbers. In San Francisco by 1930 there were approximately 4,400 more people of Japanese heritage than in 1900; in Alameda County 4,500 more Japanese; in San Joaquin County 4,000; in the San Jose region, 4,000; and in Sacramento, a whopping 6,900 more than had been the case thirty years earlier.[13] Not surprisingly, each area fielded several Nisei teams in different levels of competition. In the Sacramento vicinity alone, for instance, ten teams were routinely active. In an earlier era, Issei teams, by comparison, were not nearly in such abundance and, as a consequence, necessarily competed in municipal city leagues against whites and Mexican and African Americans.

Second, transportation had become modernized and roads improved. Between 1933 and 1940, New Deal policy makers allocated $1.8 billion for highway construction and upgrades.[14] Northern California's Nisei residents were among the beneficiaries. The Issei did not have this advantage and, apart from the occasional trip to Japan, rarely ventured beyond their communities. The Nisei, on the other hand, often strayed well beyond their home areas. In fact, apart from metropolitan locales, Nisei teams routinely participated in leagues in which one-hundred-mile round trips were not uncommon. Their ability to travel also afforded them the opportunity to compete solely against other Nisei.

Third, Issei elders saw value in a sport that many had adopted years earlier. To the elders, the game, it is speculated, "nourished traditional virtues of loyalty, honor, and courage."[15] In that manner, alongside sumo and kendo, baseball was one of the few remaining umbilical cords they had with the homeland. For many of the Issei, as baseball traveled with them across the Pacific, it came with vestiges of both the Old and the New World. That their sons continued the tradition was entirely acceptable. To observers of that era, the game's symbolic connections between generations were no surprise. "Baseball," writer Wayne Maeda remembered, "allowed each generation to interpret the meaning of the sport and yet the excitement of the game crossed generations."[16]

To an extent, baseball's generation importance was not unlike the role it played with their immigrant counterparts—migrants from Europe—east of the Rockies. Church elders and local YMCAs encouraged the practice of sport, particularly baseball, not only for the purpose of assimilation but also for "the preservation of the community itself."[17] However, Irish, Italian, and Jewish immigrant parents adopted baseball only after they arrived in America. Japanese and Latin American immigrants stand alone as the only newcomers who arrived already knowledgeable in the skills and traditions of the game.[18] As such, baseball was part of their heritage.

Fourth, the game was "American." For the Nisei, this was imperative. Patriotism was essential to their generation. This was the path, as they saw it, to eventual assimilation. Even at the Japanese-language schools, historian David K. Yoo points out, "Textbooks and teachers encouraged the Nisei to be good Americans and become fully conversant with life in the United States."[19] The Japanese American Citizens League (JACL), claimed James Sakamoto, a cofounder of the JACL and editor of Seattle's *Japanese American Courier*, fully concurred that the Nisei destiny was to become "an integral part of national life."[20] And the hope for that acceptance, they believed, had many roads. Educational achievement, of

Florin baseball team. 1934 Rural League Champions. Florin, California.
Take note of the self-built ballpark. (Courtesy of the Sacramento
State University Library Special Collections)

course, was their primary path. But to identify with American culture they also
viewed baseball as key to that quest. To that end, American themes and messages
often laced Nisei baseball. Fourth of July tournaments provided one forum for
patriotic activity. In 1936, the northern California Nisei "A" clubs, for instance,
initiated the first such event in their state. Though only four teams participated,
the *New World-Sun Daily*, a San Jose Japanese American paper that sponsored
the tournament, naturally referred to it as "an epoch in the history of Japanese
sportsdom in America." The opening ceremony even featured an airplane flight
in which the pilot dropped onto the field a baseball tied to an American and
Japanese flag.[21] The report went on to claim an attendance of some six thousand
patrons at the game.[22]

As a result of these factors, the Nisei could afford to retreat into their own
leagues and compete exclusively against others like themselves. Some, like
writer Bill Hosokawa, offered the somewhat sober analysis that "community
leagues were organized where boys of ordinary ability could compete against
each other."[23] But the actions of the community elders indicated that other factors were also present.

Comfortable and safe in their enclaves, Issei parents strongly backed all-Nisei sport programs, particularly baseball. George Yoshio Matsumoto, a player on the Sebastopol team, recalled Issei financial support at fund-raisers for the club. And at games, his father, among others of his generation, routinely "passed the hat around" to pay for umpires.[24] In Sacramento, Issei acted in a similar fashion. "They may have been poor farmers," Wayne Maeda points out, "but when it came time to donate money for uniforms and equipment, they reached down into their pockets and always came up with something to help the team out."[25]

All-Japanese athletic sites also appeared. At a time when the New Deal's Works Project Administration (WPA) program included the construction of thousands of parks across the country, many Japanese Americans, without federal or local support, built their own baseball facilities. For instance, of the eight ball clubs in the NCJBL, four of those—Oakland, San Jose, Sebastopol, and Florin—played in their own ballparks. Though many of these "stadiums" were, in fact, stitched together ball fields laced with wooden stands and improvised chicken-wire back-stops set behind churches or a community member's farm, they were sanctuaries that drew the community together on game days. Contests could be easily scheduled, particularly after morning church services. But the little ballparks also provided a sense of comfort in that the Nikkei could conduct their affairs and play their beloved game free from the discrimination they might have otherwise experienced beyond the outfield fence. In short, the parks themselves were, to a large degree, microcosms of the community itself. Unfortunately, by 1941, these games and the all-Nisei structure kept them at a distance from the mainstream at a time when suspicion about their loyalty reached its greatest height.[26]

◆ ◆ ◆

Long before 1941, however, baseball had been a strong presence in the Yamato Colony, an agricultural enclave in central California and the first such Japanese cooperative in the mainland United States. Though reports on overall athletic activities during the Issei era in that region are cloudy, greater clarity emerged during the 1920s. Koko Kaji arose as the leading proponent in the establishment of the baseball there. Kaji, whose origins are unknown, landed in the nearby community of Livingston somewhere between 1916 and 1917. Shortly thereafter, he put together amateur teams of high school–aged Nisei and during the summers played throughout the San Joaquin Valley. By 1924, and far better established, Kaji reportedly formed a club he called the Livingston Peppers. Throughout the remainder of the decade, the *Livingston Chronicle*, who dubbed their manager "Smiling Koko Kaji," followed the club's progress. Their games, said writer Kesa Noda, "were well attended and were given front page coverage in the paper."[27]

Mainstream agitation toward the Yamato Japanese also mounted during the 1920s. In character with anti-Japanese sentiments in other parts of the state, several Livingston residents, fearful of increased Japanese land ownership, formed the Merced County Anti-Japanese Association. Calling on a boycott of any further land deals with the Japanese, the group erected distinctively large signs on their municipal boundaries that read, "No More Japanese Wanted Here."[28] Although no effort emerged to oust those Japanese already in place within Merced County, those who remained in this hostile atmosphere closed ranks. Though a handful of Caucasians defended their Japanese neighbors, by the 1930s the Japanese of the Yamato Colony and beyond recognized that the majority watched them with a degree of guarded suspicion. And what they saw was not only a community of law-abiding people who exhibited a strong work ethic, but one that also held America's national pastime close to its heart.

Many Nisei inherited their love for baseball from their elders. Koko Kaji had much to do with that development, but it is likely that even had Kaji not come along, baseball's magnetism would still have captivated the Nisei youth. The Livingston Dodgers—a club that more accurately reflected Nisei from the Yamato Colony—were formed in the new era. "By the time we got out of high school we developed our own sports activities," recalled Fred Kishi, a Yamato Colony resident and a respected athlete even among area Caucasians.[29] The Dodgers, by 1934, joined a slew of other Nisei baseball squads playing throughout the San Joaquin valley. Competing in the smaller "A" level in the Central Valley Japanese League, the club acquired sponsorship funding from local merchants and community churches. Kishi reminisced that the team "played against Walnut Grove, Lodi, and other valley squads. These were all Nisei leagues and we played for probably three or four years actively in this league. Most of the Nisei players developed their expertise playing in [these] leagues."[30] So great was the love of sport that team members often assisted their mates on the farms to make time for baseball. "Every weekend we had the Livingston Dodgers," said former pitcher Gilbert Tanji. "So, every Sunday when I had a hard time getting away [from my chores at home], all the boys would come and help me with [my] work so I could take off and play ball."[31] Fred Kishi emphasized that a special chemistry brought the team together. "The players on [our] team knew each other practically from the day we were born; we went to church together, we played on Saturdays together, and we went to high school together, so it just fell into place," he said.[32] Coach Masao Hoshimo, an Issei, stressed unity both on and off the field. Kishi remembered that Hoshimo "had good psychological methods of getting us together. He made us go to Sunday school before we went to any games, so it was a very close-knit group that we had."[33] Another former player, Robert Ohki, added that "the manager always used to say, 'you guys got to go to church or we're not going to play on Sunday.'"[34]

In context, the Dodgers' baseball activities reflected the larger enthusiasm over sport within the Yamato Colony. Along with the Dodgers' Sunday games, softball also grew in popularity and, before long, Yamato residents who played that sport took on their counterparts from other locales. Basketball also found a home there, as it did in other regions. Those who competitively played that sport were not exclusively male. Young Nisei females formed some of the most active athletic squads in that region.[35]

Rivalries, of course, emerged to enliven the competition. The games between Livingston and nearby Cortez were among the most intense. Like its counterpart in Livingston, Cortez's baseball team grew out of its youth organization called the Cortez Young People's Club (CYPC). Though these associations came together as a means to promote social activities, athletics, particularly baseball, won the greatest attention.[36] As was the case in other Japanese communities throughout the West, Issei farmers carved out a baseball diamond in their properties for their Nisei offspring. "We had a great big ballpark," Yuk Yatsuya, a former pitcher on the Cortez Wildcats club remembered. "We were the only ones [in our region] who had our own ballpark."[37]

Yatsuya was a standout pitcher who, in one 1939 game, came within one pitch of throwing a perfect game against a club from Lodi.[38] Like the Livingston team, the Cortez players also tailored their work schedules to provide ample time for baseball. "We used to pick berries in the morning, then run to the game, and then we'd come back and finish the work," Yatsuya recalled. His teammate Yeichi Sakaguchi asserted, "We were obligated to the team . . . so we tried like heck to make [the games]."[39] Interestingly, Hilmar Blaine, a Caucasian who worked as a Shell Oil Company distributor and delivered petroleum to Japanese customers, was also a baseball aficionado and coached the Wildcats in the late 1930s. "He helped us get started and then he helped us get uniforms," Yatsuya fondly remembered.[40]

Because of their proximity, the rivalry between Cortez and Livingston seemed natural. Many of the boys attended the same public schools and after-school community programs. But it was also clear that the more established Yamato Colony residents took umbrage at their upstart Cortez neighbors. And, as a means to establish a firm pecking order when it came to Japanese enclaves in the Merced County region, the Livingston Dodgers took it upon themselves to carry the banner of superiority, at least in terms of baseball. "We didn't care who [we beat], just so we [beat] Cortez. We went to school with the Cortez boys and beat them maybe seventy or eighty percent of the time," Gilbert Tanji, a Yamato Colony resident, proudly remembered.[41] But nearly fifty years later, Yatsuya's competitive spirit remained, and in defense of his club's tenuous performance against his Livingston rivals, he argued that they "practiced more than we did [and] had a lot of material to pick from."[42] The Cortez Wildcats, in fact, were not alone among the teams victimized by the ever-competitive Dodgers. Between 1939 and 1941, the Livingston Dodgers compiled an impressive record of thirty-four wins to only four losses in the Central Valley Japanese League.[43]

◆ ◆ ◆

The Japanese enclave in Monterey was similar in size to that of their brethren in Livingston. However, the history of the Japanese in that coastal region predated that of their central Californian neighbors. As early as 1900, 710 Issei lived in Monterey County. Twenty years later, 1,121 inhabited the area. Some came as contract agrarian laborers, while others arrived to tap into the fishing and abalone industry. As the community grew, both civic organizations and churches blossomed. In an attempt to offset that era's anti-Japanese sentiment, a number of Japanese Associations appeared in the area to act as mediators between them and the mainstream community.[44] In Monterey, for instance, the Japanese Association formed in 1908. But, in time, cultural and social groups also organized.

By the mid-1920s, at the prodding of Issei elders, the Monterey Nisei Athletic Club came into existence. More popularly known as *minato*—the Japanese name for harbor—the club, by the early 1930s, according to chronicler David T. Yamada, became "the center of their universe."[45] From that club emerged basketball, track, tennis, and football teams. Issei support for athletics was akin to those in central California whereby private properties were transformed into athletic sites. In Monterey, one family-owned fish processing plant at night became a makeshift gym for basketball and judo teams.[46]

Monterey in the 1920s was also the site of practice grounds for the Pacific Coast League's San Francisco Seals and Oakland Missions. Inspired by the presence of popular professional baseball stars, young Nisei boys adopted the national pastime as their sport of choice. Evidence of Nisei baseball in the area appeared in the *Monterey Peninsula Herald* when it reported a game featuring a "Japanese Nine" pitcher named Frank Manaka who struck out seventeen "Redmen" in a 1930 contest.[47] In the next couple of years, communities in the Monterey Bay region also formed baseball teams that emerged from their own athletic clubs. In 1935, representatives from six regional athletic clubs met and inaugurated the region's first all-Nisei sports league—the Central California Coast County Athletic Association, the 4CAA. Though the league featured basketball and football teams, along with other sports, baseball clearly dominated their interests.

In April of that year, the Monterey Minatos christened the new league in a contest against the Salinas Athletic Club. The Minatos shut out their neighbors 6–0 behind the one-hit pitching of Jim Takigawa.[48] As with the Central Valley Baseball League, the 4CAA operated at the single A level. But the league was well organized and drew attention from outside the region. The Minatos, in particular, earned the lion's share of publicity. Not only did they win the majority of league titles, but also, at one point, featured five brothers on its roster.[49] The club regularly played against competitors from outside the 4CAA, including teams outside their enclave such as those from the nearby military presidio.[50]

Their most celebrated games came against popular Nisei squads from larger cities and whose competitive level ranked higher than their own. Clubs from both northern and southern California frequented the small port city and encountered tough competition from the Single A Minatos. The Monterey team took its games seriously. In one its most high-profile contests, a 1941 game against the state Triple A—the most competitive level—champs, the San Pedro Skippers dealt the Minatos a humiliating 13–2 beating. But the Monterey faithful did not take the loss lightly. Because a number of its stars were then in military service, the Minatos blamed their defeat on the U.S. Army. "Apparently the Army was too busy fighting forest fires to release some of the key Minato players for the intersectional battle, and the locals went into the game way under par," wrote one angry aficionado.[51]

The Monterey Minato Club captivated the attention of that region's Japanese population. While other clubs participated in the 4CAA league, the Minatos always took center stage. Furthermore, their popularity also earned them coverage in the peninsula's Caucasian press. This was uncommon. Outside the Monterey area, rarely did Japanese teams or athletes in any sport find their activities covered in their region's mainstream press. Whatever exposure they received largely came from the Japanese American press.

◆ ◆ ◆

By the 1930s, the Japanese American press had adopted a mission far different from that set forth by its key founders. Issei publishers like Kyutaro Abiko of the San Francisco–based *Nichibei Shimbun,* Michiharu Maruyama of the *Shin Sekai*—another Bay Area daily—and Masaharu Yamaguchi, Seijiro Shibuya, and Eitaro Iijima, three students who started the *Los Angeles Rafu Shimpo,* founded their newspapers for the sole purpose of providing first-generation subscribers with community news and keeping readers informed of activities in Japan. As such, they printed their papers entirely in Japanese. These journals were not unlike those found in other ethnic communities in the West, such as the Los Angeles–based *La Opinion,* which reached out to the homesick Mexican immigrants with inspirational stories about their country and its heroes. As early as 1922, Robert E. Park recognized that "The immigrant press serves at once to preserve the foreign languages from disintegrating into mere immigrant dialects, hyphenated English, and to maintain contact and understanding between the home countries and their scattered members in every past of the United States and America."[52]

As the Nisei generation grew, however, many of the papers began to offer to its readership English-language sections. Practical reasoning lay at the heart of the transformation. In a four-year span between 1926 and 1930 the population of Nisei jumped from 26.7 to 49.2 percent of all Japanese in the United States.[53] But other factors also contributed to the change. Toyosaku "Henry" Komai, one of two publishers who conceived the idea of the English-language portion for the *Rafu Shimpo,* "hoped that the new section would serve as a public forum for Nisei, awakening their social, economic, and political consciousness."[54] The arrival of English-language sections also came as a result of the Immigration Act of 1924, which brought the migration of Issei from Japan to an end. The *Nichei Bei,* for instance, adopted a bilingual daily in 1924. Two years later, the *Rafu Shimpo* did the same. The Issei newspaper echelons fully understood the long-term implications behind this change. "The support of the Issei," argued historian David Yoo, "represented an investment in the next generation and the future of Japanese America. Making space for the Nisei reinforced generational ties, even if little collaboration took place between the two staffs."[55] As the Nisei matured, their Issei elders echoed their sentiments on values and principles through the Japanese American press. "The newspapers, by making constant suggestions of proper behavior, showed that they held positions of prestige among their audiences," wrote Dorothy Ann Stroup in her 1960 thesis on the Japanese American press.[56]

The Japanese American press was more than simply a tool for Issei ideology. Beyond being a forum for values, the press grew in importance for two reasons: first, an increase in the population of Japanese Americans and, second, the continuing racial policies aimed at their community. By 1928, in the two largest California cities, Los Angeles and San Francisco, the *Rafu Shimpo* of the south had 8,013 subscribers, and the Bay Area's *Nichei Bei* 16,258.[57] Of the forty-four papers whose beginnings stemmed from the Issei era, only the *Rafu Shimpo* and *Nichei Bei* survived into the Nisei generation.[58] They provided the only news for a larger number of California Japanese Americans. As such, these publications served not only the cities where they were based but also the central coast and inland regions of that state.

The publishers and journalists of these papers also saw themselves on the front lines of fighting against racial discrimination toward their enclaves. "Children of European [immigrants] were able to merge into the mainstream and became the readers of American newspapers," claimed writer Katie Kaori Hayashi. "However, children of Japanese immigrants were isolated from the mainstream because of their color and therefore needed media that would lead the fight against racism, as blacks needed their own newspapers."[59] Having the advantage of United States citizenship did little good for Nisei when it came to racial discrimination. Many mainstream Americans in the West continued to fuel yellow peril sentiments into the late 1920s and 1930s. Most noticeable was their inability to pursue careers after having earned the appropriate credentials. "I am a fruitstand worker," recalled one a dejected Nisei. "It is not a very attractive nor distinguished occupation. . . . I would much rather it were a doctor or lawyer . . . but my aspiration of developing into such [was] frustrated long ago. . . . I am only what I am, a professional carrot washer."[60]

Faced with a rigid barrier of prejudice against them, the Nisei press set an agenda for "racial responsibility." Much akin to Booker T. Washington's late-nineteenth-century call for accommodation as a formula to eliminate racial barriers in his era, Japanese American journalists called upon the Nisei "to respond to racism be embracing life in America as loyal, hard-working citizens who would 'prove' their worth."[61]

◆ ◆ ◆

In Los Angeles, the *Rafu Shimpo* pressed the Issei to move in this direction, and in a 1926 column offered a suggestion to their readers: "How to lead youngsters can be summed up in two words, strong and right. Mental and physical toughness is above all needed for Nisei. If possible, Nisei should learn the essence of judo and kendo from Rafu Dojo masters. However, those American-born youngsters don't show an interest in either of them, so it is impossible for us to initiate them into judo and kendo. Rather we should prompt them to take whatever sports they like. Baseball is it!"[62]

In that same year, the paper reported the existence of twelve Nisei teams that included some 130 players. Playing their games exclusively on Sundays, writer Yoichi Nagata wrote, "the Southern California Japanese Baseball Association embarked upon their goal to organize a strong Nisei baseball team to strengthen their solidarity and at the same time represent Japanese and Japanese Americans in Southern California and show off their athletic ability to other Americans."[63]

The creation of a representative club was not uncommon among ethnic communities across the nation who wanted badly to demonstrate not only their "Americanism" but also the virtues of their athleticism to the mainstream. For example, about the same time that the Nisei formulated their baseball world, in New York City proper, the Jewish community touted the achievements of the Dux, a successful semiprofessional basketball club that won recognition outside the Lower East Side. Haunted by the rising anti-Semitic rants of the Reverend Charles Coughlin that reinforced mainstream stereotypes about Jews, such success as seen with track star Marty Glickman and baseball player Hank Greenberg was meaningful to American Jews. The Dux proved no less important. Irving Bernstein, who then played for the East Bronx Dux, said they "found the kinship, security, and confidence to reach beyond the physical horizons of their neighborhoods to join the mainstream."[64]

The Nippons were to the Los Angeles Nikkei community what the Dux were to New York Jews. From 1927 through the 1931 baseball season, the *Rafu Shimpo,* save small snippets on other Nisei clubs, exclusively featured the Nippons in their Sunday editions. A May 1927 visit of Japan's Waseda University baseball team was among the most noteworthy event. Though the hometown Nippons lost an 11–7 contest, the paper touted "one of the largest crowds to witness a Japanese baseball game" and concluded "most of them went home thankful that the day was well spent."[65] With such excitement before them, and armed with a new English-language section in their paper to help draw Nisei readers, *Rafu Shimpo* writers began to campaign for the advancement of athletics on a year-round basis. Only days after the Waseda-Nippons' game, one columnist wrote of the "need for a more adequately organized all year-round club." In an effort to expand beyond the Nippons, he suggested "Enthusiasts who promote other sports would do well to lend their efforts and dollars to this cause. Think it over."[66]

As the Nisei in and around Los Angeles increased in numbers by the end of the twenties and into the 1930s, so too did their activities in a variety of sports. As with other Nikkei communities across the West Coast and inland, by the mid-1930s, sports and leisure activities evolved into year-round events. "In Los Angeles, the Japanese YMCA and YWCA provided facilities for play and meetings along with programs in athletics, sewing, drama, and the like," said Paul Spickard.[67] Moreover, Buddhist and Christian churches, along with the language schools and Japanese American Citizens League, encouraged their youth to participate in athletics and related programs. "All of these organizations sponsored Nisei baseball, basketball, football, and track teams," observed Spickard.[68]

◆ ◆ ◆

In an effort to reinforce a sense of Japanese culture within the context of their American nationality, Nikkei leaders in 1934 created a festivity they dubbed "Nisei Week." In the depth of the Great Depression and in an era whereby their access to advertisements in the mainstream media was virtually nonexistent, Issei merchants needed to come up with creative measures to attract customers. Other reasons were also at play. As the Nisei grew into adolescence, many sought to relocate outside their more confined neighborhood near downtown Los Angeles. Japanese American civic leaders did not wish to see the Nisei generation forget their roots. Nisei Week was, in part, an attempt "by the older generation to get their kids to come back to Little Tokyo, and party Nisei-generated efforts to replicate mainstream American activities in their own ethnic context."[69]

Events like Nisei Week had large-scale objectives. "Nisei Week was also an occasion to pay respects to the highest elected official in Los Angeles," stated historian Lon Kurashige.[70] Festivals such as Nisei Week, were, in part, a means to build a stronger political base, particularly in local elections. Of course, the Japanese American Citizens League was often in the lead of such campaigns. In 1936, John Maeno, president of the JACL, which was in itself a relatively new organization, having been founded six years earlier, announced, "Through the medium of this festival, the JACL hopes to present, acquaint, and contact you directly with the young Japanese American citizen, his life and environment."[71] They also formed community business associations as a means to both foster economic opportunities and establish connections with their mainstream counterparts. Still, there is little evidence that their efforts resonated in a manner that won them discernible political clout.[72] In other circles, such as education, they also made little headway. Roger Daniels observed that in spite of their academic achievements, ". . . the Nisei faced a society that rejected them regardless of their accomplishments. Fully credentialed Nisei education majors, for example, were virtually unemployable as teachers in the very schools in which they had excelled."[73] Given the difficulties in building any type of bridges with mainstream society, the Nisei, by necessity, turned to the only comfort zone left to reach their goals: themselves.

Baseball provided a respite from their otherwise frustrating endeavors to reach out to the mainstream. More important, in the face of such discouragement, the game both galvanized the community and provided a stage for those who might otherwise be invisible to the larger society. In short, it helped give the enclave and its players an identity. Similarly, other "invisible" Asian enclaves sought similar attention through sports. In 1939, for instance, a Chinese American basketball team from San Francisco called the Kues, in an effort to gain exposure in mainstream America, barnstormed in a trip that took them through the upper periphery of the United States to Chicago and back, where they played against largely Caucasian and black clubs. When it was over, though they became "the equivalent of matinee idols" in the Chinese communities they had visited, historian Kathleen Yep noted that mainstream "sports coverage trivialized the Kues' athletic talent in racial and gender terms."[74] But, Yep also noted that among the dividends from the trip came "an opportunity for racial uplift" within the Chinese American enclaves. At home in San Francisco, the *Chinese Digest* wrote, "[The Kues] are spreading plenty of good will for us Chinese wherever they play by their fine sportsmanship, clean behavior, and excellent ball playing."[75]

In Los Angeles, the Japanese displayed similar affection for their sports teams. The Nippons were among those teams that baseball aficionados there rallied around. Including the 1927 contest with Waseda University, between 1927 and 1936 the Nippons hosted ten games against Japanese collegiate squads and five more with the new Tokyo Giants professional club.[76] The Giants, in their 1935 and 1936 visits to Los Angeles, were attractive to the baseball-hungry Nikkei. Along with their professional status, they also included popular players who had appeared in previous years with the university teams. Moreover, there was the novelty of competing against a foreign team whose origins linked with audiences in the Pacific Coast. As with the 1927 game with Waseda University, the *Rafu Shimpo* heralded the 1935 three-game series between the Giants and Nippons

San Fernando Aces with wives. San Fernando, California.
(Courtesy of the Nisei Baseball Research Project)

as "The Japanese World Series." In all, the Giants took two of the three games before crowds that averaged five thousand. Following the games in Los Angeles, the Tokyo club continued to barnstorm the West Coast and, much to the great satisfaction of those in Little Tokyo, upon the conclusion of their trip assessed that "the Los Angeles Nippons were the best of the Japanese Nines."[77]

While other Japanese American teams existed in the late 1920s and early 1930s, they did so largely in the shadow of Nippons. But, by the mid-1930s, as many of these teams and baseball organizers consolidated to form all-Nisei leagues, they began to appear in the *Rafu Shimpo* with more regularity. As such, the winning ways of such teams as the San Fernando Aces and the powerful San Pedro Skippers, clubs with distinctively Americanized names, rose to prominence and attracted their own baseball aficionados. Unlike the Nippons, teams like the Aces and Skippers, along with most of their contemporaries, except in a few cases, played exclusively in all–Japanese American leagues. As early as 1928, the *Rafu Shimpo* reported on a league that carried some eight members.[78] League members played in mostly public facilities, including the expansive Griffith Park, at the time a rural area on the northern periphery of Los Angeles, and the paper also observed the construction of new baseball diamonds by the San Fernando foreign-language schools.[79] As the decade progressed, excitement over baseball spanned from San Pedro to the south to as far north as Ventura County. In most of these locales, organizers had ample talent with which to provide for "A" and "B" division teams.[80]

Nikkei baseball observers in the Los Angeles region also kept an eye on the development of all-Japanese teams and leagues in northern California. In almost all walks of life throughout the history of the state, regional rivalries in the state had been intense. The Pacific Coast League clashes between the Los Angeles Angels and San Francisco Seals dramatized these divisions. In this respect, the very competitive Japanese were quite in step with the culture of the state. To that end, the *Rafu Shimpo* periodically reported scores and other athletic developments from their neighbors to the north and looked to schedule contests of their own. In 1927, the Nippons led the charge as they traveled some three hundred miles northward to take on the San Jose Asahis, a prominent Bay Area club. With the Nippons taking two of the three games in that series, the *Rafu Shimpo* proudly reported, "Every man on the squad contributed wonderfully to make the invasion a successful one."[81]

◆ ◆ ◆

Teams did, occasionally, travel to face their counterparts in other regions. They not only traveled to face other Japanese American teams, but they also competed in Japan. These exchanges were nothing new, as several of them, largely from Seattle and the San Francisco Bay Area, had played ball in the land of the rising sun. Issei-laden clubs used these opportunities to spend time with family and even conduct business. But Issei elders also impressed upon their Nisei offspring the importance of visiting the land of their family origins. What better way to make their case than to help arrange these visits through their baseball connections? For those in Los Angeles, in 1931, upon having accepted an invitation from the Japanese newspaper *Osaka Mainichi* to play a series of games against their local teams, they saw the Nippons in February of that year board a steamship bound for Japan.[82]

Throughout the spring of 1931, the club played several teams of different levels in the Osaka and Nagoya areas. As they experienced life in Japan, the enthusiasm over baseball captivated them. Catcher Ken Matsumoto's accounts that he sent to the *Rafu Shimpo* described "how the populace of Japan takes to baseball. Even kids that are barely able to walk are throwing balls around—everywhere you go they are playing baseball."[83] The Nippons completed their journey with an impressive twenty-win and five-loss record. But the trip served other purposes, as well.

For the Issei, as much as the United States symbolized opportunity, anti-Asian prejudice stood in the way of one's goals. Within this environment, many believed that their offspring might be conditioned to think of their heritage as less than honorable. To that end, they concocted ways to provide passage for their sons and daughters to visit Japan and "develop their pride in being Japanese."[84] The Issei had always been concerned with the cultural education of the Nisei. Like most first generations of those who had migrated to the United States, the sanctity of heritage was essential. To immigrant Jews in early twentieth-century New York's Lower East Side, for instance, success in America remained a goal for their children. But the pragmatic target of achievement, nonetheless, carried with it a counterbalance of a romanticized sense of cultural values imparted upon their children so that "the old people remain[ed] [their] conscience, the visible representatives of a moral and religious tradition by which the [child] might regulate [their] inner life."[85] To be sure, the struggles to find a balance between the American identity and that of one's cultural background were not confined to Jews in America. Mexicans-born parents, too, tackled the issue during the 1930s and succeeding decades. "What is happening with our children?" wrote one Mexican woman in a southern California journal. "Why do they reject our behavior? Why don't they respond harmoniously with our way of thinking? Don't they feel the warmth of our traditions and customs like we do?"[86]

Travel to Japan was the Issei effort to offset the positions that Jewish, Mexican, and other first-generation immigrants found themselves in when it came to heritage and their children. These study tours, initiated in the 1920s and known as the *kengakudan,* were intended to mold the Nisei into their perceived role as the "bridge of understanding" between two cultures. David K. Yoo pointed out, "In reality, very few of the second generation could have served as true bridges, since they lacked adequate knowledge of Japanese language, history, and culture. Nevertheless, the ties to Japan mattered particularly because the Issei could not acquire U.S. citizenship, and this fact served as a constant reminder of the vulnerability of the Nikkei in America."[87]

The Los Angeles Nippons' 1931 baseball trip, and those from other Nikkei communities in the West, provided an opportunity to many working-class Nisei youth to visit Japan and immerse themselves in their heritage. Catcher Matsumoto wrote, "One distinct feature of our first impression was our feeling of relaxation when we found ourselves mingling among the Japanese people. What a feeling that was. Never before had we experienced anything so dramatically realistic. No prejudiced feeling, etc."[88]

Matsumoto's comfort with race was an instrumental by-product of the trip. Though in high school Nisei had routinely mixed with Caucasians on all matters academic, their comfort level beyond the classroom was often tenuous at best. Numerically there were few of them. Also, their small stature increased their insecurity. Though the concept of being a cultural bridge sounded good in theory, as a practical matter, the anti-Asian racial components had, by the time of the Nisei generation, been in existence for several decades. David Yoo recounts the experiences of one southern California Nisei man: "In going through high school and college, I can't recall how many times I was cast aside just because I am Japanese. I was barred from parties, dances, swimming pools, etc. for the same reason previously given. America is for Americans and all other races are not given its [sic] chance." Known as L. Toyama, he concluded: "Americans are the narrowest-minded people in the world. They think only about and for themselves and exclude all others . . . a model to be avoided by all others."[89]

The 1931 Nippons' trip to Japan, however, revealed a slight breach in the racial barrier. Club organizers included on the team roster three Caucasian players: Jimmy Crandall, a University of Southern California pitcher; "Red" Frazier, a seventeen-year-old Major League prospect; and a former Pacific Coast League player named Bucky Harris.[90] Influence toward this personnel decision came from the Japanese organizers at the Osaka Mainichi, who believed that the competition level and attendance numbers would increase with the appearance of talented Caucasians. However, Yoichi Nagata points out, "the Nippons almost regularly included white players on their squad anyway, which was very unusual for a Nisei team."[91] Carrying these players, however, had its dividends, a point not lost to catcher Ken Matsumoto in his reports, which often made the front pages of the *Rafu Shimpo*. "The Crandall-Harris combination was claimed to be the best ever seen in Japan," wrote the enthusiastic Matsumoto as he crowed about the club's success with "the best record of all the teams that have invaded Japan."[92] But Matsumoto qualified his comments with a note on the club's cross-cultural makeup as a component of its success. "All members of the team stuck together and it was the harmony and cooperation which was responsible for the many victories the boys won."[93] Like the Nippons, other Nikkei teams in the state exhibited cross-cultural activity. Kenichi Zenimura, known as the Dean of

Los Angeles Nippons touring Japan, 1931.
(Courtesy of the Nisei Baseball Research Project)

the Diamond in many circles around California, in the 1920s not only played on largely Caucasian rosters, but also, according to writer Kerry Yo Nakagawa, captained a white club in the popular Twilight League.[94]

◆ ◆ ◆

Fresno Japanese American baseball had a distinguished stature, not so much because it could rival the number of Nikkei constituents and ball clubs found in larger urban centers, but because of Kenichi Zenimura's pioneering activities. With other clubs from Sacramento, Stockton, Alameda, and later San Jose in the league, the large Fresno Nikkei community was not as isolated as their geographical location might suggest. By the mid to late 1920s, Fresno Japanese American baseball established itself as one of high caliber, one by which others gauged their own talent level. Under Zenimura's direction, the Japanese American press lauded players and teams from Fresno and routinely measured other clubs as ranking "below" them.[95] Although through the 1920s and into the 1930s, Fresno

Nikkei baseball came to include an array of teams that played on a local basis, the core of the area's baseball fortunes continued to be the Fresno Athletic Club.

Along with their membership in the Northern California League, they took on the most high profile non-Japanese competitors in games that were well advertised. And as they had done in the late 1920s, Fresno teams of the Depression era continued to make sojourns to Japan and, in doing so, reinforced their area's reputation as a hub of Nikkei baseball talent from California.

Nisei baseball in California throughout the 1930s was a vibrant activity that had developed from the strong roots planted by the earlier generation. In this respect, the game's magnetism was as great in the rural communities as it was in larger cities. Indeed, for the Nikkei living in the union's "golden state," the national pastime created a vast network that tied them together during a period of economic stress. Pooling their assets, they formed baseball "co-ops" so that they might ambitiously pursue the game in areas outside their own realm. As the game and its leagues won the attention of the Nikkei community, it also provided farmers, shopkeepers, and otherwise low-skilled workers a chance to create and advance an identity of honor among their own. The "frustrated fruit-stand worker" of the work week could achieve prominence as a Nisei athlete, if only for a few hours on a Sunday afternoon in Fresno, Livingston, Los Angeles, or San Francisco, and all the way up to the Pacific Northwest.

5

The Courier League

Japanese youngsters could communicate
with the Americans through baseball.
—S. Frank Miyamoto, 1939[1]

One can speak of rising interest in football
and basketball as there has been, but it takes
old Abner Doubleday's orchard pastime to
bring out the papas and mamas of the rising
generation.
—Bill Hosokawa, *Seattle Japanese American
Courier*, April 10, 1937[2]

In 1927 James Sakamoto, a boxer-turned-journalist, had just returned to his
hometown of Seattle after having spent a few years in New York City. As he
scanned his old neighborhood, he noticed a development in the old haunts:
sport had taken hold of his community. Though his Japanese enclave in the
city that on Puget Sound represented a tiny portion of the overall population,
the residents there, nonetheless, were a very active minority. Neighborhood
rivalries were common and, as Sakamoto discovered, residents often channeled
their sentiments through their athletic clubs. As such, friction often arose among
those who identified with these organizations. To Sakamoto, this was a potential
red flag.[3] But the writer did not call for an end to sport. Rather, he considered
an alternative course of action: sport could be corralled as a means to unify the
Pacific Northwest Nikkei for the larger purpose of winning mainstream acceptance. Though the logistics needed to be worked out among those with whom he
shared his thoughts, never was there a question between them as to which sport
might galvanize Japanese Americans throughout the region. "King Baseball,"
everyone agreed, stood at the head of the line.

♦ ♦ ♦

Like San Francisco, Seattle was a main point of entry for the Japanese coming to the Americas in the late nineteenth century. Some forty miles to the north of gigantic Mount Rainer, white settlers founded a village next to Elliott Bay in 1852 and named it after a friendly local Indian chief named Seathl, or Seattle. In 1869, Seattle was formally incorporated as a city, and six years later steamship lines began bringing passengers and goods from San Francisco. The city and its surrounding Puget Sound region, however, experienced its greatest growth immediately following the discovery of gold in Alaska in 1897. Still, while many remained in Seattle in this period, many others, seeking fortune in the Klondike, spent only a brief period in the port city. In the meantime, as industries such as shipping, lumber extraction, fishing, and the railroad increased their operations, labor shortages were not uncommon. And like their counterparts in other sectors of the country, employers organized recruitment programs to lure prospective laborers from Japan. Enticed still further by Japanese labor contractors already in the United States, by 1900 a small stream of young Japanese males embarked upon sojourns that eventually landed them in Seattle. "It was by good chance that the Japanese came to Seattle about that time, for the city itself as a frontier community was in the throes of expansion," explained S. Frank Miyamoto in his 1939 study of the Seattle Japanese community. "Building and commerce were going forward at an unusual rate, and there were not enough workers to go around."[4]

Seattle was, for the Issei travelers in the late nineteenth century, a popular port of entry to the United States. Though some thirty-four Japanese workers appeared in the region in 1878, a little more than five thousand were found thinly spread in a large radius in and around Puget Sound.[5] During the first decade of the twentieth century, however, as a result of fewer economic opportunities in their homeland and the passage of the 1907 Gentlemen's Agreement, Issei laborers looked to Seattle as a place for settlement. Consequently, with a rising population in that town, Issei entrepreneurs recognized the increased demand for food service, hotels, and laundromats. Moreover, those who farmed in such places as the White River valley, just south of the city, saw an increase in crop prices. Indeed, between 1900 and 1910, the Japanese population in Seattle rose from 3,212 to 7,497.[6] By all measures, the decision to settle in that region appeared sound. But, as in California, resistance to the Issei also appeared in the Evergreen State.

Taking a page from the growing national resistance to immigration, in 1921, Washington joined other states in adopting alien land laws. On the heels of the state mandate, in case known as *Ozawa v. United States,* the U.S. Supreme Court ruled, in 1922, that Japanese immigrants were ineligible for citizenship. In fact, the *Ozawa* decision was the last of several court challenges the Issei embarked upon on behalf of their rights. Indeed, the Seattle-based Northwest American Japanese Association, having immediately taken on Washington's 1921 alien land law, was among the most active in this regard. Their efforts notwithstanding, by the end of 1922 the legal setbacks they suffered proved devastating.[7] "The land law decisions have dealt a severe blow to Japanese immigrants, spiritually as well as materially . . .," claimed the San Francisco consul.[8] The *Rafu Shimpo* stated that "The extreme dejected spirits of the Japanese . . . cannot be concealed."[9] Seattle's Japanese leaders remained incredulous. From a strictly legal and constitutional position, they were shocked at the continuing outcomes of the court decision. "Not only Japanese farmers, not only leaders of the Japanese associations, but also many Americans in the legal profession and Japanese government officials thought in this way," wrote the journalists of the *Taihoku Nippo*.[10]

Socially and economically confined, Seattle's Issei operated within the boundaries of their community. By the mid-1920s, the majority of their establishments were found in *Nihonmachi*—or Japantown—a bustling neighborhood just south of the downtown area. For the Japanese living in the Pacific Northwest, Nihonmachi was their capital city. It was the center of their social, cultural, and political activities. The Nippon Kan Theatre, for instance, stood in the middle of the community and featured not only dramas and musicals, but one might also witness political debates, church fund-raisers, and even judo matches. But there were also few secrets in the close-knit community. Gossip and cliques were common. And varied opinions regarding local issues often contributed to rivalries among the urban residents. Compounding these dynamics, the Nisei born during the first decade of the twentieth century grew into young adults and established their own turf. They shared their vision in community meetings and, for some, displayed their competitiveness through sports. It was into this environment that James Yoshinori Sakamoto returned.

◆ ◆ ◆

After his 1903 birth in Seattle, Sakamoto spent his entire childhood there and excelled in high school sports. At eighteen years old he moved to northern New Jersey and eventually took a job as English-language editor of the *Japanese American,* based in New York City. For extra money he competed as a prizefighter.

Though proficient in the ring, the slightly built Nisei sustained injuries to his eyes that eventually led to complete blindness.

Sakamoto returned to Seattle in 1927 and, though only twenty-four, set upon an agenda that came to identify a guiding philosophy for Nisei in America: assimilation. To be sure, the movement toward assimilation had grown in recent years. The Issei had struggled with varying degrees on the extent of proper adaptation to life in the United States. But, in part a result of a 1911 incident in Bakersfield, California, whereby the small Japanese immigrant enclave split as a result of their differences regarding commemoration of the emperor's birthday, the idea of a permanent settlement in America gained new traction as a feasible option for the newcomers. [11] As the first generation struggled with adaptation, they did so with the haunting notion that to move toward an assimilationist position also invited accusations of "disrespect" and, worse yet, disloyalty to the fatherland. Kyuturo Abiko, the prominent and influential publisher of San Francisco's *Nichibei Shimbun,* argued that pragmatism dictated the assimilation position. As observed by historian Yuji Ichioka, assimilation to those like Abiko "meant that they should prove to the world that the Japanese as a people were capable of adapting themselves to live and work outside of Japan." To do less would be "archaic."[12]

Indeed, to the descendants of the Meiji, "archaic behavior" was the antithesis of strength and clearly out of step with Japan's destiny in the global arena. After all, between 1895 and 1907, Japan had waged two successful wars against China and Russia, respectively. It also set up Korea as a protectorate. Most important, though the infamous "unequal treaties" were no longer in existence, memories of it remained fresh in the minds of the Meiji generation. To show that they could rise above hardship, even in a foreign land, was a matter of respect and honor. Therefore, those who positioned themselves behind Abiko's school of thought argued that assimilation was, in fact, the only model by which to effectively display Japanese greatness.[13]

With that in mind, Japanese city and rural leaders prodded their constituents to adopt an American external persona that they called *gaimenteki doka.* In all things visible, to the extent that they were able, they took on American appearances in clothing and habits. In 1911, the Japanese Association of America reinforced this thinking when, upon launching a "campaign of education," it brought in from Japan two dignitaries, Nitobe Inazo and Shimada Saburo, with extensive experience in United States culture. Both were sent on lecture tours throughout the West to implore their immigrant audiences "to learn English and adopt American concepts of morality."[14] Although not all Issei adopted in its entirety the gaimenteki doka, enough of them did move in this direction so that, within a few years, the Issei community held a more "Americanized" profile. This was particularly true in such urban areas as Los Angeles, San Francisco, and Seattle.

◆ ◆ ◆

Gone for five years, Sakamoto returned to his Seattle community, which was distinctly more Americanized than it had been when he had left for the East. Years of practicing the gaimenteki doka among the Issei were augmented with increasing numbers of Nisei in each household. But the portrait of an "Americanized" community belied distinct cultural differences below the surface. First of all, though the Issei had, years earlier, adopted American characteristics for the sake of assimilation, the exercise did not call for them to internally abandon their Japanese values and principles. Thus, as reflected inside their communities, with cuisine, and in their use of language among themselves, the Issei remained Japanese. For their part, the Nisei, though they had attended cultural language schools in their youth, few could speak or read Japanese with any efficiency as they matured. Moreover, growing up in households that impressed upon them American characteristics further separated them from their heritage. Finally, the majority had never been to Japan and, as such, could only relate to it through the tales of their parents.

The Japanese-language press in the United States during the 1920s reflected the cultural differences within the community. Though on many fronts, their administrators were practitioners of gaimenteki doka outside their work, through 1925 publishers of these papers printed their issues exclusively in the Japanese language. Kyuturo Abiko, however, understood the changing demographics, and in that year an English-language section began to appear in his paper, by then referred to as the *Nichi Bei*. Other papers followed his lead. Still, the dailies remained heavily laden with news of Japan and offered few or no American viewpoints.[15]

With his eyesight all but gone because of his days in the ring, James Sakamoto devoted himself to civic activities and reasoned that the Nisei, like himself, were at a point where their presence called for greater recognition. Community service was not a new arena for the former boxer. Only one year out of high school, in 1921, Sakamoto helped found the Seattle Progressive Citizens' League, an organization designed to fight Seattle's antialien land law then in place plus other prospective anti-Japanese legislation, some of which led to the infamous *Ozawa* cases one year later.[16] By 1927, as Sakamoto and others like him saw it, the stakes for their generation had increased, as did their sense of responsibility. Impressed upon by their elders, and reinforced by activists in their age group, Sakamoto was one of many Nisei who identified themselves as a "bridge of understanding" between their culture and that of mainstream Americans. Loyalty to the United States, of course, was imperative in this pact. "The bridge concept," observed historian David Yoo, "moved beyond the mere status of interpreter and required the Nisei to be contributors to American life and to take up the responsibilities of U.S. citizenship."[17]

Schooled in this manner, Sakamoto took action and, with sparse funding, he and his wife, Misao, pieced together a newspaper designed exclusively for Nisei readership. In January 1928, the paper he christened the *Japanese-American Courier* made its inaugural appearance in the Nikkei Seattle community of Beacon Hill. Sakamoto's *Courier* became the first paper from the American Japanese community to be printed entirely in English. From 1928 until 1942, though it never gained the subscription numbers of his competitors, Sakamoto's newspaper (much more akin to a newsletter in contemporary terms) provided a window for which to observe Nisei positions on their identity and, in his time, amplified his thoughts concerning the direction for those of his generation. In large part owing to his prodding, community leaders throughout the West came to Seattle in 1930 and subsequently formed the Japanese American Citizens League (JACL). Six years later, the organization elected him president for a two-year term.

Declaring that "American born Japanese," a label that he used in lieu of the more "foreign" sounding Nisei, had "obligations and duties," the publisher preached a continual message of "undivided allegiance" and "full-blooded Americanism."[18] To Sakamoto, the onus lay with the Nisei to forge the path to assimilation. His paper lacked any forum, other than direct letters to the publisher himself, for readers to air their concerns. Thus, though he reported the general news of the community and printed civic announcements, Sakamoto's designs for his paper were to echo the call for unity. "Only if the second generation as a whole works to inculcate in all its members the true spirit of American patriotism can the group escape the unhappy fate of being a clan apart from the rest of American life," he wrote.[19] To that end, the *Japanese American Courier*, Sakamoto made obvious, was the heartbeat of the Japanese in the Pacific Northwest. And, more than simply boasting written words, the publisher encouraged the use of his newspaper's facilities to organize community strategies and activities, such as sports.

◆ ◆ ◆

Of course, the Seattle Nikkei community had been athletically active long before Sakamoto's newspaper came into existence. And, thanks to Frank Fukuda, by 1928, baseball had increased its visibility among those in Sakamoto's world. The Issei elders had been very competitive in their younger days. By the late 1920s, as they settled into a more sedentary life of raising their families, playing baseball was a torch they easily, and gladly, passed on to their offspring. What could be more "American?" some thought. And they would be unique Americans, at that. "Being Japanese by descent but American by birth, the Nisei were suited ideally to become a future bridge of understanding between two nations to dispel the ignorance which had been . . . the fundamental cause of the exclusion movement," observed Yuji Ichioka.[20] Frank Fukuda, as explained earlier, put the concept of *kakehashi* (bridge of understanding) to work on the baseball diamond when he arranged matches between his Asahi clubs and their Japanese counterparts. Thus, the Seattle Japanese community, prior to Sakamoto's return, was very active in its athletic endeavors and incorporated baseball as a means to display the virtues of the second generation to those in Japan.[21] The question to the leaders of the new generation was: could these same virtues be displayed on the home front in a manner that transcended the community itself?

Sakamoto, a former professional athlete, fully realized the potential that came with sport as a mechanism for unity among the Nisei. Of course, among the very competitive Japanese, athletics occasionally did divide the community. To this, the *Courier* publisher warned in his first issue, "there is too much politics in sport . . . and too much sports in politics."[22] Though he recognized the propensity of civic leaders to protect their turf, Sakamoto, nonetheless, moved forward with plans for an "athletic union" in the hope that it would overshadow the "petty jealousies" that, in his opinion, weighed down his enclave.[23]

The Courier Athletic League came alive within a short time after the paper began operations. Sakamoto drew up a constitution, made available his limited office space for meetings, and recruited local leaders who he believed could be, for this new institution, "representative of a sportsmanlike and high code of ethics."[24] Following the announcement of this venture, Sakamoto's invitation, wrote S. Frank Miyamoto, ". . . drew an intriguing combination of members—Buddhist and Christian churches, YMCAs, and Japanese-language schools, . . ."[25] As they brainstormed how best to service the athletic appetites of their constituents, it grew apparent that what they had before them was a product whose attraction would be year-round and reach into areas well beyond their Seattle neighbor-hoods. The paper, wrote the publisher, would act as a "purely non-partisan connisseur [sic] of athletic events of the Japanese community."[26] Ironically, and probably to much chagrin on Sakamoto's part, the paper's priorities seemed misplaced. Organizers like "Sparky" Hide Kono, caught up in their enthusi-asm for sport, saw Sakamoto's call for unity as an afterthought. Kono wrote, "I understand [the *Courier*] is to be a paper not only in the interest of sports itself, but to establish a better Japanese American relation."[27] Following the lead of the ambitious and patriotic Sakamoto, the new league officials constructed athlet-ics around the notion that Courier League sports would be those distinctively "American." Thus, as the institution developed, basketball, football, and volley-ball, sports that crossed gender and age lines, won *Courier* sanction. Of course, the lion's share of attention went to baseball.

◆ ◆ ◆

"One can speak of rising interest in football and basketball as there has been," wrote Bill Hosokawa, among the young Nisei journalists who advanced their experience as writers under Sakamoto's auspices, "but it takes old Abner Double-day's orchard pastime to bring out the papas and mamas of the rising genera-tion."[28] Indeed, throughout the 1930s, the national pastime presented a magnetic attraction among the entire Nikkei community. The "Nipponese ball fans will be out in howling droves to cheer and jeer with the vociferous enthusiasm only dyed-in-wool lovers of baseball can display," reported the *Courier*. "And how the Nipponese love their baseball."[29]

That baseball took center stage was no accident. To be sure, it was popular. But Sakamoto's concerns transcended the game. At the time that the *Courier* came into existence, sport among the Nikkei, beyond baseball, was already a fixture in the Seattle area, and at times a divisive one. Football, in particular, drew the publisher's attention, and ire. Still simmering from a game held weeks earlier between two of the community's most prominent athletic clubs, Nippon and Taiyo, that resulted in aggressive unsportsmanlike behavior, the *Courier* lashed out: "Too many fans become over enthusiastic and in showing their loyalty to their club, they are wont to indulge, without heed to discretion, in reckless denunciations of opposing club members and players."[30]

The passive nature of baseball, however, made it much better suited for Saka-moto's leanings toward unification. Initially, the publisher pressed to construct a single "all star" type of team, but gave way to the organizers who opted to form, instead, an all-Nisei league. For the young Nisei at that time, this was not unimportant. "I made the high school [baseball] team when I was a fresh-man. I played the whole season, every game, every inning," remembered Kenji Kawagawa. "But outside the ballgame, [Caucasians] weren't friendly with you. So I realized that was not the kind of situation I'd give my efforts to. So, after my freshman year, I quit [the high school team]. I [wanted] to play Sunday ball with my [Nisei] friends."[31]

But Issei support was also apparent. "The older people were interested. In those days most people didn't have cars and there were not too many activities available [outside the community]. So they came to the games to watch their young ones play. It was community involvement," said Kawagawa.[32] With the game already having established itself since the first decade of the 1900s as an acceptable practice, along with the lure of sunny weather following months of Pacific Northwest rainfall, Nikkei baseball aficionados anxiously gravitated to the new leagues. Indeed, affection for the game came from both generations. "Baseball served to bring together the two generations and lessen the generation gap between the immigrant fathers and their American-born sons," observed historian Gail Nomura. "In baseball the immigrant fathers could come together with their sons in a shared passion."[33]

In its modest beginnings, the baseball division of the Courier League featured ten teams, all from Seattle proper, in 1928. By 1941, its final season, the league had expanded to exceed thirty teams and four different classifications based on skill level.[34] Moreover, these Nisei young adult clubs who, in one manner or another, participated as affiliates of the Courier League could be found as far east as Wapato, Washington, approximately two hundred miles from Seattle, and as far south as Portland, Oregon. As the league caught on, in any given year more than one thousand players participated, and the *Courier* sponsored traveling all-star clubs that played in Oregon, California, and Japan and hosted Japanese clubs who toured the United States mainland.

The *Courier* echoed the affinity the Nikkei held for the national pastime. Afi-cionados routinely expressed their sentiments about the game and its heritage within their community. The popular "Sports Cope" section of the paper, for instance, in 1933 drew from baseball icon Frank Fukuda names of Issei play-ers to be listed on their "Northwest All-Time, All-Star Diamond Aggregation." "Advancing the nostalgia," the paper wrote, "A roll call of the names recalls the days of the old Nippons, Mikados, Cherries and Asahis, those prewar [World War One] and wartime days when the players would rather play ball than eat.

These were times when the first generation nines ruled the diamond roost. . . ."[35] *Courier* writers also included brief stories of Major League players, commentary on professional baseball, and even touted the "rosy" scenario of possibly seeing Japanese teams in the Major League.[36]

◆ ◆ ◆

Of course, as the league matured, rivalries developed in and out of the Seattle area. At the outset of the league's existence, the Nippon Athletic Club and Taiyo Athletic Club, whose origins were in the Issei period, were the two most prominent organizations. Each club, in fact, had established athletic traditions beyond baseball and drew Nikkei sports aficionados when they competed for local honors. But their rivalry, Sakamoto observed, also led to uncomfortable rhetoric and tart exchanges among their devotees. Only a week into its existence, the paper warned that "Too many fans become over enthusiastic and in showing their loyalty to their club they are wont to indulge, without heed to discretion, in reckless denunciation of opposing club members and players."[37] Still, in spite of the rivalry, the two clubs were rallying points when it came to competition outside the community. Their propensity to challenge opponents, particularly those of Caucasian background, was a source of pride for the Nikkei. Both clubs participated in Seattle municipal leagues, something that most Japanese American teams in all sports rarely did. At the conclusion of the 1928 baseball season, even though the Nippons finished with a 12–17 record and the Taiyo finished at 7–9, the *Courier* seemed satisfied with the "creditable showing" of each against Caucasian opponents.[38] Both clubs also participated in athletic exchanges with similar associations in Japan as a sign of goodwill and, as such, won the blessings of the *Courier*. Athletic competition "to and from Japan," the publisher determined, "is a much wiser method of promoting international friendship than treaties or pacts."[39] Referring to his own club as "mediators" between Japan and the United States through sports, Taiyo president George Okada, in 1933, associated athletics with "high moral character." The actions of the Taiyo and Nippon Athletic Clubs reflected, in many ways, the principles set forth by Sakamoto in how he envisioned the Nisei future in America. Though at times, the competitive spirit of their athletes and supporters deviated from their ideals, both clubs provided a model of integrity and strength by which others who came to participate in the Courier League were expected to follow. Within a few years, Nisei "clubs" that participated in the league started to appear in other King and Pierce County townships. By the mid-1930s, in such places as

Auburn, Eatonville, Fife, Kent, and Tacoma, Nisei baseball teams, along with those from other sports, participated on a year-round basis as members of the Courier League. Indeed, by that time, on an annual basis, athletic clubs from beyond the Puget Sound area also visited Seattle.

The Pacific Northwest Baseball Tournament, initially referred to as the Silver Cup Tournament, was the Courier League's most popular event. In step with the principles of patriotism, the first event took place in 1931 and was held annually on the Fourth of July weekend. By then, the paper was already in its fourth year of operation, subscriptions had reached well beyond Seattle proper, and its readership lived in Nikkei communities throughout the Pacific Northwest. Given that half of the paper was devoted to sports news, to no one's great surprise, teams from Oregon and Idaho, as well as those from rural eastern Washington, anxiously sent in their applications to request participation in the tournament. "Thousands of Japanese Americans from Washington, Oregon, and Idaho came by car, train, and boat to the tournament," wrote Gail Nomura. "It was the biggest social gathering of the year for the Japanese American community of the Pacific Northwest."[40] Playing on a variety of fields, largely public parks and high schools, out-of-town players most often stayed in the homes of relatives and friends. In other cases, fans opened up their own dwellings to the players. In this realm, Nomura's claim that the tournament was a "social gathering" was accurate.

Through the years, players wearing uniforms with such names as "Fife Nippons," "Wapato Nippons," and "White River" flocked to compete in the tournament. Other clubs like the powerful Asahis from Vancouver, British Columbia, and the heralded Taiyo Athletic Club were also regular participants. Of course, postgame social gatherings did not preclude the intense competitive spirit that accompanied the games. Indeed, local Seattle baseball aficionados, as expressed in the *Courier*, made no secret of the high estimation of their own clubs. In 1934, for instance, journalist Bill Hosokawa wrote, "Why according to scores are Puget Sound teams superior to aggregations from other districts or are they? Is the brand of ball in other districts of a lower standard?"[41] Many of those teams from those "other districts" came from Oregon, such as the ones from Portland.

◆ ◆ ◆

In the eyes of some, by the mid-1920s, Portland's smaller population—301,815, compared with Seattle's approximate 365,000 residents—gave the appearance of a subpar status to its neighbor in the north, where ball of a "lower standard" might be played.[42] Indeed, Gordon B. Dodds, the author of the definitive study on Oregon history, in reference to the region's two largest cities, claimed that ". . . the Alaska gold rush, and defense industries in the First World War enabled Seattle to attain regional primacy over Portland by 1920."[43] But Portland and its Nikkei residents had much to tout. Nestled along the Willamette River where it meets the Columbia, as early as the first decade of the twentieth century, Portland was home to a small community of Issei who had gravitated there to work in the lumber industry. By 1928, in a community called Nihonmachi that sat along the Willamette River waterfront near downtown Portland, the Nikkei maintained a bustling neighborhood of small shops, hotels, and other services. Like their counterparts in Seattle, the Portland Japanese inhabitants, too, had a newspaper, called the *Oshu Nippo*. Shinsaburo Ban, a labor contractor, started the paper in 1906. Three years later, Toyoji Abe took over as editor, and in 1917 Iwao Oyama, an ambitious young editor from Japan, became its chief until the government shut down its operations in 1942.[44] Like James Sakamoto, Oyama's paper was primarily a one-man operation and carried the format of a contemporary newsletter. Unlike Sakamoto, Oyama, an Issei, was bent much more on reporting the news or providing announcements for Nihonmachi residents. As such, even sports coverage was much more tepid than was found in the *Courier*. Nonetheless, athletics in the Portland Nisei community and beyond were very much in evidence.

"Nearly all Nisei participated in sports. Besides the fun and competition, we met people who would become life-long friends," recalled John Murakami of his days as a youth in Portland.[45] Organized athletic activities emerged from a number of sources. At times the Japanese Association put together programs for area youth. The growing Japanese American Citizens League also sponsored basketball tournaments. But churches, too, played a role. The Buddhist church, in particular, not only boasted the largest contingent of followers, but also was critical in its capacity as a social nucleus for the Nisei. "[The church] served not only a religious function, but was also a body for discussing vocational and civic problems. In addition, it gave the Nisei a chance to get to know each other socially and to have a good time," writer Barbara Yasui observed.[46] Baseball was an imperative tool in this quest.

Though teams appeared on and off through the Issei years, it was left to Frank Fukuda, as already noted, a legendary figure in Pacific Northwest Nikkei baseball, to organize the game on a larger scale among Portland's adolescent Nisei. In 1927, he moved to Portland. While working as a principal of a language school, he came in direct contact with many of the area's Nisei, and, as he had done in

Seattle, the popular coach helped organize a number of baseball programs. Hiro Takeuchi, then a young Nisei out of the Gresham-Troutdale Japanese enclave who played for Fukuda, recalled, "Everyone respected Mr. Fukuda. He taught us important fundamentals about how to play the game and how we should conduct ourselves as gentlemen. He was a coach and a teacher and my friends and I learned a lot from him."[47] Fukuda continued to work with local baseball enthusiasts until he moved on to Wapato, Washington, in 1931.[48]

By then, baseball activity in northern Oregon was, nonetheless, sparse. Though there was much enthusiasm among the Nisei, their small population hindered development of a large-scale league akin to what was, by then, a thirty-plus-team Courier League in Seattle. Hence, to compete against other Nisei clubs, teams along the Columbia River had to branch out in search of opponents for their Sunday baseball. In this manner, the seeds for further regional networking were planted. Though some of their elders had, in earlier times, developed economic alliances, the national pastime took these contacts to a different level. These baseball connections brought metropolitan and rural residents together. On Sundays, Portland clubs inevitably planted their spikes into the turf of Gresham-Troutdale, Hood River, Salem, and even Wapato, Washington.

But not all Nisei clubs competed against one another. The Nippon Giants were the most powerful of the Portland teams. Formed in 1933, this organization took in the best Nisei talent the region had to offer. Moreover, the Giants competed in Portland's municipal city leagues, where they routinely finished high in the standings throughout the 1930s. Kats Nakayama was among the team's founders. Born in Seattle in 1906, Nakayama grew up in a region where baseball took center stage in recreation among the older Nisei. Indeed, Nakayama was all of twenty-two years old at the time that the famed Courier League came into existence. As such, he had ample opportunity to hone his baseball skills amid a community that actively pursued the national pastime. In 1933, with work scarce in a Depression-enveloped Puget Sound region, he left the area and found work in a Portland grocery store.

The economic conditions, however, did not temper his appetite for baseball and, through contacts he made in his Buddhist church, Nakayama looked to recruit skilled ballplayers to form a blue-chip team. In a short time, he and his cohorts christened themselves the Nippon Giants, and for the remainder of the decade, they routinely took on strong, Caucasian teams in the Portland area. Ralph Takami, a star high school player, carried the club in its earliest years, with his pitching skills. Indeed, college scouts gravitated to the Nisei star, and nearby Oregon State College awarded him an athletic scholarship.[49]

In addition to their athletic talent, some of the Giants utilized the bilingual abilities acquired in their adolescence. As batboy to the club, Jerry Inouye recalled, "When they played Caucasian teams, the Giants would speak in Japanese to each other to send signals. They always caught the white players off guard; sometimes going over strategy right in front of the Caucasian players' face."[50] Nakayama, proud of his club's success, pointed out, "We didn't lose too many games too often."[51] When they could, the club also competed in the *Courier's* fabled Pacific Northwest Baseball Tournament. In 1936, with an undefeated record, they brought back the tourney's Silver Cup to Portland.

◆ ◆ ◆

By the mid-1930s other Nisei clubs in northern Oregon had formed. Eventually, five teams spanned the region from Salem to Hood River, along the Columbia. Though not as talented as the Giants, the newer teams were no less competitive. Moreover, they arose from different sources. In Portland, for instance, the Midgets, a name adopted in the manner of self-deprecating humor, were more than a baseball club. They began as a social organization. To be courted for membership was a matter of honor. "I was excited to be asked to join the club. I wanted very much to meet new people," remembered Jerry Inouye.[52] Athletes were among the organization's founding members and, eventually, came to form a baseball club. "Sundays became exciting during the summer. Baseball was not only fun, but it also was a way of bonding with the other Nisei," said Inouye.[53]

John Murakami was the leader of the Midgets. Born in Sherwood, Oregon, in 1919, Murakami came to Portland with his family when he was seven years old. His Issei father, involved in agriculture, never took to sports, but not so his son. "There used to be ballgames in the local park in Lake Oswego. And when my father and I went to sell produce, I used to look forward to driving past that park so I could see them playing. I just knew that when I got old enough that that is what I wanted to do," Murakami recalled.[54]

Murakami even held hopes of playing at the professional ranks until his dreams were dashed when he was sixteen. From time to time, professional scouts held well-publicized tryouts. Like so many other boys who harbored Major League dreams, Murakami participated in a 1935 exhibition of players and felt confident that he gained the notice of scouts. "I played real hard that day and then, after the game, they made us all stand in a single line as they spoke to each player," he said. With his heart pounding, his mind dared to consider the possibility of a professional career. The scout, however, scanned the player's small stature and Oriental features, and took but a second to determine Murakami's fate. "He said, 'You might as well forget it kid, you'll never play professional ball.'" The young player endured further frustration when his parents prohibited him from playing on the high school team. "I wanted to play high school ball real badly, but my parents thought that was just out of the question."[55]

Murakami found solace in the Buddhist church, where, coincidentally, he met others who shared the same passion for baseball. By the time he turned eighteen, he had expanded his baseball interests and eventually joined two of the area's more popular teams, the Oseis and the Mikados. Murakami and his brother Jumbo became blue-chip players and spurred others to compete. "Sundays was a day we looked forward to. We could participate in athletics and then socialize afterwards," said Murakami.[56] Baseball, some Nisei sheepishly admitted later, took priority over church services during those occasions when teams traveled to such spots as Hood River and Wapato. "Well, the ministers didn't like it, but it wasn't an every-week occurrence either; only once or twice in a season. I think they were willing to forgive us."[57]

As the nation struggled through the difficult depressed economy, the Portland Nikkei community found respite in the familiar confines of the national pastime. For Nisei like Murakami, who were then young adults, "the thirties was the beginning of a fun time for us. We were old enough to drive and some of us started to date," said Murakami.[58] For baseball games, Murakami gladly got behind the wheel. Using a grocery-store pickup truck as their mode of transportation, the Midgets, dressed in their flannel uniforms, weekly piled into the back for what could be up to three-hour drives. "Johnny [Murakami] was our chauffeur," claimed Jerry Inouye.[59]

In Gresham-Troutdale, on the western periphery of Portland, there existed another Nisei club that competed against the Midgets, the Fujis. Long before urban sprawl, the Gresham-Troutdale communities were largely composed of Issei farmers who not only supported an athletic club but also provided funding and resources for construction of a small baseball diamond. "We were proud of that home field," said former player Hiro Takeuchi. "We had a real home-field advantage because our ground was rougher than the other parks."[60] The young players, like Takeuchi, revered the game. "We worked real hard during the week do we could play ball on Sundays. My dad even said that baseball took priority over the farm. He loved it."[61] Like the inner-city Giants, the Fujis, too, traveled to Seattle to participate in the *Courier*'s Northwest Tournament. "It was exciting for us to go there. We were just country kids and it was a great thrill. And we never got blown out up there," Takeuchi proudly stated.

Salem, which sat about fifty miles south of Portland, also had a Nisei club active in Oregon's northern periphery. Baseball was "really the only thing [the Nisei] had going [in sports]," said Tats Yada, who, ironically, made a name for himself as a local football star. Indeed, so small was the community that some players who eventually joined the Yamatos came from twenty miles away to compete on a weekly basis. In addition to the lack of local talent in Salem proper, competition was sparse—so sparse that the Yamatos even turned to playing the inmates at the nearby state prison. The shortage of opponents dictated this move and, as Yada noted, "[we always] ended up playing there because, of course, they couldn't go on the road and play us at our field."[62]

Like the Fujis from Gresham-Troutdale, the Yamatos built their own field. "There were no stands or anything else except a backstop and a lot of space," Yada explained.[63] The Yamatos, however, got their biggest enjoyment from playing other Nisei teams to the north. Because many of the team members lived in areas far outside even medium-sized towns like Salem, the baseball games, especially against other Nisei clubs, had the added importance of networking and socializing. Yada claimed that without those baseball trips, "we'[d] been stuck in Salem. Instead, we were able to meet other Nisei and share time with them." But Yada made it clear that, socializing aside, the Yamatos were there "to win." In 1937, they did exactly that when they completed that season in first place and brought to their small farming community the Portland Japanese Association Baseball League Tournament trophy.[64]

The Japanese people of Hood River were even more isolated than those in Salem. Though the community's founders sought to create a close-knit agricultural colony, like that found in central California's Yamato enclave, the reality was much different. The heavily forested region, rugged terrain, and unsettled weather through much of the year made it difficult for the region's Nikkei to regularly come together. Nonetheless, the Issei elders formed farming cooperatives and developed language schools to enrich their Nisei youngsters on Japanese culture. Sport also tied the loosely knit community together and, in 1935, young Nisei adults formed the region's first Nisei athletic club. Ray "Chop" Yasui took the lead in creating a baseball squad. "Everybody enjoyed our teams because of him. He chattered, kept everybody loose, and joked with the fans," recalled star pitcher Kay "Schoolboy" Kiyokawa, as he was known. "Our district would have been more isolated had it not been for baseball."[65] Homer Yasui remembered, "Baseball was the biggest draw. A lot of families came together during those games."[66] Indeed, players from throughout the Hood River valley came together each Sunday to compete and enrich friendships. "Chop" Yasui also kept the club busy by scheduling games against local clubs and others, including Native Americans on the Warm Springs Reservation, sixty miles to the south, and in Ontario, which, in the 1930s, was a six hour drive to the east on the Oregon-Idaho border.

Hood River also featured some interesting baseball facilities. For instance, the club played some of its home games in a redesigned rodeo arena in nearby Parkdale. Kiyokawa recalled, "I guess the rodeo didn't go over so good, so we played baseball there instead."[67] At another time, they used the bottom of an old gravel pit for their diamond. "The city excavated a hole," said Kiyokawa. "The field was large enough, but the infield still had gravel in it. There was no turf."[68] Homer Yasui added, "It was a terrible field. But it was all that we had."[69] Kiyokawa and his teammates took everything in stride. "You erect a backstop, place the bases and play."[70]

By the late 1930s, Kay Kiyokawa was clearly the star of Nisei baseball in Hood River. Small in stature, the southpaw nonetheless stymied opponents with an assortment of pitches that became legendary throughout the Columbia region. Of his rival in Hood River, John Murakami recalled, "He threw a ball that barely came across the plate. But you could not hit that pitch. If you hit it you just flied out. He was the hardest guy to hit."[71] Jerry Inouye added, "Oh ya, 'Schoolboy' Kiyokawa was tough. In fact, Hood River always had good talent. They were farm boys. I think they were stronger than us."[72] One Gresham player, according to Kiyokawa, struck out seven straight times to the lefty, "and I still remind him of that at our golf tournaments today."[73] Kiyokawa's skill won him a scholarship to Oregon State College and, as a result of World War Two, he transferred and pitched for the University of Connecticut.

Baseball's magnetism also infected young Nisei women, many of whom were themselves competitors in the vast array of softball leagues.[74] Players who sought to exaggerate their accomplishments learned quickly that their female fans were not in the dark when it came to their own knowledge of the game. Such was the case when, in one instance, John Murakami, in an attempt to win favor with one young woman, proudly announced that he had collected three hits. "No you didn't," she responded. "You only got two hits and a fielder's choice."[75] In many respects, the baseball games were akin to modern-day dating services. The love of baseball crossed gender lines, a factor that added to the game's popularity. To say the least, females' attendance made an impression on the players. One young Portland woman, John Murakami related, "[drove] herself and her parents all the way to Wapato to see the ball games. I thought that was really something that a young woman would drive that distance."[76]

The game expanded social networks, and courtships were not bound solely to neighborhood enclaves. "Some of the Wapato guys married some of the Hood River girls. And some of the Hood River guys married some of the Ontario girls that they met at and after the games," said Kay Kiyokawa.[77] Postgame socials proved as enjoyable as the games themselves. Jerry Inoyue remembered, "Those guys in Hood River were good hosts. They always had sandwiches for us after the game."[78] Sometimes, however, the socials had awkward moments. "When our [Gresham-Troutdale] club visited Wapato, they put on a dance for us after the game. What they didn't count on was that none of us knew how to dance," said Hiro Takeuchi.[79]

Baseball's value to the Japanese of northern Oregon clearly went well beyond competition. In a region where their communities often lay distant from one another, the games brought people together for the first time. "Meeting others was the most important aspect of the game to me. For instance, without a team, we in Salem would have never gone to Hood River," said Tats Yada.[80] Kay Kiyokawa claimed, "We were close to the Gresham players. And those association[s] which began with baseball have remained through life."[81] "We [in Hood River] were country bumpkins. Coming to Portland was a wonderful and thrilling experience for me because they had taxis, buses, trolley cars, and elevators. To young men like us, this was big time," said Homer Yasui.[82] Hiro Takeuchi added, "We just loved our sports. [And] the fellowship that came from [our baseball] was really important."[83]

◆ ◆ ◆

James Sakamoto was correct. Sport did help to unify the Nikkei in the Pacific Northwest during the 1940s, and baseball was their most popular attraction. The Courier League was an enormous success in its mission to galvanize Japanese Americans and strengthened the Nikkei network from Seattle to Portland, and to the eastern fringes of Wapato, Washington, and Ontario, Idaho. The league not only provided a platform for players and teams to display their talents but also to display their patriotism by virtue of their popular Pacific Northwest Tournaments held on the Fourth of July. This was especially important for the Nisei, a generation christened to be the "bridge of understanding" between two cultures. In this realm, the practice of baseball presented one opportunity to meet this challenge and be the link that their Issei elders had envisioned. Thus, by the end of the decade, many among the Nikkei in Seattle and throughout the West believed that they had successfully positioned themselves to win favor as bona fide Americans in the eyes of open-minded Caucasians.

Their track record in education lent itself to this belief. By 1940, census records and other surveys revealed that along the West Coast, the Nisei high school graduation rate was 10 percent higher than their white counterparts.[84] Inside the classroom, they were equally impressive. Educational journals in the 1930s displayed articles that pointed to the Nisei "eagerness to learn." Said David K. Yoo of these observations, "The second generation did well in school and often won the esteem of their peers and teachers—showing the possibilities of Americanization at work."[85] This sense that they might be close to assimilation also appeared on the athletic field. Jim Yoshida, a high school sports star in Seattle, played "alongside White, Black, and Chinese teammates,"[86] wrote Paul Spickard. Said another high school student, "I always mingled freely with American children while I was in school and never encountered any difficulties. Some of my best friends were American [Caucasians]."[87]

But there were disturbing factors at play, as well. When it came to professional and economic opportunity, the Nisei were held to a different standard. "Fully credentialed Nisei education majors were virtually unemployable as teachers in the very schools in which they had excelled," said Roger Daniels.[88] In California, though, according to a Stanford University survey, some 40 percent of Nisei aspired to professional positions, but in Los Angeles by 1940, only 3 percent of men and 5 percent of women held such jobs.[89] In one remarkable instance, after having won an oratorical award in Los Angeles, the winner, a Nisei student, learned that the American Legion, which sponsored the event, opted to send the second-place winner, a Caucasian, to represent Los Angeles in the national finals.[90] Racial discrimination clearly overshadowed Nisei merit. "The second generation, who showed real signs of assimilation in dress, language, and other measures, met with much of the animosity that had been directed at their parents," said David Yoo.[91]

And, for all its success, the Nisei baseball leagues in Seattle and beyond also had challenges when it came to assimilation. For instance, though the proponents of Nisei baseball achieved their quest to better unify the entire Nikkei people, the overall hostility toward the Japanese tempered their efforts to close gaps between themselves and the mainstream community. As such, the Nisei "golden age" of baseball, owing to voluntary or involuntary reasons, was primarily a segregated game. Rarely did they compete beyond the boundaries of their race. Nor did they attain visibility beyond their own foul lines. To illustrate that point, between 1935 and 1941, the *San Francisco Chronicle,* which routinely listed box scores of approximately fifty to sixty semiprofessional and amateur teams each Sunday, reported the results of only three Nisei games within that six-year period. Much of the same also held true with the *San Jose Mercury-News* and the *Stockton Record.*[92] Frustrated with this lack of response, Japanese Americans turned to their own community papers to attain some semblance of recognition for their achievements on the ball diamond. Thus, by 1941, on many counts, their crusade to assimilate ran into a brick wall. And, sadly, for them, it could not have come at a worse time.

While the Courier League and other Nisei ballplayers throughout the West competed during the 1941 season, diplomatic tensions between Japan and the United States increased. With Europe already embroiled in battle, and Japan's alliance with the Axis powers by virtue of the 1940 Tripartite Pact already in place, most observers agreed that war in the Pacific was inevitable. This explosive chemistry had already impacted sport. Upon threat of a boycott stemming from Japan's aggressive behavior in Asia, the International Olympic Committee moved that summer's Olympic Games from Tokyo to Helsinki, Finland. The news proved a major disappointment to some Nikkei leaders, like Kenichi Zenimura, who had hoped to marshal in baseball as a sport on the Olympic roster.[93] In anticipation of military activity, leaders in the Japanese American Citizens League strongly encouraged other Nisei to adamantly display their patriotism. "The time has come upon us when we must prove ourselves as Americans," announced the organization's president, Thomas Iseri, who seemingly ignored the decade-long crusade to assimilate themselves in all walks of life.[94] The inevitable came on December 7, 1941, when Japanese bombers attacked the United States naval base at Pearl Harbor, Hawaii. The next day, President Franklin D. Roosevelt presented to Congress his declaration of war against Japan. In tiny Hood River, Oregon in the Japanese community hall that was adjacent to the gravel pit where for so many years their kin lovingly played the national pastime, a group of Issei elders were in the midst of practicing for a talent show when a policeman burst into the room. "We are at war. You Japanese shouldn't be together. Stay home," he said, according to Chiho Tomita. "So we quit the show. No more show.

Everybody confused."[95] In a matter of hours, Tomita and others learned that the government had christened a new designation for them: "enemy aliens."[96] With the attack on Pearl Harbor, the Courier League effectively came to an end, as did any semblance of normality in the lives of Japanese Americans. Indeed, for all of them, a nightmare had begun.

6

Barbed Wire Baseball

Some inland points to settle may roam
As leave they must their coastal home
The rest of us in turn will enter
The barracks at some reception center
—"We Shall Meet Again," Fusaye Obata[1]

Hey, you guys, take your [baseball]
uniforms and whatever you have.
—Robert Ohki, on the eve
of incarceration, 1942[2]

In the days that followed December 7, 1941, many in Japanese American communities were somber and anticipated that evacuation orders might soon arrive. Since the attack on Pearl Harbor, rumors abounded about what might happen to them. Those who knew anything about the current military leadership in the West felt unease about those who sat at the top. John L. DeWitt, the unassuming lieutenant general and head of the Fourth Army, whose held a low level of respect among his peers, commanded the region from his post at the Presidio in San Francisco. Since the Pearl Harbor attack, DeWitt was a picture of uncertainty and routinely issued curfew orders based more on rumors than on hard evidence. Indeed, DeWitt's erratic management style "was a headquarters at which confusion rather than calm reigned, and that the confusion was greatest at the very top."[3] Throughout January, the general's paranoia also was a microcosm of the events occurring outside his Presidio headquarters. Mainstream newspapers, political operatives, and Caucasian community leaders acted similarly, and some even argued that a Japanese "fifth column" operated in the country's western region. As hysteria increased, they lobbied strongly for federal action to corral possible saboteurs. In this uneasy environment, DeWitt and other like-minded military associates deliberated for the sole purpose of convincing the president and congressional members that all ethnic Japanese in the West were a national security risk. United States citizenship, argued DeWitt, carried no weight. "A Jap's a Jap. . . . You can't change him by giving him a piece of paper," the general charged.[4]

◆ ◆ ◆

Leaders in the Japanese communities, particularly the Issei, largely recognized the inevitability of their fate. In anticipation of federal crackdowns, many destroyed artifacts and keepsakes that provided cherished memories of their heritage. Along with a Japanese flag, "Papa," recalled Jeanne Wakatsuki Houston in her book *Farewell to Manzanar*, ". . . burned a lot of papers too, documents, anything that might suggest he still had some connection with Japan."[5] Nisei, on the other hand, clung to their evaporating hope that citizenship might save them from the peril their elders faced. To that end, at every instance, they exhibited their patriotism to anyone who wished to listen. "We are loyal to the American flag, but race hatreds are being stirred up in a fascist pattern," announced Larry Tajiri in Los Angeles.[6] In the immediate days after Pearl Harbor, the Japanese American Citizens League's Los Angeles chapter even reached out to Franklin D. Roosevelt for his then "fair treatment" of their circumstances.[7] In a clear case of denial, Nisei there declared that "Our faith that American sportsmanship and tolerance would triumph over hysteria and mob action in a time of war has been justified in the calm and considerate treatment given to American citizens of Japanese ancestry."[8] In further attempts to display their loyalty, the Nisei sponsored various civic programs, such as "Defense" bowling tournaments, to collect money for American troops.[9] Paul Uyemura, director of the JACL in Los Angeles, urged Nisei there to contribute in any manner they could. "Don't be a slacker. Let's all of us not in the ranks do our share to help Uncle Sam," he stated.[10]

In Seattle, James Sakamoto, the stalwart devotee of Nisei patriotism, saw both his beloved *Seattle Japanese American Courier* and the sports leagues that he sponsored come to an end in January 1942. Since 1928, athletics had played a large role in the organization's popularity, drawing thousands of Nisei from throughout the Pacific Northwest to the hundreds of rosters that existed on a year-round basis. More important, Sakamoto and his associate journalists, many of whom acquired invaluable experience while with the *Courier,* never lost track of the working principles behind their support of athletics: unity and patriotism. That this display of their virtues on the baseball diamonds, basketball courts, and other athletic venues seemed lost to the mainstream at a time of crisis was greatly disappointing. Instead, the larger presses in their area and throughout the West greeted them with columns that called to attention their race in lieu of their citizenship. Earl Warren, then attorney general of California and who, in later years gained fame as a champion for civil rights during his days as Chief Justice of the U.S. Supreme Court, in January 1942 believed that with Nisei, "by and large there is more potential danger" to American national security.[11] In another case, historian Roger Daniels revealed that the County Supervisors Association of California pushed forward a resolution to place all Japanese living in the United States into "concentration camps under the supervision of the federal government."[12] In Portland, Oregon, the city council gave its full support to this California position.[13] But not all non-Japanese were in lockstep with sentiments to incarcerate the Nikkei. Writing for the *Bainbridge Review*, a small daily on Bainbridge Island in Puget Sound near Seattle, Walt Woodward, the paper's editor, wrote in his column "Plain Talk," "These Japanese Americans of ours haven't bombed anybody. In the past they have given every indication of loyalty to this nation. They have sent, along with our boys, their own sons . . . into the United States Army. . . . Let us so live in this trying time so that when it is all over, loyal Americans can look loyal Americans in the eye with the knowledge that together, they kept the Stars and Stripes flying high."[14]

James Sakamoto, on the other hand, took a different approach. As one of the leaders of the Japanese American Citizens League, to display his allegiance to the union, he adopted a position of cooperation with the curfew. Indeed, in the months leading to Pearl Harbor, the editor pressed harder the issue of loyalty and, with JACL sponsorship, lobbied for "Americanism Day" programs.[15] Following the attack on Pearl Harbor, Sakamoto knew that the sunset of the *Courier* was before him. In his remaining issues, pleas for tolerance gave way to statements of super patriotism. Nothing helped.

A number of Nisei resisted General DeWitt's curfew, such as Minoru Yasui, an attorney from Hood River, Oregon, whose older brother was Raymond "Chop" Yasui, a catalyst in advancing area baseball. Like Gordon Hirabayashi in Seattle, Minoru Yasui challenged the constitutionality of the curfew and spent nearly a year in solitary confinement. Along with Hirabayashi, Yasui's case reached the U.S. Supreme Court, where the justices held for the government on grounds that the curfew was a "measure necessary" for the protection against sabotage.[16] The High Court's decision in the Hirabayashi case was particularly revealing. A unanimous court held that "military necessity" justified the use of the curfew and, in effect, validated the executive order. Among the reasons that Chief Justice Harlan Stone viewed the Japanese in America as potentially capable of "espionage and sabotage" was his perception, based on government briefs, that there had been "relatively little social intercourse between [them] and the white population."[17] Stone's position, and that of the High Court, ultimately eroded any hope that the existence of America's concentration camps might soon come to an end.

The Nikkei community was, in fact, the portrait of a dual existence: an isolated enclave that struggled to find balance between the Japanese spirit drawn from its past and an unconditional duty to display its loyalty to the United States. In certain respects, the "bridge of understanding" concept, practiced initially in the late 1920s and designed to, in part, temper Caucasian concerns and ignorance about Japanese culture, ironically worked against them. Never fully accepted by the mainstream and, indeed, shunned by many of its leaders and laws, their isolated existence ultimately doomed them at a time most critical in their years in the United States.

Japanese American baseball in this period exemplified the Nikkei conundrum. Designed to give its youth an opportunity to play the national pastime in a secure and controlled environment, leaders of their leagues rarely omitted any display that spoke to American patriotism. They even held tournaments on the Fourth of July to help trumpet their sense of loyalty. Hence, their sense of duty to the United States was never in doubt. Unfortunately, only these leaders, aficionados in the stands, and the Nikkei press saw these displays and fully grasped the meaning and purpose of the "bridge" concept. Thus, apart from a few teams and players, the entire structure of Nikkei baseball existed in virtual isolation from the very group with whom they hoped to someday fuse.

◆ ◆ ◆

All efforts to display their patriotism proved fruitless. "Fair treatment" aside, Roosevelt gave in to proponents of evacuation and signed the presidential mandate to bring that about. Ironically, one of the rationales that led to Japanese incarceration involved baseball. As the federal authorities pondered the extent of evacuation, John H. Tolan, a congressman from California, led a series of West Coast hearings taking testimony from officials and citizens about their security concerns. With General DeWitt pressing for a mass evacuation to include enemy aliens from Germany and Italy, along with the Japanese, Tolan's committee to investigate "National Defense Migration," following mid-February hearings held in Los Angeles, Portland, San Francisco, and Seattle, revealed the overwhelming anti-Japanese sentiments by those cities' authorities. Among the most compelling arguments to single out the Japanese occurred when, in San Francisco, attorney Chauncey Tramutolo presented a scenario to the committee where he pointed out that should the government incarcerate parents of famous athletes, like the DiMaggios, it would have a negative impact on troops. "To evacuate [people like the DiMaggios] would . . . present . . . a serious situation. Many of the people affected by the existing order have boys and girls in the armed forces. . . . I believe that it would be destructive and have a tendency to lower morale . . . ," Tramutolo insisted.[18] While the Japanese in the United States, too, by 1941 had an extensive baseball history and other "American" activities to attest to their assimilation, none of that made it into the proceedings' dialogue. To Bill Hosokawa, the hearings exhibited a classic dual standard. "Literally and figuratively, the Nisei had no Joe DiMaggio whose baseball's brilliance all but obliterated the fact of his Italian immigrant heritage. No one would dream of suspecting Joe DiMaggio's father, much less the great Yankee Clipper himself, of disloyalty toward the United States even though the elder DiMaggio was an alien," wrote Hosokawa. He added, "Unlike the Issei, the elder DiMaggio had the privilege of naturalization. Up to 1941 he had not chosen to exercise it."[19] More concisely, Roger Daniels pointed out, "For Europeans, guilt was individual; for Asians, it was collective."[20] On February 19, 1942, President Roosevelt signed Executive Order 9066. The order gave General DeWitt—whose charge included the Western Defense Command, a vast sector that stretched from the Pacific coast to Utah—the authority to remove all ethnic Japanese from the West Coast and into parts of western Arizona. "We were ready for the worst, but hoped that there would be no evacuation," remembered Robert Ohki, who played with the Livingston Dodgers in central California. "[Then] all of a sudden they put out this order. They never warned anybody. We didn't know how long we were going to be gone."[21]

◆ ◆ ◆

In the next few months, Japanese American families grappled with both the practical matter of relocation and the trauma that accompanied questions of their loyalty. Given that in many areas they faced a limited amount of time for which to evacuate, Japanese Americans literally threw their belongings together in preparation for relocation to, in many cases, undisclosed locales. The first leg of their journeys took them to one of sixteen assembly centers, strewn largely across the Pacific Coast states and into Arizona. While some, such as those in the Los Angeles, central California, and King County in Washington State, for example, landed close to their home regions, others started their incarceration two states away. From some locales in the Pacific Northwest, evacuees were sometimes moved to the Pinedale Assembly Center near Fresno, California, which was six hundred to seven hundred miles away. Under the supervision of the newly created Wartime Civilian Control Administration (WCCA), these encampments, for the most part, were situated in county fairgrounds. Rudimentary facilities, like horse stalls in some cases, became dwellings. "It was such a God-forsaken place," recalled one resident upon her arrival to the Pinedale assembly center from her home in the White River valley of Washington state.[22] Such statements were but the tip of the iceberg. Tamie Tsuchiyama, who landed at the Santa Anita, California, Assembly Center, a converted racetrack, recalled that "most of the Nisei were extremely resentful of being 'shoved into jail.' They felt that the U.S. government had no right to 'imprison' its own citizens in 'concentration camps.'"[23] "The most bitter Nisei seemed to be those who had recently graduated from high school or had been in college when war broke out," wrote David. K. Yoo. "Older second-generation members tended to be more philosophical, having more experience with the virulence of race prejudice. . . ."[24] Though camps varied in terms of construction layout and size, their consistency was a much greater commonality. Bill Hosokawa, who found himself in the Puyallup, Washington, assembly center called "Camp Harmony," observed the U.S. Army's own description of these sites: "Physically, all Assembly Centers are more ideally suited for troop use than they were for the housing of families."[25] In some cases, like at the Santa Anita and Tanforan, California, sites, new residents found themselves in structures that were not only not well suited for families, but better suited for livestock.[26]

Created largely to monitor the evacuation, the WCCA came under the watchful eyes of Karl R. Bendetsen, a strong proponent of internment and ally of General De Witt. Tom Clark, later to serve as an associate justice on the U.S. Supreme Court, who then worked in the Justice Department, assisted Bendetsen in organizing the process. To make strategically sensitive areas "Jap-free," assembly centers were designed to serve as temporary stations, while the blueprint for more "permanent" structures lay on the table of government authorities.[27] As the Japanese settled into their new surroundings, the WCCA slowly transferred its authority to another newly created government body: the War Relocation Authority (WRA). The WRA, more beholden to civilian authority than was the WCCA, eventually remained the sole authority of the center and for concentration throughout the war.

◆ ◆ ◆

For all the animosity aimed at the Nikkei, there were instances where those sympathetic to their plight rose above the fray. Sport often afforded some Samaritans an opportunity to exhibit their courage. For instance, evacuation deadlines varied in different locales, and in some cases even cut into the early part of baseball season. In the Bainbridge Island community, some did take heed of Walt Woodward's earlier call for tolerance and sought to ease the plight of their neighbors of Japanese descent, with whom they had been friends and associates. At Bainbridge High School, the Spartans started their 1942 campaign only days before Nisei students were scheduled to evacuate their homes. With a handful of them on the squad, Coach Walter "Pop" Miller started all six Nisei boys. "[I]t was their last appearance before being evacuated. How they wanted to leave with a victory! And how their fellow teammates wanted to win for them," wrote Woodward.[28] Paul Ohtaki, a resident there, recalled, "Coach Miller didn't care about the score. He just wanted all of the Japanese Americans to play their last game for Bainbridge and enjoy themselves. We lost 15–2, but Pop Miller's kindness will be remembered."[29]

In the southern California community of Arroyo Grande in San Luis Obispo County, the Nisei received valuable assistance from Vard Loomis. Loomis, whose family had befriended Japanese Americans through their agricultural business operations, enjoyed the company of his neighbors. Elected as 1931 class president at Stanford University and a star pitcher on the baseball team, Loomis returned to Arroyo Grande after graduation and, upon assuming his role in the family business, joined the local Nisei baseball club and coached for the remainder of the decade, until the evacuation. Though this relationship made him a target from resentful Caucasians in the days following Pearl Harbor, Loomis openly looked after the Nisei interests, even to the point of caring for one disabled Issei who could not immediately join his family at the assembly center.[30]

◆ ◆ ◆

Adjustment to their new surroundings was not an easy chore. First, as government officials saw the incarceration as a "military necessity," none were prepared to announce when that "necessity" might come to an end. In essence, for all anyone knew at that time, incarceration could conceivably last a lengthy period.

Also, as difficult as it was to organize up to eighteen thousand plus in some centers, as was the case at the Santa Anita Race Track, once they had settled in, most had little to occupy themselves. "'Time is on My Hands' could well be tabbed the theme song of about 75 per cent of the Japanese and Japanese-Americans quartered at the North Portland assembly center now that action at the evacuees' home has settled to a more even keel," reported the *Portland Oregonian* in May 1942.[31] According to Emil Sandquist, director of the center, the sparse number of jobs rendered "better than 1200 [evacuees] with not much to do."[32] Between monitoring the movement of some 120,000 people, preparing livestock facilities for human habitation, and making arrangement for center bureaucracies, little thought had initially been given to resident activities. But, trying as it was, the tenacious Nikkei took it upon themselves to create a livable circumstance in the midst of the most difficult crisis they had experienced during their existence in the United States.

Almost immediately, journalists among the evacuees launched center newspapers. Though they were, in reality, largely newsletters, the information they dispersed created a sense of community among the newcomers. With the blessings of WCCA officials, the papers provided information about everything from camp rules to messages designed to raise morale. Residents turned to such center papers as the *(Merced Center) Mercedian*, the *Pinedale Center Logger*, the *Portland Evacuazette*, among others. In some centers, including Stockton, California, professional journalists such as Fred Oshima, a veteran with the *San Francisco Nichibei Shimbun*, took charge of the center's *El Joaquin*. In other instances, however, freelance writers and students saw these jobs as apprenticeships for future careers. The papers' creators worked tirelessly to cover activities at their respective centers. The most frequently read stories involved competitive sports.

Though incarcerated, detainees' enthusiasm for sport remained high. In fact, their circumstances increased their interest in athletics. "Once we got into camp, everything fell into place," remembered Fred Kishi.[33] "We had to get something going," added Yeichi Sakaguchi.[34] In each center, those who had organized community athletics during the 1930s gravitated toward each other for the purpose of requesting equipment, laying out facilities, and creating teams and leagues to both satisfy their competitive appetites and temper the trauma of evacuation. The latter of those goals was the least difficult to attain.

At the Portland Assembly Center, Ralph Takami, a Nisei whose credentials as a former player at Oregon State College had earned him local prominence, directed the athletic programs. By mid-May, the new residents had converted former fairground parking lots into baseball diamonds and three games had "been in progress simultaneously."[35] That same month, two states away at the Pinedale Assembly Center near Fresno, another Oregon baseball legend, Ray "Chop" Yasui, given limited recreational space, initiated an ambitious men's softball program that featured thirty clubs in three divisions and competed on a daily basis. In June, Yasui's program added twenty-two women's clubs.[36] In other centers, by the late spring, evacuees quickly organized baseball and/or softball leagues, and in many cases, popular personalities of the past took charge. Along with Ralph Takami and Ray "Chop" Yasui, sportswriters, like reporter Fred Oshima of the *Nichei Bei* and baseball icon Kenji Zenimura, came onboard to help in the construction of athletic programs.[37] "Selling" the game, as portrayed by the Fresno Assembly Center's *Grapevine,* was not a problem. "Baseball is not just another game to the average American," wrote "Dusty" in his "Diamond Dust" column. "It is a source of great enjoyment to millions of Yankees, whether actual players or morely [sic] kibitzers."[38] Ironically, the columnist, who was an internee, closed with a patriotic theme commonly found in the writings of other like-minded Nisei. "A baseball leader," he wrote "in any community in the country is always respected as an American because it is one sport that grows with this country."[39]

At the Stockton Assembly Center, Oshima utilized his journalistic skills in the marketing of athletics. As with other center newspapers, coverage of athletics commonly took up half of the news reported in the journals' four to six pages. To that end, not only did these papers provide information and solace for the many bewildered and demoralized evacuees, their often ambitious efforts to help organize activities, especially sports, were augmented by the colorful descriptions they used in reporting these events. Incarceration and civil liberties as topics of discussion fell by the wayside in lieu of "hot title" races designed to interest the captives. "Tonight's game between the Yogolais and Chains is of great importance to them as far as championship hopes to them are concerned," reported the *Evacuazette* at the Portland Assembly Center.[40] The rhetoric Nisei journalists then used to describe the games they covered was not simply hyperbole but a means by which to help market the contest. To be sure, when such papers as the *Stockton El Joaquin* reported that "2000 fanatic fans" attended a July 4th all-star game, it is likely that reporters like Oshima accurately depicted both the numbers and atmosphere.[41] Reporters at these sites, themselves incarcerated, recognized the importance afforded by the diversion of sports. As such, these journalists understood the need for momentary respite from the difficult circumstances they and their fellow residents faced in their new lives behind barbed wire.

In the limited space of the sports sections, the attention given to baseball often overshadowed the coverage of other spring and summer sports, such as men's and women's softball, basketball (often played on dirt courts), and volleyball. This did not go unnoticed. Writing for *The Mercedian,* at the Merced Assembly Center, Mack Yamaguchi routinely fielded criticism that his reports favored one sport over others. The journalist, only three months into the center's existence and often scrambling to make *The Mercedian* operational, replied, "It is almost impossible to give each organization just publicity at present."[42] Even as baseball and other summer games came to their conclusion, sports programs remained "overcrowded."[43]

The *Fresno Grapevine* fielded no such complaints when it promoted an all-star game to honor Kenichi Zenimura. Everyone at the Fresno Assembly Center knew him. His longtime promotion of baseball, along with the legendary 1927 game when he competed against Babe Ruth and Lou Gehrig, won him the admiration of the Nikkei in and out of the Fresno region. Having been notified that the assembly center was closing and that all residents were being shipped out to the Gila Relocation Center in Arizona, for the purpose of raising the spirits of the glum evacuees, athletic coordinators hastily organized and all-star game that featured a testimonial to the baseball icon. "Many a fan will feel the heart-tugs, as Ken Zenimura . . . is honored this evening to bring down the curtain on his long Fresno career."[44] Zenimura, in response to his appreciative fans, was thankful "for your sincere cooperation in advancing baseball activities during the past five months."[45]

While Nikkei community leaders did the legwork to organize athletic programs at the assembly centers, they did so only in the capacity as advisors to Caucasian directors of these programs. A large factor in this stemmed from the government's belief that Japanese Americans lacked the components for true "Americanism." Karl Bendetsen, the army colonel who served as director of the Wartime Civilian Control Administration, accepted this school of thought. Though he grew up in Aberdeen, Washington, and adjacent to a Japanese enclave, Bendetsen never befriended his neighbors. Thus, in the mind of the WCCA director, the Nikkei were, in fact, a Japanese "nation" lodged in the West Coast. "They carried on their own culture; their own educational system," he argued in an interview long after the conclusion of the war. "Their Shinto religious beliefs predominated and these beliefs coupled with the isolation which arose out of the legal restrictions of the applicable laws of the U.S. and California, Oregon and Washington states then in force, combined in influence to generate a separate way of life," he determined.[46] To the colonel, the Japanese in America could not be trusted. "The ones who are giving you only lip service are the ones always to be suspected."[47] Indeed, at no time during his tenure at the WCAA did Bendesten demonstrate any semblance of fair play or justice when it came to the Japanese under his authority.

Bendetsen's impressions of Japanese Americans both translated into policy and characterized the feelings of others in charge. For many officials in the WCCA, and later WRA, who served onsite at the assembly centers and internment camps, they came into their positions with preconceived myths as a result of decades-long stereotypes and wartime hysteria, not to mention inherent prejudices, about the people to whom they would administer. Additionally, many who worked out of Washington, D.C., grew up in regions far from the West and had no working knowledge of it, let alone the people of Asian background. For these people, their notion of "Oriental" came largely from the popular Charlie Chan movies of the 1930s. Indeed, among the most sinister of villains during their childhood was Charles Middleton's "Ming the Merciless," of the famed *Flash Gordon* movies. Also, their training in government generally came from their experience in the New Deal policies of that era, not in anything we might, in contemporary times, refer to as multicultural studies. Still others earned their "stripes" in the Deep South, where their own personal prejudices might have biased them in all matters regarding people of color. As such, on many levels, the administrative personnel of these agencies came to regard the evacuees as a group that was less than "American."

Though some, like Milton Eisenhower, the first head of the WRA, had misgivings over the necessity and validity of the incarceration, and even argued that some 85 percent of the Nisei were "loyal" Americans, the director never went on record attesting to their defense as Americans, nor did he ever challenge General John L. DeWitt's condescending contention that a "Jap's a Jap."[48] He also took the remarkable position that those American citizens among the Japanese who had educational training in Japan, known as Kibei, be "repatriated" if they "[preferred] the Japanese way of life."[49] On some balance, he did suggest that President Franklin Roosevelt himself make a "strong statement" on behalf of the Nisei. Roosevelt, preoccupied with the war, never addressed the recommendation.[50]

After only about four months on the job, Eisenhower resigned and his position went to his former boss in the Department of Agriculture, Dillon S. Myer. Like others in the agency, the new director knew little about the 120,000 people who were under his charge. In his memoirs, Myer recounted, "Neither I nor most of my staff were well informed regarding the problems we faced. We lacked information about the evacuees and their history. We were generally uninformed regarding the anti-Oriental movements on the west coast and the pressures, rumors, and fears that had led to the evacuation."[51] One gets the overall impression that, at the outset, Myer and his staff ran the entire operation by the seat of their pants. In many respects, the evidence from those at the sites and in Washington bears that out. For certain, the variables that came with the aforementioned administrators were among those that affected even the athletic programs.

By the end of the summer in 1942, evacuees were ordered to leave the assembly centers and enter one of the ten concentration camps. Once there, they faced, in less than a year, a second time with which they had to re-create a community in a strange environment. At this stage they fell under the scrutiny of the WRA, endured often drastic weather patterns, and experienced an uncommon sense of geographic isolation. "All ten sites can only be called godforsaken," wrote historian Roger Daniels. "They were in places where nobody had lived before and no one has lived since."[52]

◆ ◆ ◆

At the administrative level of the War Relocation Authority, John H. Provinse played an important role. An academic who held a Ph.D. in anthropology, in the early 1930s he had served on the faculty at the University of Arizona and in several federal administrative positions elsewhere, including one in the Bureau of Indian Affairs. In 1942, Provinse joined the WRA as its chief of community management. Convinced, like his boss Dillon Myer, that the agency's base knowledge of Japanese Americans was, at best, thin, in May Provinse touted the idea of employing social scientists whose expertise included Asian culture in the United States. During the chaotic evacuation process of 1942, Myer only granted Provinse the authority to bring John F. Embree, a professional anthropologist, on board.[53] But civil disturbances at the Poston, Arizona, and Manzanar, California, camps advanced his position. In November at the Poston site, a combination of poor living conditions and frustration with the camp's bureaucracy, particularly after an incident involving the arrest of two men for the alleged beating of another, led to a general strike that effectively shut down camp operations.[54] Less than a month later at Manzanar, tensions between various factions of Issei, Nisei, and members of the Japanese American Citizens League culminated in violence that enveloped the entire encampment.[55]

As a result of these events, Provinse reiterated the need to employ more social scientists who could help carry out a policy of "no repressive" engagement with the incarcerated. The events at Poston and Manzanar convinced others at the WRA that Provinse's suggested merited immediate attention. Thus, with the blessings of Director Myer, the Community Analysis Section, armed with several more experts and assistants, under the auspices of Provinse's larger bureau, came into existence in 1943.[56] Their charge was to establish better lines of communication between the evacuees, the agency, and on-site directors. As reported by Edward H. Spicer, himself a trained anthropologist and analyst at the camps, "One of the most successful roles of [the analysts] was as participant in meetings between the camp director and his assistants and various evacuee administrative groups, such as the block managers, and evacuee committees organized for particular purposes. Here the role was not simply the reporter of information but participant in decisions affecting operations."[57]

An examination of memos and correspondence that came from analysts throughout the ten camp sites revealed not only a profile of the conditions the evacuees endured, but also directives that either came from the WRA or from on-site authorities. To be sure, many of those who ran the camps characterized their roles not only in terms of simply being overseers, but also as keepers of a camp designed to assimilate the residents. The term "Americanization" was repeatedly echoed in their reports, sometimes from the Nisei themselves, who served in operational capacities within the camps. Following a purge of those Nisei who refused to serve in the armed forces, the so-called "no, no" respondents, in a 1943 correspondence to Provinse from the Jerome camp, Al Tsukamoto wrote, "We have adopted a policy of stressing American style programs rather than suppressing the Japanese style activities. I hope that with the pro Japanese element eliminated, we will progress toward our goal of Americanization of our activities with more speed."[58]

G. F. Castleberry, project director at the Jerome camp, concurred with Tsukamoto's observations in that the segregation of pro-Japanese evacuees paved a path in the assimilation of those who remained in Jerome. But Castleberry went further and offered salaries only to those activity instructors who had training in American sports. "All judo instructors have been removed from the payroll," he wrote to his superiors.[59] Indeed, working on the premise that even the Nisei were, somehow, subpar as Americans, authorities included in their programs "educational opportunities for Americanization not only for the school children, but for the adults, as well." In the eyes of Director Myer, the mission on the camps, as indicated in his letters to members of Congress, was to increase the Nikkei sense of patriotism. "Every child in school is enrolled in classes such as American history and similar classes whose purpose is to give children knowledge and attitudes about American traditions, ideals, and backgrounds."[60]

The WRA's "Americanization" programs were employed with the presumption that its targets were not Americans to begin with. To compound the woes of the evacuees, the program's monitors lacked a practical knowledge of Japanese American life. As such, when the evacuees forwarded a list of requests, administrators were surprised at what they saw. "Heart Mountain has sent in a rather elaborate list, weighted down with sports equipment, which it claims is minimum for physical education and recreation programs, correlating the school and community program," John Provinse told his superiors.[61] "This far exceeds the allotment of athletic equipment in the preliminary minimum school list."[62] He went on to advise the agency that the JACL had earlier pressed him about "the inadequacy of recreation equipment at the various projects."[63]

WRA officials learned that sport was an activity that required no coaxing. As the bureaucrats muddled through their cumbersome efforts to establish protocols, organizers among the Japanese wasted little time before creating activities that they could start right away. As was the case in their prewar communities and assembly centers, camp newspapers took the lead. Within weeks after their arrival, the *Heart Mountain Sentinel, Rohwer Outpost,* and *Tulean Dispatch* were founded. These papers, initially used to convey agency policy, eventually expanded their operations and served as the heartbeat for those interned. Though camp newspapers rarely challenged the dictates of the WRA, they did provide general information about various matters within the camps and occasional stories about Japanese American war heroes. Because the reporters and editors of these newspapers fell outside the realm of constitutional provisions that, beyond the barbed wires, protected mainstream journalists, Nisei newspaper staff people, in recognition of their tenuous circumstances, gingerly expressed their opinions when it came to the WRA and the war itself. Reporters' opinions were less ginger when it came to their depiction of those with whom they disagreed. For instance, at the Heart Mountain, Wyoming, camp, in response to the actions of a draft resistance movement called the "Fair Play Committee," the *Heart Mountain Sentinel* described the members as "deluded youths," "warped-minded members" who "lacked both physical and moral courage."[64] While the camp newspapers operated under careful editorial guidelines when it came to the WRA itself, they expressed no such hesitancy when it came to their most popular feature: the sports section.

◆ ◆ ◆

Early historical studies of America's "concentration camps" did little or nothing to illustrate the role of sports in evacuees' lives. Some suggested that camp newspaper coverage of athletics was an "innocuous" aspect of life inside the barbed wire.[65] But to describe Japanese American sports in that fashion completely ignores their prewar athletic heritage, assembly center activities, and sports' level of importance reflected by their requests for equipment to the WRA administrators. To the evacuees, sport was not an "innocuous aspect of life"; it was an essential component to their mental and emotional survival in the camps. In the camp newspapers, only stories about their brethren at war rivaled athletics in terms of attention. Given that camps were, in effect, hastily thrown together cities where, in some circumstances, social scientist analysts describe them as "simply ghastly," sport and its coverage was prominent.[66] As the evacuees settled into their new environs by the late summer and fall of 1942, within weeks organizers among the Japanese started the process of initiating recreational activities. Announcements of meetings and sign-ups for teams appeared in the camp newspapers. Moreover, that these papers were able to advance circulations to populations of, in the case of the *Tulean Dispatch,* 18,785 new residents in such a short span of time was remarkable.

In June, at Poston, the *Chronicle* described a softball game that drew, by their estimate, 4,500 observers.[67] At Amache, though, on October 27, in an apparent oversight, WRA administrator Edward B. Marks in a letter to John Provinse wrote that at the Colorado camp he saw "no organized activities worth mentioning and no leadership." By November 18, the *Granada Pioneer* reported the existence of thirteen football teams, and sign-up for boys' and girls' basketball.[68] Interestingly, most of the football clubs were those made up of players from temperate California communities. At Arkansas, the *Rohwer Outpost* started operations in mid-October. A little more than two weeks later, sport coverage of the camps' football season took up half of the four-page paper.[69] By November 18, the paper announced that each block within the approximately 8,400-person center had a girls' volleyball team.[70] Throughout the winter of 1942–1943, as reflected in the camp newspapers, athletic activities were in abundance. While it was conceivable

Panoramic view of Tule Lake Stadium in 1944, with multiple guard towers
behind the outfield. (Courtesy of the Nisei Baseball Research Project)

that the newspapers, had they not been censored, would have expended their
coverage of war-related news, sport, it is safe to say, would have maintained a
prominent presence in the news. The basketball, football, and volleyball teams
and leagues did exist, and in great numbers. From the earliest days of each camp,
sport was a constant routine. Moreover, as they pursued the aforementioned
sports in one fashion or another, the groundwork was already being laid in advance of the most popular sport: baseball.

◆ ◆ ◆

"'King Baseball' will again take the limelight as THE summer sport," announced
Bill Hata in his sports column in the *Topaz Times News Daily* in mid-April 1943.[71]
In anticipation of a season with many participants, camp officials announced the
construction of twelve baseball diamonds in various areas around the camp.[72] At
other sites, baseball got a similar enthusiastic reception. At Jerome, Arkansas,
by April 28, twelve teams were ready for competition. A short time later, the

The Guadelupe (Calif.) Nisei baseball club. Champions of the Tule Lake Camp, 1944.
Tule Lake, California. (Courtesy of the Nisei Baseball Research Project)

Jerome baseball activities, as reported by the more developed *Rohwer Outpost*, carried the potential to "draw 2,000 to 4,000 for each game" in an encampment whose census was approximately 8,500. In Rohwer, at the outset of May, six baseball clubs started play.[73] Three weeks later, five more teams joined the new camp league.[74] At the northern California Tule Lake site, in mid-May the *Daily Tulean Dispatch* enthusiastically reported "Tule Lake's baseball picture, softball, . . . takes in over 100 teams and approximately a thousand participants. Utilizing some twenty softball fields and two well-conditioned hardball diamonds, league games are held every night and hardball games are held all day Sunday."[75] And at the Minidoka camp in Idaho, baseball organizers presented to WRA officials plans "to organize a baseball team to represent the project in semi-pro out-of-project games." The government analyst in attendance noted that the evacuees committee was made up of "former outstanding diamond stars of the Pacific northwest."[76] An apparent rejection of the proposal did not douse their baseball fever, as the report noted the announcement of a May commencement for a 1943 season.[77] Arguably the most ambitious campaign to initiate a baseball season took place at the Gila River, Arizona, camp where the legendary Kenichi Zenimura, from Fresno baseball fame, organized a thirty-two-team league.[78]

But baseball activities did not come about without great effort. First of all, at some camps, such as in Rohwer, WRA officials did not initially envision any athletic fields, and believed a "good question would be where Japanese Americans [can find] land to place fields."[79] Thus evacuees, whose capacity to organize had earlier been questioned by many WRA officials, with little support took it upon themselves to build the diamonds. At most of the sites, the landscapes were hardly suitable for the national pastime. Uneven terrain, sagebrush, and rocky soil greeted those who, upon their arrival, hoped to organize baseball leagues. For instance, though at their previous site at the Merced County Fairgrounds, where a decent, grass-filled diamond existed, complete with covered stands, no such luxuries were seen at the Amache camp. "We had to make the baseball diamond and there were no stands, no seats, no nothing, so the crowd just stood around the field and watched the game," recalled Fred Kishi.[80] Fields were generally carved out of firebreaks, rarely had backstops, and sprouted little or no grass. At the Poston, Arizona, camp, one government analyst who, in astonishment, guessed that "there are more participants in sports in Poston than in other cities of this size," observed "playing fields are in the firebreaks with makeshift backstops made from pieces of boards and fence wire."[81] Just south of Poston, at the extremely arid Gila River encampment, the venerable Kenichi Zenimura, impatient with the WRA's cumbersome red tape, took it upon himself to build a ball diamond. In a nearby firebreak, he "diverted water from a laundry room to nourish grass for an outfield. He built stands from wooden poles taken from the enclosing fences. [And] he poured flour to make chalk lines."[82] By 1943, "Zenimura Field" was ready for play and tended to regularly. "I remember watching this little old brown guy watering down the infield with this huge hose," said actor Pat Morita. "He used to have his kids dragging the infield and throwing out all the rocks. Jeez, I was glad I wasn't them. They worked like mules."[83]

Uniforms, in the absence of retail outlets, were sparse. While many wore the outfits that they had donned in their prewar leagues, others employed their creative skills to stitch together new jerseys. As related in Kerry Yo Nakagawa's profile on Japanese American baseball, a Tule Lake resident said, "The pants were potato sacks that came from the farm. They were heavy cotton, bleached white. Two or three ladies sewed them on for us and they looked real professional."[84]

There and in other instances, ballplayers took materials from their government-issued mattresses and converted them into baseball jerseys and pants.[85]

Bats and balls, too, were in short order and a source of great frustration. At Topaz, despite an enthusiastic April 15, 1943 announcement from organizers about the creation of a baseball season, owing to "lack of equipment," games did not commence until July 27.[86] Similar circumstances occurred at other camps, whereby actual play was not reported until a month or two after the initial announcements. As frustration mounted, the WRA stumbled in its attempts to explain their lack of preparation. For instance, following complaints that baseball equipment requested in February 1943 had not yet arrived to selected camps by July, Dillon Myer awkwardly replied, "The fault lies not necessarily with the WRA, but rather with the lack of clarification [in the original order] and the absence of materials that could be used in the construction [of equipment]."[87] Others, like Edward B. Marks, who had earlier stated his doubts about the organizational skills of the Japanese evacuees, in May 1943 sheepishly admitted to his own bureau's oversights. "We recognize that lack of recreational equipment had handicapped the development of the recreation programs, not only at Heart Mountain but also at the other centers. At the same time the evacuees have shown a great deal of ingenuity in creating resources of their own and a lively program is being carried out at all the centers," he wrote.[88] At the core of the WRA's inability to efficiently run camp recreational activities was, as earlier noted, the ignorance of decision makers when it came to a firm understanding of the Japanese Americans as a people. The surprise that administrators exhibited when they encountered the Nikkei enthusiasm for sports simply illuminated this lack of knowledge. And it was, in fact, reflected in their planning. "The recreational program had not been instigated in a formal overall [WRA] plan," admitted Charles F. Ernst, director of the Topaz camp. Indeed, Ernst, clearly caught off guard, could hardly believe that "one person, two or three maintenance workers [had] organized approximately sixty baseball teams utilizing a completely volunteer resident leadership."[89]

Apart from the "ingenuity" of the evacuees themselves, and the seemingly hapless WRA, several religious groups, along with pacifist organizations, offered help and supplies to help temper the plight of incarcerated Japanese. Along with books, blankets, and other items, groups like the Women's Christian Fellowship collected athletic equipment for the various camps.[90] In fact, as early as February, church-affiliated organizations send out notices for "equipment and supplies

Jerome Camp. Jerome, Arkansas. The batter, George Omachi, went on to become a Major League scout. (Courtesy of the Nisei Baseball Research Project)

[that are] urgently needed in Japanese Relocation Centers."[91] Groups like these often met with evacuees themselves, "assessed the needs of the internees and cobbled together efforts to fulfill them."[92] By mid-summer of 1943, months after slogging through problems associated with the WRA, and following their own hard work to continue a time-honored practice, this time behind barbed wire, hurlers finally threw the first pitches.

Internment, or barbed wire, baseball was a combination of competitive and spirited play, entertainment, tradition, gambling, challenging environments, therapy, and unity. Camps were generally divided into blocks and, in most cases, entire prewar communities remained intact. As such, players who had competed in 1930s Nisei baseball either stayed together as teams or fused with players from leagues with whom they had earlier competed, a factor that brought comfort. "These players and [or] team knew each other practically from the day we were born. We went to church together, we played on Saturdays together, [and] we went to high school together," said Fred Kishi of the Dodgers from Livingston,

California, who found themselves competing at Amache.[93] Though the reported attendance was prone to exaggeration, photos of the games, nonetheless, reveal extraordinary turnouts for the contests played in firebreaks on the periphery of the camps. Spectators, some for want of entertainment, crowded around the ball diamonds that were in areas "just cleared [of] sagebrush" that "was equivalent to a little league stadium," said Kenji Kawaguchi of Seattle, who played his baseball at the Minidoka camp in Idaho.[94] An abundance of spectators, sometimes making up one-fourth of the entire encampment, attended the makeshift fields or sat on small dunes at self-proclaimed "Yankee Stadiums."[95] Attending a game at the Minidoka site, one government analyst observed about the spectators, "The crowd was very enthusiastic and noisy. There were different degrees of familiarity shown towards the players. Some of the players were addressed by their first names or nicknames. The older players were usually addressed in more formal terms, such as 'good one, Atsukata San!'"[96] Players were not unaware of the nicknames with which baseball aficionados and camp journalists had christened them, many of which had their origins in prewar leagues. But, considering that the evacuees came from various locales, the degree of familiarity and sensitivities sometimes caught spectators by surprise. Mack Yamaguchi, from Livingston, on the rare occasion when a public address system was available, in the interest of entertainment, had a propensity to dress up the names of players. But, in one instance, after referring to Sam Muto, as "Sad Sam," a name he took from a popular San Francisco Seals player at that time, at the game's conclusion, Muto let out some steam and, with some aggression, told Yamaguchi that "he didn't like that a bit."[97] Muto made such an impression that Yamaguchi, a writer for the camp's *Irrigator* newspaper, never again referred to the player by that name.[98] Of course, these types of sensitivities and competitiveness also, at times, led to fights. Block, regional, and personal rivalries were as rampant behind barbed wire as they had been in their prewar leagues. Referring to the players they saw as being "testy," in mid-July 1944, only a few weeks into the season, the *Granada Pioneer* reported that "things get somewhat out of hand and usually end up with fists flying."[99] In fact, it should be noted that by 1944, those who engaged in brawls were not the young men of the camp, many of whom had left for military service or off-site work camps, but players well past their thirties. At the Tule Lake Center, tensions rivaled those found at the other camps. "We weren't on very good terms," said Bill Matsumoto of the grudges between Californians and evacuees from the Pacific Northwest. "More than one time we [as players] got chased out of the ballpark because the fans got so carried away. The cardinal rule was that we would talk back to the fans." The argumentative exchanges often took place over close plays and, at times, some aggressive fans "would come after you with bats. There were times we just had to go home and run like hell."[100]

While games between the evacuees themselves drew great attention and illuminated their tremendous competitiveness, contests that featured camp "all-star" squads against Caucasian squads ignited a sense of ethnic spirit. At Minidoka, in a May 1943 game in which a white team made up largely of schoolteachers faced the evacuees, though the final resulted is not written in the report, the government analyst who observed the game made sure to describe the combatants as "the Niseis and 'all-American' boys."[101] The analyst added an estimation of some 2,500 to 3,000 in attendance in a game threatened by rain showers. Nonetheless, the spectators "watched the game very attentively and with great enthusiasm."[102] At other camps, like Rohwer, "Kango" Kunitsuga, who monitored baseball at his and other camps, compared Nisei baseball skills with that of Caucasians. "Minidoka's all-star team has slaughtered two outside semi-pro teams and expects to enter the annual Idaho state semi-pro tournament," he wrote. He went on to point out that the Tule Lake internees had beaten a Klamath Falls, Oregon, semipro team, 16–0, and promptly concluded that "the record speaks for itself."[103] Kunitsuga's spirited columns, it might be noted, undoubtedly had the support of Fred K. Oshima, his sports editor at the *Outpost* who, in his days at the *Nichei Bei* in San Francisco, had been a crusader for Nisei athletics.

By the summer of 1944, as Allied forces made great strides in the war that, in turn, lessened domestic tensions following the paranoid reactions over the Pearl Harbor attack, WRA officials relented to the evacuees' request to leave their encampments to compete in baseball games against teams from other camps. To be sure, Nisei athletes did occasionally compete against teams outside the camps. But this happened on a very limited basis and with communities that were local to the camps. The baseball organizers at the Amache and Gila River camps, however, participated in one of the most extensive trips in this realm. To be sure, baseball trips had been common in their prewar community life. But, these were brief holiday weekend contests and not under armed guard. Moreover, these trips represented for many of the evacuees, for the first time, first-hand knowledge of teams and leagues at camps other than their own. "We didn't know how the teams or competition were in the other internment centers," said Fred Kishi.[104]

In August 1944, a team of "all-stars" from the Colorado camp embarked upon a nearly month-long road trip that included stops at Gila River and Poston.[105] In spite of their unbridled enthusiasm, the Kenichi Zenimura–led host team proved too much for the visitors, as the Amache squad lost all eight contests under the hot sun at Zenimura Field.[106] Leaving Gila River at the end of the month, the team stopped at the Poston site for an additional eight games, where they fared better and won five before they returned "home."[107] "The ballplayers would usually travel in small groups of five or six so that we would not create attention," recalled Howard Zenimura, who added that they traveled on Greyhound buses. "None of the citizens of the different towns and cities we passed through paid us much attention."[108] These exchanges took place with other camps on and off through the following year and, ironically, concluded with a Tule Lake team competing at the Topaz camp; these games occurred only days after the United States dropped atomic bombs on two Japanese cities.[109]

Inside the camps, as baseball contests were met with enthusiasm and competitive play, the teams and leagues often experienced a depletion of talent. Though in many cases, internment baseball captured the spirit of the game as it was played in their prewar life, it did not necessarily represent the most skilled players among the Nisei. A number of players, including Fred Kishi, a standout athlete from Livingston, California, less than a year after their arrival at the camps joined the military. "By June 1943, I was in military intelligence school in Maryland," said the ballplayer.[110] Others, like college students, were permitted to leave and complete their education at schools outside the western military zone, while farm workers got temporary respites from incarceration to help fill a need for field hands.[111] Still others attained "leave clearances." Approximately seventeen thousand evacuees, after being thoroughly vetted, left their respective centers to settle in cities including Chicago, Salt Lake City, and Denver.[112] That many of the "leave clearance" players were between the ages of eighteen and thirty, prime years for athletes, watered down the talent level found in the leagues. Considering the scope of the impact internment had on the Nisei, from his post at the Rohwer camp, "Kango" Kunitsuga lamented in the *Outpost* that "the mass evacuation of Japanese from the west coast cut short many brilliant sports careers of Nisei athletes. It seems that just when the Nisei were hitting the sports pages on the big dailies, the catastrophe hit them and hit 'em hard it did."[113]

The aforementioned drawbacks, along with the continued struggles for equipment and financial support, continued into 1945 and hindered the life of "King Baseball" in several camps. Also, not every camp had the likes of a Kenichi Zenimura, whose ambition, legacy, and skills of persuasion won him the latitude to build a baseball program that was arguably the strongest in the camps. For all the affection that Japanese Americans felt for the national pastime, softball often rivaled the game because in terms of space and equipment, softball was more accessible. In fact, at Manzanar in California, women, who themselves actively pursued sports in each camp, formed a softball league that was easily the most popular at that site.

Overall, however, during their period of incarceration, baseball remained a strong attraction for the Nikkei. The 1945 season was their last behind the barbed wire of the camps. On August 6, the *Enola Gay*, a U.S. bomber, dropped the atomic bomb on Hiroshima, resulting in the deaths of at least ninety thousand residents within four months. Three days later, the city of Nagasaki suffered a similar fate, with at least fifty thousand killed. On September 2 Japan formally surrendered to the Allies aboard the *USS Missouri* and the war came to an end. By then, the evacuees in America's concentration camps were drifting back home.

7

Catching Up

It would be great to see an Asian American
get an opportunity to manage in the major
leagues. But frankly, I don't know if anyone
really gives a damn.

—Lenn Sakata, September 2007[1]

If I'm seen as a stepping stone for Japanese-
Americans and equality in baseball, I'm glad
to carry that torch.

—Don Wakamatsu, November 2009,
 upon being named manager of the
 Seattle Mariners[2]

Throughout much of 1945, residents from the ten concentration camps slowly packed their belongings in preparation to leave their imprisonment. Their release came as a result of the U.S. Supreme Court in the case called *Endo, Ex Parte*. Though in previous cases, such as *Hirabayashi v. U.S.* (1943) and *Korematsu v. U.S.* (1944), the plaintiffs, who had challenged the constitutionality of their curfew and incarceration, failed to win their freedom, Mitsuye Endo's legal argument did the trick. A California state worker before the attack on Pearl Harbor, Endo in July 1942 filed a habeas corpus petition in federal district court challenging the government's detention based on the question of her loyalty. Not until November 1944 did the case reach its conclusion. However, when it did, the justices viewed the internment of the Japanese less favorably. "Whatever power the War Relocation Authority may have to detain other classes of citizens, it has no authority to subject citizens who are concededly loyal to its leave regulations," read Justice William O. Douglas, for the majority.[3] With that January 2, 1945, decision, the process of release began.

In consideration of their trials, tribulations, and re-entry into mainstream society, the government allocated a $25 subsidy for each to restart their lives.[4] But, the return to their prewar communities had its drawbacks, and many approached their newfound freedom with caution. At the Minidoka camp, for instance, Seattle hotelkeepers funded the return of one of their own so that he might observe the conditions that lay before them. "He reported that there was much anti-Japanese hostility in Seattle, and some hotelkeepers delayed returning," wrote historian Roger Daniels.[5] Similar examples of anti-Japanese sentiment were widespread. "No Japs Wanted" signs were common and many Japanese homes were vandalized. Nor could the former evacuees turn to local courts for satisfaction. In Placer County, California, in a case that involved a group of men who had confessed to firing shots at the home of a returning evacuee while attempting to dynamite it, a jury there, nonetheless, acquitted the defendants and then praised them for their actions. More remarkably, two of the men were AWOL from the army.[6] At Livingston, California, in seven different incidents, vigilantes fired gunshots into the homes of Japanese who had recently returned from internment. So shaken were the dwellers that they "lined their bedrooms with mattresses, rice sacks, and sheet metal."[7]

In other incidents, "the Hood River, Oregon, American Legion Post removed the names of all sixteen local Japanese American servicemen from the public honor roll, and American Legion posts from Seattle to Hollywood barred Nisei veterans from membership."[8] Joe Meyer, the town's mayor, led the charge: "We must let the Japanese know they're not welcome here."[9] Asayo Noji's family was among the first to return to their Hood River home. For them and others, staying alert for possible repercussions to their bold presence was a twenty-four-hour chore. "We were so frightened! I jumped at every sound! Even at night, I did not sleep well. When we saw a stranger, we were unduly alarmed for we did not know what to expect," she recalled.[10] Ruth Wakamatsu, whose mother-in-law, Hisa, arrived in America years earlier as a picture bride, recalled, "My sister-in-law and I went shopping downtown, got a cart, filled it up with food, and a man said 'We're not trading with you.'"[11]

◆ ◆ ◆

In such a difficult environment, in most places Nikkei baseball came to a virtual halt. This was a first in their world, for the Japanese in America had played continual ball since 1905 and had even done so through internment.[12] However, throughout much of 1945 and into 1946, evacuees concerned themselves with the transition from camp to home. While they encountered hostility from outside their ranks, they also saw turbulence inside their circles. This was the case for James Sakamoto. As the chief Japanese supervisor at the Evacuation Administration Headquarters of the Puyallup, Washington, assembly center "Camp Harmony," Sakamoto fell from grace among the residents for questionable decisions that they believed better suited the interests of the WCCA.[13] Furthermore, Sakamoto and many of his cohorts in the Japanese American Citizens League (JACL) needed to patch up their reputations as a result of their preinternment collaborations with the Federal Bureau of Investigation. Sakamoto, the famed publisher of the Seattle-based *Japanese American Courier,* whose paper had sponsored the region's greatest overall sports programs, was, by 1945, a broken man. A leading founder and voice for the JACL, his ambitious calls for Nisei loyalty came back to haunt him during the internment phase, because many at the Puyallup Assembly Center where he resided believed he had cooperated much too generously with authorities. Already handicapped by his blindness, Sakamoto, with his newspaper defunct, returned to Seattle unemployed. With little voice left in the community, he found work at the St. Vincent De Paul group as a telephone solicitor. In December 1955, twenty years after the height of his prominence, he died after a car struck him while he crossed a street on his way to work.

Ray "Chop" Yasui, a baseball organizer in Hood River, Oregon, prior to the war, also had no time for the game upon his return home. Unlike Sakamoto, however, Yasui experienced trouble from his Caucasian neighbors. At a time when he so often had been preparing for opening-day ceremonies to celebrate yet another baseball season, a neighbor named Kent Shoemaker greeted the former player and coach with a petition that he had circulated in the area. Shoemaker, a member of the local American Legion, in an attempt to force Yasui and other Nisei to sell their properties, gathered several signatories to a note that read: "You Japs . . . have been told by some that you would be welcomed back in Hood River. This is not true, and this is the best time you will ever have to dispose of your property."[14]

Kenichi Zenimura, another fabled pre–World War Two sports figure, had a different postwar experience than did Sakamoto and Yasui. Upon his release, Zenimura made it clear that once resettled in his Fresno home, he fully intended "to make a team to play in the league in the city."[15] The old coach had always seen baseball as a "bridge of understanding" between cultures. In the 1920s and 1930s, the "Dean of the Diamond" had organized "goodwill" baseball trips to Japan, Korea, and Manchuria. Plus, his Fresno Nikkei teams had routinely played against collegiate and Negro League clubs. Thus, in his eyes, there was no better time than the immediate postwar period to implement this process to "speed up" healing between the Japanese and the mainstream enclave in his beloved Fresno area. "It is much easier to make efforts of starting a better understanding between us in the field of sports than trying to talk your way through the rough spots," said Zenimura.[16]

True to his word, upon his return to Fresno, Zenimura began to lay the groundwork to resume Nikkei baseball and encouraged the Nisei among them to hit the diamond. His talented sons, Kenshi and Kenso, not only played at then Fresno State College, but also later joined the Hiroshima Carp in the Japanese professional circuit. So, too, did Fibber Hirayama, a Zenimura protégé at Gila Bend, who played alongside the Zenimura brothers in Japan.[17] But for all Zenimura's idealism, not even baseball could shield Japanese Americans from postwar animosities. Ironically, only miles from where Zenimura operated, in the small community of Sanger, Nisei high school players encountered verbal assaults. "[Caucasian fans] would taunt us with racial slurs while we were playing" recalled player Dan Takeuchi. Nonetheless, as part of the "healing" process, Takeuchi and his Nisei teammates played through the season "to let others know that we were going to go on very positively."[18]

◆ ◆ ◆

Outside Fresno, Nisei baseball also slowly re-emerged. A few teams appeared in northern California, most notably in San Jose, where the Zebras in the immediate postwar years eventually challenged Zenimura's powerful Fresno teams for Nisei supremacy in California. The most illustrative example of baseball's perseverance in the hearts of the Nisei came with the report of veterans from the heroic 442nd Nisei combat unit. While stationed in Italy waiting to return home, the players in their ranks formed a baseball club and, in May 1946, reportedly compiled an 8-0 record in an army league.[19] Back in the United States, by 1947, several Nisei communities in northern California formed the ten-team Northern California Nisei Baseball League, which encompassed clubs in the Bay Area, Monterey peninsula, and central California.[20] In southern California, the San Fernando Aces reconvened and in Santa Barbara, the Nisei Athletic Club, with not enough Nisei teams to form a league, opted to play in a city league.[21] The Japanese American press, too, reported on some of these teams, but with considerably less attention than it had prior to the war. All agreed that the larger chore of stabilizing their community and restoring the dignity of its members needed to take priority.

Of course, the effort to rehabilitate the Nikkei image proved a monumental task. To start with, a National Opinion Research Center poll taken in 1946 revealed that 66 percent of survey respondents believed that both the first- and second-generation Japanese in the United States had acted as spies for Japan.[22] Furthermore, from 1945 through 1960, in particular, the mainstream impressions of the Japanese were largely shaped by what they saw in the movies and on television, much of which augmented long-held stereotypes of the Japanese that predated World War Two. In an atmosphere that, in the wake of anti-Communist red baiting, saw an increase in patriotic fervor, movies such as *The Sands of Iwo Jima*, which debuted in 1949 and starred popular actor John Wayne, did little to temper the lingering resentments against anything Japanese. So mindful were movie marketers of this sentiment that in 1951, at the premiere of the film *Go For Broke!*, a movie that depicted the U.S. Army's 442nd Division, a highly decorated Japanese American unit noted for its gallantry in the recent war, only the Caucasian actor Van Johnson appeared in posters and other advertisements promoting the film.

The very images that painted those of Japanese ancestry in a negative light also came from some Nisei themselves. As television made its mark in the 1950s, there were among the Nisei some who used their training in sumo wrestling to make a profit when professional wrestling joined the television lineup across the nation. Masaru "Charlie" Iwamoto, a Hawaiian-born Nisei who adopted the stage name "Mr. Moto," became one of the most well-known wrestlers on the professional circuit. But what drove his popularity was the anti-Japanese sentiment of the audience. "It was just great being able to root against the Japanese," said Mike LaBell, a promoter who personally liked Iwamoto but also recognized the drawing power of the stereotype he advanced. "It was mainly the Anglo population that we were asking to 'Come on down and let's kill this Jap.'"[23] With the lure of money, professional wrestling, wrote Brian Niiya, "was also probably one of the only occupations of any sort where being 'Japanese' was not only not a detriment, but may have actually been an asset."[24] Advancing the stereotype for wrestling fans, "Mr. Moto" routinely entered the ring dressed in a kimono, clogs, and wearing small round glasses. And he was not alone. An Oregon Nisei and relative to the Hood River Wakamatsu family, George "The Great Togo" Okamura, also fed into the so-called Japanese profile. In the ring and showered with boos, the wrestler prayed to a small Buddhist altar at the outset of each match.

Of course, outside the ring, these antics came at a cost. In one 1949 incident in Fresno, while Kenichi Zenimura sought to temper animosities in that locale, on

November 18, police were called on to protect The Great Togo from a revenge-seeking mob, whom the wrestler had angered after he had thrown his Caucasian opponent out of the ring.[25] A few years later, Charlie "Mr. Moto" Iwamoto also was attacked. After a match in Florida, a fan assaulted Iwamoto with a stick as he sat and drank coffee at a restaurant. Iwamoto's partner, wrestler Tinker Todd, jumped in to help Iwamoto while the assailant, who claimed to have been a participant in the infamous Bataan Death March, shouted, "Damn Japs! Damn Japs! I'll kill every damn Jap I can get my hands on."[26] The animus directed toward Japanese Americans like Iwamoto did not necessarily galvanize all Nisei against their critics. Larry Tajiri, editor of the *Pacific Citizen,* took the position that the popular and entertaining athletes themselves had done a disservice to the second generation. In a 1952 column, of the Nisei wrestlers, he wrote, "The right of the Nisei wrestlers . . . to continue in their arduous profession does not extend to them the right of provoking prejudice against their fellow Nisei."[27]

◆ ◆ ◆

As the Nisei grappled with the restoration of their image, baseball's image also underwent change when, in 1947, the first black player, Jackie Robinson, entered the Major League and broke the so-called "color barrier." Not since the period of the 1880s had professional baseball been integrated at this level. Thus, with Robinson in the uniform of the Brooklyn Dodgers, Americans awoke to a game now more open to players of all ethnic persuasions. Jackie Robinson, of course, did not fail his admirers. He completed his rookie season with a .297 batting average, led the club in home runs, and led the National League in steals. Moreover, he was easily the most exciting ballplayer in the Major League and became a symbol of hope for a generation of Americans who viewed baseball as a microcosm of their belief in the principles of fair play and democracy. "My favorite player was Jackie Robinson largely because he integrated baseball," said author Jules Tygiel, who, at seven years old, did not even see the Dodgers' star until nine years after he broke the color barrier. "I was not sure what this meant, but I knew it was wonderful. I thus learned my first lesson in politics and race relations."[28]

Nisei ballplayers also had direct connections with Jackie Robinson long before he joined the Dodgers. Raised in a South Pasadena, California, neighborhood not far from Japanese American enclaves, the future baseball pioneer often crossed paths with the Nisei. Shig Kawai, in his recollections as a teenager, testified that Robinson routinely joined sandlot games with Kawai and his pals.[29] More notably, while at Pasadena Junior College, Robinson and his teammate Shig

Takayama, a local Nisei baseball standout, were paired off as roommates and in many settings experienced segregation together.[30]

The Jackie Robinson episode triggered not only an opportunity for other blacks, like Larry Doby, whom the Cleveland Indians signed in the summer of 1947, but it also "emancipated" black Latino ballplayers. In 1948, Cuban Minnie Minoso joined the Indians. Baseball's changing profile also mirrored similar activity in race relations outside the ballpark. Between 1945 and 1950, President Harry Truman desegregated the military, initiated a study on racial discrimination in federal offices, and established a Civil Rights Division in the Department of Justice. In the courtrooms, Thurgood Marshall, who headed the Legal Defense Fund of the National Association for the Advancement of Colored People (NAACP), was making headway in several cases that ultimately prompted the U.S. Supreme Court to rule in favor of integrating the public school system in a case known as *Brown v. Board of Education of Topeka* (1954). In lesser but still significant headlines, U.S. Hispanics, too, launched their crusades for justice beginning with the 1946 case named *Mendez v. Westminster School District,* a case in which the federal court ruled that ethnicity, on its own, could not be a factor used to discriminate. Thus, as the Nikkei slowly settled back into their routines, by the 1950s, there seemed to be reason to hope that in terms of race, divisions between groups might no longer be as rigid as in the past.

The Issei, among others, readily understood the trials and tribulations of racial discrimination. And, in spite of the seemingly changing dynamics in race relations, three years after the end of the war the California's attorney general's office continued to seek the confiscation of Issei assets linked to their properties under the 1913 Alien Land Act. However, in 1952, the California Supreme Court, in a case known as *Fuji v. State of California,* held in favor of the plaintiff, which effectively deemed the land act unconstitutional. In another notable twist during that same year, Congress, caught up with the anti-Communist rants of the McCarthy era, voted to enact the McCarran-Walter Act. One provision created fewer impediments toward deportation and revoking the citizenship of an individual if found guilty of subversive activities. However, the law also ended the total exclusion of Asian immigration to the United States and their restrictions on attaining U.S. citizenship. For the Issei, the discriminatory measures that had blocked them from U.S. citizenship had ended. "The year 1952 thus marks the end of an era for the Japanese Americans," historian Roger Daniels observed. "Just ten year after the evacuation the last legal discrimination against Americans of Japanese ancestry disappeared."[31]

◆ ◆ ◆

By then, baseball among the Nikkei also sprang to life. Though the *Pacific Citizen* reported very little baseball activity in 1947, by the summer of 1949 the paper devoted an entire page to sports.[32] The *Nichi Bei Times,* which had only sparse coverage of baseball immediately after the war, also started to report on games with the type of ambition reminiscent of prewar years. In an effort to draw upon the nostalgia of their readers, in July 1950 the paper promoted an "Old Timers" Fourth of July tournament held in nearby Santa Clara, as it had done for so many other such tournaments in the years prior to Pearl Harbor. Though the reporter observed that the war had stolen much of the "vitality" from the Issei and older Nisei baseball aficionados, he nonetheless encouraged fans to go out and cheer for their sentimental favorites. The "tournament" turned out not to be a tournament at all, but a doubleheader between a Stockton Nisei war veterans team and one from the Florin area near Sacramento.[33] Within the next ten years, however, the Japanese American press, which had been instrumental in its promotion of the national pastime in the Nisei era, reported on games with less frequency, a gauge indicating that baseball's "golden age" among the Nisei was in its twilight years.

In the meantime, throughout the early 1950s, Nisei baseball took its last significant swing. In Fresno, as promised, Kenichi Zenimura brought baseball back to its competitive format as he collected variations of "all-stars" who routinely traveled to other towns and displayed winning baseball in games and tournaments throughout the state. Other Nisei-laden clubs also demonstrated a prowess for the game, such as the Skippers from San Pedro, California, who challenged their Fresno counterparts for state dominance.[34] San Jose's Japanese American baseball demonstrated a strong postwar heartbeat, as well. Like their Fresno brethren, baseball in San Jose had a long and distinguished prewar past, with particular attention given to the community's featured attraction on the ball field: the Asahi. Having changed the fabled club's name to the Zebras, the team survived the internment period as it competed in the harsh environment of Heart Mountain, Wyoming. Shortly after their return from Heart Mountain and other camps, the Zebras trotted back onto the field and played games beginning in June 1946.[35] One year later, they were among the clubs that joined the newly formed Northern California Nisei Baseball League (NCNBL).[36] Before the end of the decade, they established themselves as one of the state's most powerful Nisei clubs and enjoyed several celebrated contests with the Kenichi Zenimura–led Fresno teams.[37]

By 1956, the profile of Japanese American baseball changed as teams largely consisting of either young Nisei or Sansei no longer played in leagues exclusive to their ethnicity. In the Sacramento area, for instance, the *Pacific Citizen* listed a club called the "Placer JACL" playing in the Placer-Nevada League.[38] It was with some irony that a Japanese American team competed under the name of a community that, only nine years earlier, acquitted assailants who had fired gunshots at the former evacuees. With exclusive Japanese American baseball leagues all but gone, the *Pacific Citizen*, as the decade came to a close, rarely reported on any baseball. By the 1960s, the paper no longer featured any sports. The *Nichi Bei Times*, for its part, continued to report on sports, but like the *Pacific Citizen*, by the early 1960s baseball disappeared from its coverage.[39] Of course, some Nisei players remained active in baseball and even made it into the professional ranks.

Tsueno "Cappy" Harada, a Nisei from Santa Maria, California, was part of baseball at several different levels. Born in 1921, Harada, like other young Nisei, played the game as a youth. By the time he reached high school, he displayed enough potential that in 1936, his local amateur team invited him to play against the touring Tokyo Giants when they came to his hometown. Harada played at the semiprofessional level and even caught the attention of the St. Louis Cardinals.[40] But any chance to advance further ended when the war intervened.

Like many other Nisei, Harada enlisted in the military and was assigned to the army intelligence division in the Pacific Theater, where he saw some action and was twice wounded. Harada remained with the forces occupying Japan, and General Douglas MacArthur, who was in charge of the occupation, handed him the task of initiating sports programs. Harada's position made him an instrumental figure in Japanese baseball fortunes. In step with the *kengakudan* of his heritage, the Santa Maria native, along with Lefty O'Doul, the popular manager of the Pacific Coast League's San Francisco Seals, arranged several baseball goodwill tours, one of which included celebrities like Joe DiMaggio and his wife, the actress Marilyn Monroe. By the 1960s and no longer in the military, he remained active in baseball circles. In 1964 Harada helped engineer the signing of Japan's first entry into the Major League, pitcher Masanori Murakami, who joined the San Francisco Giants later that season. One year later, the minor league Lodi Crushers of the California League hired Harada as its general manager, the first Japanese American to be named to such a post.

Cappy Harada's rise and influence within the ranks of professional baseball, along with the emergence of Murakami in the big leagues, were significant steps for those Japanese Americans who entertained thoughts of playing baseball as a career. However, only in Japan could they find work. Wally Yonamine, a Nisei from Hawaii, was arguably the most prominent Japanese American to play in the Japanese leagues. A star athlete in the high school ranks, Yonamine initially earned his stripes in professional football when, in 1948, he joined the San Francisco 49ers and played one season in the National Football League. Injured during his rookie season and faced with an uncertain future on the professional gridiron, Yonamine turned to playing baseball, and this decision eventually landed him on the roster of the Yomiuri Giants.

◆ ◆ ◆

Born on the island of Maui on June 25, 1925, under his birth name "Kaname," the future slugger got his early education in baseball by watching Filipino plantation workers play the game on company teams. As a young boy, his entire world was his local community. "We lived in the country so I didn't know who was Joe DiMaggio. I didn't even know who Babe Ruth was," he later recalled.[41] By 1939 and then a teenager, Yonamine started playing in one of several amateur leagues and, like so many others, hoped to play for the legendary Asahis in Honolulu Stadium.[42]

Yonamine came from a Hawaiian Nikkei baseball environment that had a rich legacy. Rooted in the late-nineteenth-century plantation society, baseball activities among Japanese Americans there grew though the decades. By the 1930s, as in the mainland, Nikkei teams were in abundance. Some barnstormed the United States and Japan. By the end of the decade, several of these players landed on professional rosters in the new leagues in Japan while two, Kenso Nushida in 1932 and Jimmy Horio in 1935, joined the Sacramento Salons at the Triple A level. At the amateur level, Hawaii's Japanese Americans, as studied by Karleen C. Chinen, "supported AJA baseball in a big way, accounting as they did for 75 percent of the Hawaii Baseball League's gate receipts as early as 1936."[43] With the United States at war by 1942, the AJA postponed play, because most players had enlisted in the armed services. The Asahi club, too, curtailed games, and in the few instances where they did play, mindful of the possible repercussions regarding their team name, they renamed club the "Athletics."[44]

As on the mainland, Hawaiian Nikkei baseball resumed soon after the war came to an end. Unlike their brethren on the mainland, Japanese Americans

Wally Yonomine.
(Courtesy of the Nisei Baseball Research Project)

on the islands were not incarcerated. As such, with their communities intact, Nikkei baseball aficionados quickly organized their teams and games. Two well-known clubs, the Rural Red Sox and the Asahis, regrouped to play in 1946 and 1947, respectively.[45] And in 1948, an all–Japanese American interisland tournament resumed, one that began on an annual basis in 1936 but was interrupted by the war. The championship game, held in Honolulu Stadium, drew four thousand spectators.[46]

In 1948, Yonamine joined the Athletics, and during this season he fine-tuned his baseball skills. Prior to that, he had already made a name for himself when he played football for the 49ers the previous year. Ironically, the Hawaiian sports star joined the NFL team at a time when his brethren on the mainland had only just returned home from having been incarcerated in various regions in the United States. "It was right after the war and the Nisei had just come out of the relocation camps," he said. "So when I went to the 49ers, the Japanese Americans in San Francisco were very happy that there was a Japanese playing on the team. I was a bit of a hero to the Nisei in California."[47]

After a failed attempt to return to the NFL, Yonamine signed on to play minor league baseball in Salt Lake City in 1950, and then, upon the prodding of legendary San Francisco Seals coach Lefty O'Doul, the Hawaiian signed a contract to play for the Yomiuri Giants in Japan, and became the first highly acclaimed Nisei player to compete there professionally after the Second World War.[48] From 1951 to 1961, Yonamine demonstrated his skills to Japanese baseball fans. As a rookie, he batted .354; he later captured three batting titles and won the 1957 Central League's Most Valuable Player award. Following a playing career that included a .311 lifetime batting average, he remained in Japan to both coach and manage clubs.[49] But his career in Japan was not always a comfortable one. There, Yonamine experienced tart behavior from some Japanese baseball fans, many of whom undoubtedly motivated by memories of wartime traumas. In a manner akin to Jackie Robinson's experience in the Major League only a few years earlier, fans routinely booed the bespectacled American, launching catcalls regarding his foreign status. Irritated by his aggressive play, fans pelted him with rocks and, in some cases, threatened bodily harm.[50] "The Japanese didn't like me because I was a Nisei and because they thought I was a dirty player," he recalled.[51] "Hawaii e kaere (Go Back to Hawaii)," he heard on a daily basis.[52] But, Yonamine maintained his composure and eventually won the respect of the Japanese. In 1994, the Hawaiian Nisei entered the Japanese Baseball Hall of Fame alongside Sadaharu Oh, Japan's all-time home run leader.

Like Yonamine, other Nisei also played professional baseball in Japan. Howard and Harvey Zenimura, sons of the famed Kenichi, signed on to play for the Hiroshima Carp during the 1950s, as did their friend from Fresno, Satoshi "Fibber" Hirayama. Jiro Nakamura and Hank Masuba, among others, also joined the rosters of minor league teams in the United States. But, not until the rise of the third generation, the Sansei, did Japanese Americans finally see one of their own in the United States Major League.

Ironically, nearing the eve of that event, another era came to a close. On November 5, 1968, while en route to a birthday party for one of his granddaughters, Kenichi Zenimura, then sixty-eight years old and still working, was killed when a drunk driver slammed into the baseball icon's vehicle.[53] Since 1920, when he first arrived in Fresno, the Issei from Hiroshima made his mark not only in that community's baseball circles but also throughout the Pacific Rim. His contributions not only helped create a positive image of the Nikkei people, but his determination to employ baseball as a means to offset the trauma of incarceration paid dividends in challenging the face of injustice. His efforts created good will between nations previously at war and helped open the door for talented Nisei and Sansei ballplayers to enter the college and professional ranks on both sides of the Pacific. Following a brief and modest obituary in the *Fresno Bee,* which described him as "one of the oldest amateur baseball players in his time and considered the dean of Nisei baseball in America," the Fresno Buddhist Church hosted a service that drew a "standing room only" crowd to pay homage to the legendary player and coach and bid him farewell.[54] Had Zenimura lived another seven years, he would have borne witness to a landmark event in the history of Nikkei baseball. In that distant year, Chiura Obata, the great watercolorist and University of California professor who had founded the first Issei ball club in 1903, passed away, but not before seeing one of his own reach a major milestone in Nikkei history.

◆ ◆ ◆

On May 20, 1975, Ryan Kurosaki, a relief pitcher born in Hawaii, joined the St. Louis Cardinals. While this came with no great fanfare, when he took the mound late in the game, he became the first Japanese American to play in the Major League. By doing so, he joined a distinguished list of other pioneers such as Moses Fleetwood Walker, Esteban Bellan, Jackie Robinson, Minnie Minoso, and Masanori Murakami. "I was just blessed to become the first player of my ancestry to reach the big leagues," he said.[55] But this milestone occurred in quiet. None of the Japanese American papers reported the monumental event, nor was there any apparent praise from inside the Nikkei community. As a matter of perspective, the loud response accompanying Jackie Robinson's entry occurred at a time when blacks continued to face discrimination in all dimensions. Kurosaki's ascendancy to the Major Leagues, on the other hand, did not carry the weight of a civil rights achievement. A large factor in this might be that his Sansei generation had reached of degree of acceptance from the mainstream community and did not experience the degree of discrimination or hardship as had earlier generations.

Growing up in Kaimuki, Hawaii, Kurosaki was part of a generation that had reached a dream their Issei ancestors and Nisei elders had envisioned: assimila-

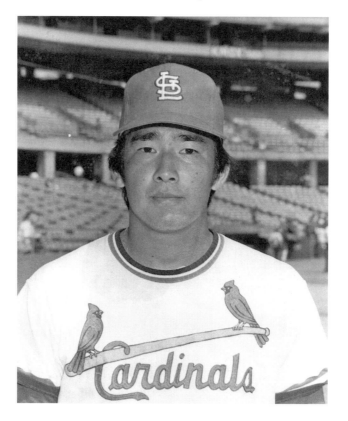

Ryan Kurosaki.
(Courtesy of the Nisei Baseball Research Project)

tion. Doors that were closed to their parents and grandparents now were swung open to those who were largely born after the period of internment and into one of tremendous postwar change. Federal and state budget surpluses in the 1950s and 1960s led to an increase in highways bills. With greater and easier highway access, bedroom communities emerged adjacent to larger urban centers. This was particularly apparent in California, where "large-scale tract developments occurred as such 'instant' cities as Westchester and West Covina in southern California and at Burlingame and Lafayette in the north," observed historian Andrew Rolle.[56] Additionally, the signing of the 1958 National Education Defense Act expanded enrollments and many academic programs at colleges and universities. For the Sansei, these developments created opportunities for advancement.

The geographic and economic possibilities led many Sansei to feel less inclined that their elders to remain in traditional Nikkei enclaves. Though the Nisei interacted far more with Caucasians than did the Issei, because of the racial climate and economic limitations of their day, they largely remained either within or on the periphery of their neighborhoods such as Little Tokyo in Los Angeles and Nihonmachi in Portland. The Sansei, on the other hand, established their own world well apart from the community and on a distinctively individual basis. "Even for those who remained near other Japanese Americans, involvement in Japanese community institutions became, for most Sansei, a weekend activity at best," stated Paul Spickard.[57] No longer functioning communities, San Francisco's Nihonmachi and Los Angeles' Little Tokyo, he went on, "became instead tourist attractions for out-of-town visitors in search of ethnic flavor."[58]

The new Nikkei profile did not deter the Sansei from their ambitions to attend college and attain professional careers.[59] As a result of their tenacity, they helped alter and advance positive images of the Nikkei that ultimately brought them closer to the mainstream. "By any criterion of good citizenship that we choose," stated the *New York Times* in 1966, "the Japanese Americans are better than any other group in our society, including native-born whites."[60] As the nation entered the mid-1970s, some observers painted the Japanese Americans with a new brush that described the once besieged Nikkei as a "model minority."[61]

Made as a tongue-in-cheek criticism of initiatives found in Lyndon Johnson's Great Society program, William Petersen, a social science professor at the University of California at Berkeley, coined the "model minority" phrase in 1966. To Petersen, Japanese Americans, above all other minorities, were achievers whose actions should be emulated by other "non-achievers" such as Mexican Americans, African Americans, and others.[62] But not all in the Nikkei community bought into the praise. In an era where challenge to the status quo often manifested itself in the form of uprisings, journalist Helen Zia claimed that Japanese Americans worried that their ability to overcome difficulties could work as a wedge issue "against other disadvantaged groups."[63] As such, Zia observed, the Nikkei faced an awkward scenario: "should [they] accept, if not embrace, this 'good' stereotype as an improvement over the 'inscrutable alien enemy' image of the previous hundred years."[64] By the 1970s, the Sansei rejected all stereotypes and adopted an "Asian American" profile. Still, the "model minority" label was a lightning rod for those who debated the issue of merit among the nation's ethnic groups. For the first time in their history, observations regarding Japanese

Americans led to arguments regarding the degree of their positive attributes. Also, notable individuals had attained mainstream leadership positions.

Daniel K. Inouye, a Nisei decorated war veteran from Hawaii who had served in the 100th Infantry Battalion of the 442nd Regimental Combat Team, in 1963 became the first Japanese American to win a seat in the U.S. Senate. Two years later, another Nisei from Hawaii, Patsy Mink, became the first woman of color elected to the U.S. House of Representatives. In 1962, Hawaiians sent Masayuki "Spark" Matsunaga, another who had served in the 442nd Regimental Combat Team, to the U.S. House of Representatives and, in 1976, into the U.S. Senate alongside Inouye. And in San Jose, California, in 1971, voters elected Norman Mineta their mayor. Sansei, too, were making their mark. Los Angeles television station KNBC promoted Tritia Toyota, a Sansei from Portland, Oregon, to anchor their prime-time evening news in one of the country's largest markets.

◆ ◆ ◆

Japanese American baseball players, too, as seen with Kurosaki's Major League debut, were participants in construction of this new identity. As had happened in the early twentieth century when Issei sojourners first arrived on the West Coast, the national pastime was a key ingredient in the creation and stability of their young community. Now, as their descendants approached the end of the twentieth century, a time when, by most gauges, the Japanese American community had grown thin, Kurosaki's uneventful appearance in the big leagues was one of the first important stepping-stones in the new collage of Japanese American identity.

Ryan Kurosaki's Major League career was not a long one. After his 1970 graduation from Kalani High School in Honolulu, the young Sansei left the islands to pitch for the University of Nebraska. After a three-year college career, the St. Louis Cardinals drafted him, and he pitched successfully in their minor league system. Following his Major League debut against the San Diego Padres, he appeared in only six more games, compiled a 7.62 earned run average in thirteen innings, and was sent back to the minors, never again appearing in the majors. Ironically, a high school teammate of Kurosaki's, Lenn Sakata, enjoyed a much more fruitful career.

Two years younger than Kurosaki, following his own high school graduation in 1972, Sakata left Honolulu and landed in Spokane, Washington, where he attended Gonzaga University on a baseball scholarship. In 1976, the Milwaukee Brewers signed Sakata to a contract, and the following year, he made

Lenn Sakata. (Courtesy of the National Baseball
Hall of Fame Library, Cooperstown, N.Y.)

his big-league debut. The Hawaii-born Yonsei enjoyed an eleven-year Major
League career and, in addition to the Brewers, played with the Baltimore Orioles, Oakland Athletics, and New York Yankees. The 1982 season was his most
productive, when he drove in thirty-one runs for the Orioles and played in 135
games. One year later, he helped the club reach the World Series and was the

first Japanese American to appear in the fall classic. But his career did not come without problems regarding his size, which harked back to a long-held profile of Asian people. At five-foot nine, he faced routine taunts about his frame. "I used to hear a lot of cracks about my size. . . . Because I was small, people thought I was weak. So, at times, I think, I tried to overcompensate by trying to hit home runs," he recalled.[65] Sakata ended his playing career in 1987, but remained in professional baseball as a coach and manager at the minor league level.

◆ ◆ ◆

As Kurosaki and Sakata helped Japanese Americans attain visibility in the Major Leagues, others outside the ballpark brought closure to a disturbing chapter in their history. In the 1980s, a group known as the National Council for Japanese American Redress (NCJAR), along with the National Coalition for Redress/ Reparations (NCRR) and the National Committee for Redress (NCR), made substantial gains through the courts and legislative circles, winning both financial remuneration and a formal apology from the federal government for incarcerating Japanese Americans during the Second World War. Gordon Hirabayashi and Fred Korematsu, whose wartime lawsuits had challenged the constitutionality of internment, were part of the NCJAR. Armed with information uncovered by Peter Irons, a law professor at the University of California at San Diego, that the federal government in 1942 had purposely withheld data from the U.S. Supreme Court as it considered the validity of internment order, by adopting the legal strategy of *coram nobis*,—writ of error—Hirabayashi's case was retried and overturned. "It was a strong victory," said the vindicated Nisei. "So strong that the other side did not appeal."[66] The NCJAR pressed on, and as a result of their determined lobbying, on September 19, 1987, as the country celebrated the two-hundredth anniversary of the U.S. Constitution, both the House and Senate passed the bill for redress and reparations. One year later, President Ronald Reagan accompanied his signature with an official apology for the government's actions against Japanese Americans in World War Two. "No payment can make up for those lost years. What is most important in this bill has less to do with property than with honor. For here we admit wrong," said the president.[67]

By the 1990s, Japanese Americans were fine-tuning their new identity. The Nisei campaign for reparations and redress, along with Hirabayashi's vindication, resonated for those Sansei activists who had participated in the Asian Power movements of the 1960s and 1970s, and made an impression on the fourth-generation Yonsei. Paul Spickard observed, "Many Sansei activists worked in the redress campaigns and cultural exhibitions, and their parents' newfound ability to talk about redress brought other Sansei back in touch with their ethnic communities for the first time in years."[68] The vindication that accompanied the closure of the internment phase stimulated a desire to better document and promote the history of the Japanese in America. To that end, a group of Nikkei from the business community in Los Angeles' "Little Tokyo" joined local veterans from the decorated 442nd Army unit and in the 1980s successfully lobbied for state and city funds to construct a museum there. After years of construction and collection of artifacts, the first wing of the Japanese American National Museum, one devoted to the Issei heritage, opened in 1992. In the meantime, the museum's second phase, designed to give attention to the Nisei history, had begun. As the curators gathered many donated artifacts and oral histories, a Fresno Sansei filmmaker named Kerry Yo Nakagawa took it upon himself to highlight Nisei accomplishments on the baseball diamond.

◆ ◆ ◆

Born in nearby Fowler on July 17, 1954, Nakagawa grew up in a community with a rich Japanese American baseball legacy, and he belonged to a family whose involvement in the game spanned four generations. "Grandpa Sentaro Nakagawa played on the plantations in Hilo, Hawaii," he recalled.[69] Three of his uncles, who played alongside the fabled Kenichi Zenimura, competed against Babe Ruth and Lou Gehrig when the famous Yankees pair barnstormed through Fresno in 1927. And his father, Dyna, was an exceptional all-around athlete in the region.[70] As the euphoria for capturing Japanese American history gained steam in the larger Nikkei world, Nakagawa was determined not to let the Nisei baseball story fall into the shadows. He said, "As I coached my son in little league, I realized he needed to hear the stories of all the great pioneers in our family that sacrificed so much for his generation."[71] By the mid-1990s, their history had drawn only scant attention from writers. In an effort to change this, Nakagawa drew upon regional sources made available to him, collected artifacts, and conducted oral interviews. Calling this operation the Nisei Research Baseball Project, in 1996 he christened it with an exhibit that opened at the Fresno Art Museum.

By the end of the decade, interest had grown about the history of baseball and the Japanese American community. Following the Fresno Art Museum exhibit, and with help from Gary Otake from the Japanese American Historical Society in San Francisco and a team of scholarly advisors, Nakagawa created a traveling exhibition called "Diamonds in the Rough" and it appeared in several museums, including the Japanese American National Museum, the museum at the state capitol in Sacramento, and the Baseball Hall of Fame in Cooperstown, New York. In step with the "cultural bridge" concept of yesteryear, Nakagawa also took the exhibit to the Baseball Hall of Fame in Tokyo. The filmmaker made available to the public a thirty-five-minute documentary titled "Diamonds in the Rough: Legacy of Japanese American Baseball" narrated by actor Pat Morita, his godfather.[72] The year 2001 brought publication of his book, *Through a Diamond: 100 Years of Japanese American Baseball*.

In the meantime, Major League ball clubs began recruiting Japanese nationals with more frequency. Until 1995, when Hideo Nomo joined the Los Angeles Dodgers amid great fanfare, only Masanori Murakami had been in the big leagues. However, after Nomo's rookie season and through 1999, seven more players came from Japan. And from 2000 through 2008, twenty-eight Japanese players joined big-league teams. Sensing a more welcoming attitude toward players of Japanese heritage, beginning with the San Francisco Giants in 1996, Kerry Yo Nakagawa lobbied successfully to hold celebrations recognizing and honoring the Nisei players of prewar years. The first celebration was touted a "Field of Dreams." A thrilled Paul Osaki, executive director of the Japanese Cultural and Community Center of Northern California, on July 20, 1996, at San Francisco's Candlestick Park, declared, "It's a day long overdue, but fortunately it is not too late. You are our heroes. . . . You are American heroes and today we say, thank you."[73] Other ball clubs, like the Los Angeles Dodgers and Seattle Mariners, followed the Giants' lead.

The mark of Nikkei baseball was also seen in the edifices of the Major League's new era of retro stadiums. In 1955, architect Gyo Obata, son of the prominent artist and founder of Nikkei baseball Chiura Obata, founded HOK, a design and architectural firm that by the 1990s had created blueprints for several new big-league stadiums, including Baltimore's Camden Yards. By the end of the decade, HOK won the contract to design the new home for the San Francisco Giants, then called Pacific Bell Park. Critics raved about the design, and as the project neared completion, Obata admitted that he reminisced about his father's love of the game. "He would have loved [the new ballpark]. He would have wanted to sit right behind the catcher," he said.[74]

To be sure, the Japanese American identity continued to be reshaped by the 1990s. As the Nikkei declined as a discrete geographical community, as was the case with earlier generations and the increase of intermarriage, the issue of Japanese American identity revisited them. Protocols regarding the "purity" of the Nikkei appeared in several community events. "Cherry Blossom" beauty pageant applications, for instance, started to vary on the bloodlines necessary for Nikkei women to participate.[75] Nikkei amateur sports leagues also reframed the eligibility of those who wished to compete. Contrasted with pre–World War Two leagues that were exclusively Japanese American, rules in the nineties were altered to allow increased participation. ". . . [T]hey [expanded] the definition of who is Japanese to include mixed-race Japanese Americans and, in so doing, [shifted] the criteria for membership and participation," observed sociologist Rebecca Chiyoko King.[76] In this manner of redefining themselves, Nikkei leaders of this generation were able to forestall any further decrease in their numbers and clout in the larger society.[77]

But while the surge of historical rediscovery and a new Asian profile swept the national pastime, by the year 2000, Japanese Americans continued to remain well outside the professional baseball ranks, a fact that did not escape the attention of Lenn Sakata. Since his 1987 retirement as a player, Sakata remained in professional baseball in the capacity of coach and/or manager for several teams both in the United States and Japan. Indeed, between 2001 and 2007, the former big-leaguer won three titles as manager of the San Jose Giants in the California League.[78] "I have been very fortunate to stay in the game this long and meet so many different people and broaden my perceptions of race relations," he observed.[79] His gracious comments, however, betrayed a growing sense of frustration. As big-league clubs continued to romance Korean and Japanese players (and even players from Australia), Japanese Americans drew decreasing attention. Since Sakata's retirement, only one Sansei, Atlee Hammaker, and two Yonsei, Don Wakamatsu and Onan Masaoka, reached the majors.[80] Moreover, since 1998, apart from Sakata, Wakamatsu stood as the only Nikkei in the management level in the minor leagues. By 2007, Sakata grew more candid with his thoughts. "Historically there haven't been many Asian American players in the big leagues. I remember we got really excited when Ryan Kurosaki, a pitcher from Hawai'i, played for the Cardinals for six weeks in 1975. There haven't been many others since. It would be great to see an Asian American get an opportunity to manage in the major leagues," he said. "But frankly, I don't know if anyone really gives an damn."[81] As the 2007 baseball campaign drew to an end, few could predict that in a short time, for the Nikkei, their fortunes were about to change.

◆ ◆ ◆

At the start of the 2008 season, Don Wakamatsu was an unassuming bench coach for the Oakland Athletics. Ironically, his new job in Oakland lay only a few miles away from Hayward, where he grew up. Born in Hood River, Oregon, in 1963,

Wakamatsu's paternal family background read like a textbook of the Nikkei past. His Issei great-grandmother, Hsia, from Hiroshima, had come to the United States in 1911 as a picture bride. His Nisei grandparents, in 1942, were sent to the Tule Lake concentration camp, where his father was born into an environment surrounded by barbed wire. And his father, a Sansei, like so many others of his generation, married outside his ethnicity to a woman of Irish background. "I have mochi (Japanese rice cakes) on one side and potatoes on the other," said Wakamatsu.[82] The Wakamatsu family also included an uncle who laid claim to some fame: George "The Great Togo" Okamura, the popular wrestling villain of the 1950s. Though no baseball players appeared in his family tree, young Wakamatsu was a star at Hayward High School and went on to play at Arizona State University, here he earned All-Pac 10 honors as a catcher. Through it all, he dreamed of a career in professional baseball and idolized Lenn Sakata, who "was a big influence on me."[83]

In 1985, the Cincinnati Reds drafted the catcher, and in the next few years he bounded around the minor leagues with various clubs. In 1991, the Yonsei finally got an opportunity to play in the majors with the Chicago White Sox. But his stay at that level was only for eighteen games and he returned to the minors where he continued to play until 1996. Wakamatsu remained in the minors as a coach and manager for several organizations and in 2008, he returned to Oakland as a bench coach for the team of which, as a young boy, he had been a fan. "My uncle took me to my first game ever to see the A's in the 1973 playoffs," he recalled.[84]

By coincidence, Wakamatsu's 2008 tenure in Oakland brought him into contact with Kurt Suzuki, a Yonsei from Hawaii and starting catcher for the club. Of his coach, Suzuki said, "He is the reason I read so much about Japanese-American history. We talked more about that than we talked about baseball."[85] Wakamatsu concurred, "From the very first day that we met, Kurt and I connected. Because of our Asian American connection, we already had a belief in each other."[86] Suzuki remembered that "Don already knew about our culture and that meant a lot. People forget that Hawaiian players spend most of the year away from home. So even though Don is from here, it helped a lot."[87]

Prior to the end of that season, Wakamatsu watched history made before his eyes when, in a July 17 game against the Texas Rangers, pitcher Shane Kenji Komine, from Hawaii, took the mound in the eighth inning. With Suzuki, for the first time there was an all-Nikkei battery in the majors. In the meantime, Wakamatsu grew concerned that there might be little hope for him to advance into a managerial position. Twice, with the Athletics and Rangers, he applied for such job openings, but to no avail. However, though he dutifully tended to his duties in Oakland, another team in American League Western Division, the Seattle Mariners, was in the midst of a forgettable season.

Seattle had a distinguished baseball past. Dating back to 1903, professional baseball had been part of the Puget Sound environment largely through its affiliate in the Pacific Coast League. Dubbed the Rainiers, the team was a popular fixture in the region, as was the national pastime, in spite of the constant rainfall that dogged much of the season. Playing in ancient Sicks Stadium, Seattle landed a Major League expansion franchise, the Pilots of the American League, for the 1969 season. Poor attendance, bad financing, and a woeful team led the owners to pull out of the Pacific Northwest after just one year, and they took the team to Milwaukee.

In 1976, the American League awarded Seattle another expansion team, which locals named the Mariners, and the team meandered for several years, playing in the expansive and exceedingly plain Kingdome. Though the team showed signs of competitiveness through the decades, its most productive year came in 2001 when, behind several key players like Edgar Martinez and a Japanese standout named Ichiro Suzuki, the club completed the regular season by tying a Major League record 116 wins. Though the team lost the American League championship series to the New York Yankees, they remained competitive through the 2007 season, one in which they won eighty-eight games. Thus, Seattle's baseball aficionados looked forward to the 2008 campaign with similar expectations. However, the team suffered a disastrous season and lost an embarrassing one hundred games, earning them the distinction of being the first to lose that many after bankrolling $100 million for their players. At the end of the season, the Mariners' high command made it clear that Jim Riggleman, the latter of two managers that year, was not in their plans for the following season. In November, the club made a dramatic decision on who was to replace Riggleman.

"A new day for Mariners," the *Seattle Times* reported in its sports section headline.[88] On November 19, the club announced that it had signed Don Wakamatsu as manager for the 2009 season. "Wak," as his friends called him, became the first Nikkei to rise to the level of big-league manager. The Mariners' general manager, Jack Zdurienck, told the press, "He [Wakamatsu] got hired because he's a good baseball guy."[89] Having toiled as a minor league coach and manager, followed by positions as a bench coach, the Yonsei finally got his chance. "What we're going to try and accomplish here is to win now, and establish a tradition of winning," he told the press in a manner characteristic of other new managers.[90]

Within a few miles from where Frank Fukuda, the Issei baseball mogul who, exactly one hundred years earlier, introduced the national pastime to the Japanese in the Pacific Northwest, Wakamatsu broke new ground for the legacy of Japanese American baseball. In his initial press conference as the Mariners' manager, he spoke thoughtfully of his role to his cultural identity. "I am proud to represent some of the things [my parents and grandparents] went through," speaking of their trials and tribulations. "If I'm seen as a stepping stone for Japanese-Americans and equality in baseball, I'm glad to carry that torch."[91] Warmly greeted with hundreds of letters from well wishers, Wakamatsu was struck by one from a teenage boy, who wrote, "I'm so proud of you. I am sixteen years-old and now I believe that I can do some things, too."[92]

The new manager always seemed mindful of his cultural history as he routinely spoke of his family experience. In his boyhood recollections, the government's reparations check sent to his father triggered his interest in the story of internment. "I didn't understand what the check was for," he told reporters. Curious as he aged, he followed up with more questions for family. "I delved into my past, going back to visit my grandma, learning more about my family. They went through a lot of things. It meant something, and I thought I ought to know more about it since I wasn't exposed to it much as a child."[93] The Hood River native also learned that "I had three uncles who served in the 442nd [army unit]."[94] Wakamatsu's own baseball role model reflected his desire to learn who he was. "[Lenn Sakata] was the one guy I followed. For me, there was always that issue of looking for that identity."[95]

Japanese Americans, of course, were ecstatic. "I think Don Wakamatsu will become an adopted son and a source of pride for all of us," said Beth Takekawa, executive director of the Wing Luke Asian Museum in Seattle. "He will find many instant supporters within the community."[96] In Oakland, Wakamatsu's former protégée, Kurt Suzuki, used the popular film *The Karate Kid* to describe his mentor: "He's like the Mr. Miyagi of baseball."[97] And miles from any Major League park, in California's central valley, Wakamatsu's hiring was a regular topic of conversation. "Boy, how about that?" Chris Masuda asked Robert Taniguchi, both in Merced. "You could tell that my friend was real happy," recalled Taniguchi, a one-time JACL governor of the Central California District and a JACL board member.[98] Interestingly, both the *Nichi Bei Times* and Kerry Yo Nakagawa's Nisei Baseball Research Project, in their praise of Wakamatsu, referred to him not as a Japanese American or any generation identified with the Nikkei but as an "Asian American."[99]

Kurt Suzuki.
(Courtesy of the Oakland Athletics)

Lenn Sakata, too, was pleased at Wakamatsu's good fortune, but remained wary that the new manager of the Mariners might also be the last Nikkei to make it to that level. "It's not like [we] fall out of the trees in baseball," he said. And pointing to the fact that unless the number of Asian Americans in professional baseball increases, he prophesied that "[Don] becomes a little footnote in baseball history that'll be so small eventually the only ones who'll care are the ones who care to care."[100]

Outside Nikkei circles, however, and some sixty-plus years past a time when generalizations about Japanese people in American were prevalent, distinctions between American-born Japanese and those from Japan remained cloudy in the baseball world. Following the appearance of Hideo Nomo in the mid-1990s, Ichiro Suzuki, the heralded star from Japan, signed on to play for the Seattle Mariners in 2001 and had a banner season that earned him both the American League Rookie of the Year and Most Valuable Player awards. Suzuki's continued success throughout the decade, as well as that of his fellow countryman, Hideki Matsui, who starred with the New York Yankees, catapulted the Asian baseball presence in the big leagues to a new level. Indeed, by the end of the decade, no longer did American baseball aficionados consider players from Japan a novelty in the majors. But, as reflected in some of their taunts, nor did they identify the difference between those who were Japanese or American-born. Sitting only a few feet from Kurt Suzuki during a 2009 game between the Oakland Athletics and Toronto Blue Jays, one fan recalled, "I questioned his Japanese patriotism by asking him why he used the name 'Kurt' as opposed to a traditional Japanese name like 'Hideki' or 'Kristy.' To my amazement, [later] I discovered that Kurt was not from Japan, but was actually born and raised in Hawaii, . . . and speaks with a perfect American accent."[101]

Suzuki, by then, was a two-year veteran, having debuted with the Oakland Athletics in the middle of the 2007 season. Born in Wailuku, Hawaii, in 1983, in a family where his Issei great-grandparents had migrated to the islands from Japan, his high school baseball skills won the attention of both scouts and university recruiters. In 2002, the Yonsei landed at California State University, Fullerton, on a baseball scholarship and he soon became the team's starting catcher. In 2004, he was named first-team All-American, won the prestigious Johnny Bench Award as the best catcher in Division I college baseball, and helped his team win the national championship with the game-winning hit in the final contest. The Oakland Athletics signed Suzuki following the 2004 season and he debuted with the big-league club three years later. Earning a reputation for his durability behind the plate, he became one of the most popular and dependable players on the squad. So confident was the club's brass in his potential that, in 2010, they signed him to a four-year contract worth a guaranteed $16.25 million.

◆ ◆ ◆

At the start of the 2009 baseball season, three Japanese Americans, Travis Ishikawa of Seattle and on the San Francisco Giants, Kurt Suzuki, and Wakamatsu all donned Major League uniforms. Having dispensed with the "Asian American" terminology, the *Nichi Bei Times* touted the "*Nikkei* Baseball Trifecta" because of their San Francisco Bay Area connections. "Bay Area *Nikkei* baseball fans have a lot to look forward to this season, as all eyes are on a trio of Japanese Americans who could be headed for milestone years in the majors," they proudly reported.[102] To an extent, the appearance of the players in and from the Bay Area brought the Japanese American baseball story full circle. When in 2000 the Giants opened their new home, then called Pacific Bell Park, Gyo Obata was among the designers whose blueprint contributed to the architecture of the beautiful park that lay only miles from where his father and his team, in 1903, had thrown the first ball, initiating Nikkei baseball in the United States.

Now, 104 years later, journalists from mainstream newspapers gravitated to Wakamatsu and extended him the visibility unseen to the Nikkei from prior generations. The Japanese American press, for its part, saw the new Mariners' manager as a role model for the Nikkei community. Touting the new skipper's baseball virtues, *Rafu Shimpo* journalist Jordan Ikeda echoed in his column the principles that had been indelible components of Japanese American strength throughout their history in the United States. "With accountability, hard work and honor, a new era of baseball is upon Seattle," he concluded.[103]

Don Wakamatsu's rookie season as a manager was, indeed, a success. Liked by his players and fans, he guided the club to third place in the American League West with 85–77 win-loss record, and he kept the team in contention until the season's final weeks. The club's eighty-five wins was a twenty-four-game improvement from their 2008 finish and represented only the thirteenth time in Major League history that a club ended a season with a winning record after they had lost more than one hundred games the previous year. For his part, Wakamatsu earned serious consideration as American League Manager of the Year and ultimately finished fourth in the balloting.

But the honeymoon between Wakamatsu and the Mariners came to an end during the 2010 season. Hindered by early season injuries to several key players, the club, which Seattle baseball fans hoped might challenge the Angels for supremacy in the West, started the season slowly. As the team struggled into the summer, Ken Griffey Jr., the aging superstar, as well as Chone Figgins, a high-priced free agent, grew disgruntled as they failed to produce. Tensions increased after Griffey abruptly retired in June, and Wakamatsu dropped Figgins down

Don Wakamatsu.
(Courtesy of Ben VanHouten)

in the batting lineup. On July 23, a scuffle between Figgins and the manager broke out in the Mariners' dugout after Wakamatsu pulled the infielder from the game for lack of hustle.[104] On August 9, with the team mired in last place, Seattle general manager Jack Zduriencik fired Wakamatsu. Disappointed at the outcome, the Yonsei man, looking spent, responded to reporters in a manner in step with a heritage that called for warriors to act with respect and honor. "I am not bitter about anything. I'm thankful. Real thankful," said the humbled but dignified former manager.[105] Later, upon reflection, the intuitive Wakamatsu remarked of his firing, "I try to keep things in perspective. I got fired from a public position, but my grandparents were forced to live in a horse stall when they were interned. So, how bad can my circumstances be?"[106]

By the end of the 2010 campaign, at least five players, including Kurt Suzuki and Travis Ishikawa, the latter who played in that year's World Series for the champion San Francisco Giants, were on Major League rosters. And, in the minors, others waited for their chance to move up. Wakamatsu, too, returned to the majors when the Toronto Blue Jays hired him as a bench coach for the 2011 season. Though the majority, because of mixed marriages, were no longer "pure" Nikkei, as were their predecessors, they nonetheless carried the noble legacy of Japanese American players who, in the face of adversity and antagonism, treated the national pastime with reverence and devoted play. For the contemporary Nikkei, their sense of duty beyond the diamond and to their community remained apparent. "Hopefully, I've opened the door for others and I want to do more and represent Asian Americans for future generations," said the pioneering Wakamatsu.[107] Kurt Suzuki added "We feel like we're ambassadors for people of our culture, our community."[108]

When Jordan Ikeda trumpeted a "new era in Seattle," he did so in reference to the 2008 hiring of Don Wakamatsu. However, Ikeda's premonition was also true for the Nikkei community who included baseball as a bridge to reach those outside their circles and to demonstrate their love of country and culture. By the end of 2010, on the diamond and beyond, the Nikkei were no longer outsiders looking in. Their level of respect found in community, government leadership, and on baseball diamonds was on par with others in mainstream America. Thus, it might be said that encompassed in the spirit of more than a century of baseball and its partnership in the evolution of the Nikkei and their identity, a new era had commenced for all of them, as well.

Notes

Chapter 1. Baseball in Nikkei America

1. Gary Otake, "A Century of Japanese American Baseball," Japanese American Baseball History Project, 3.

2. Kerry Yo Nakagawa, *Through a Diamond: 100 Years of Japanese American Baseball* (San Francisco: Rudi Publishing, 2001), 134–35.

3. Ibid., 140.

4. Ibid.

5. Yeichi Sakaguchi interview, August 19, 1991, Cortez, California.

6. Brian Niiya, ed., *More Than a Game: Sport in the Japanese American Community* (Los Angeles: Japanese American National Museum, 2000), 21.

7. Wayne Maeda, *Changing Dreams and Treasured Memories: A Story of Japanese Americans in the Sacramento Region* (Sacramento, Calif.: Japanese American Citizens League, 2000), 149.

8. Otake, "Japanese American Baseball," 3.

Chapter 2. The New Bushido

1. Donald Roden, "Baseball and the Quest for National Dignity in Meiji Japan," *American Historical Review* 85 (June 1980): 520.

2. Gerald R. Gems, *The Athletic Crusade: Sport and American Cultural Imperialism* (Lincoln: University of Nebraska Press, 2006), 32.

3. Peter Duus, *Modern Japan,* 2nd ed. (Boston: Houghton Mifflin Harcourt, 1998), 61. Duus claims, "Some historians argue that . . . long-term trends were pushing Japan in the direction of radical, perhaps even revolutionary change. Whether such was the case is a question not easily answered, since pressures toward a change from within were suddenly overwhelmed by a series of decisive shocks from without . . ."; Andrew

Gordon, *A Modern History of Japan: From Tokugawa Time to the Present* (New York: Oxford University Press, 2008). Gordon concurs with Duus and claims, "From the early 1800s through the 1860s, the very process of dealing with the pushy barbarians created modern Japanese nationalism." As such, Gordon argues, ". . . the Tokugawa claims to be Japan's legitimate defender began to wither."

4. Kenneth B. Pyle, *The Making of Modern Japan* (Toronto: D.C. Heath, 1996), 60.

5. Ibid., 62.

6. W. G. Beasley, *The Modern History of Japan,* 2nd ed. (New York: Praeger Publishers, 1974), 152.

7. Pyle, *Making of Modern Japan,* 67–68.

8. Ibid., 69.

9. Benjamin G. Rader, *Baseball: A History of America's National Game* (Urbana: University of Illinois Press, 1992), 11.

10. Steven M. Gelber, "Working at Playing: The Culture of the Workplace and the Rise of Baseball," *Journal of Social History* 16 (June 1983): 3–22.

11. Edward M. Burns, *The American Idea of Mission: Concepts of National Purpose and Destiny* (New Brunswick, N.J.: Rutgers University Press, 1957), 16.

12. Roden, "Baseball," 517.

13. Peter Levine, *A. G. Spalding and the Rise of Baseball: The Promise of American Sport* (New York: Oxford University Press, 1985), 100.

14. Rader, *Baseball,* 46.

15. It should be noted that baseball, prior to its appearance in Japan, had already been in existence in Asia. Author Gerald R. Gems, in *The Athletic Crusade: Sport and American Cultural Imperialism* (Lincoln: University of Nebraska Press, 2006), notes that in 1863 baseball clubs were seen in the Chinese city of Shanghai.

16. Gems, *Athletic Crusade,* 31.

17. Mariam Johnston, "Gorham Man's Gift to Japan: A National Pastime; Horace Wilson Took His Japanese Students Out to Play in 1872 and Planted a Love of Baseball." *Portland Press Herald,* May 20, 2007, available at http://pressherald.mainetoday.com/story.php?id=106835&ac=PHspt (accessed January 15, 2009).

18. "Hiraoka Hiroshi," Baseball Reference.com, available at http://www.baseball-reference.com/bullpen/Hiraoka_Hiroshi (accessed January 15, 2009).

19. Kenneth B. Pyle, *The New Generation in Meiji Japan: Problems of Cultural Identity, 1885-1895* (Stanford, Calif.: Stanford University Press, 1969), 39. It should be noted that the Darwinian model did not appeal to all of the Japanese policy makers who ruled in that era. Inoue Tetsujiro, for instance, wrote extensively on this ambivalence. The principles of Spencerian theory, to Inoue, were alarming. "His fears," Pyle points out, "were based on the conviction that Japanese could not survive competition with the superior races of Western countries" (Pyle, *New Generation,* 110).

20. Roden, "Baseball," 513.

21. Ibid., 519.

22. Beasley, *Modern History of Japan*, 154.

23. "History of Kendo." All Japan Kendo Federation, available at http://www.kendo -fik.org/english-page/english-page2/brief-history-of-kendo.htm (accessed September 18, 2011).

24. Roden, "Baseball," 519.

25. Ronald Story, "The Country of the Young: The Meaning of Baseball in Early American Culture," in David K. Wiggins, ed., *Sport in America: From Wicked Amusement to National Obsession* (Champaign, Ill.: Human Kinetics, 1995), 125.

26. Roden, "Baseball," 517.

27. C. Howard Hopkins, *History of the YMCA in North America* (New York: Association Press, 1951), 322. The high number of converts in the 1880s, it should be noted, were driven not so much by the desire to become full-fledged Christians but as another means to eventually dissolve the "unequal treaties." Indeed, as Hopkins pointed out, in the 1890s "when all efforts to end the treaties failed, a serious antiforeign animus developed, with rising resentment shown against missionaries and Christianity." (321–32)

28. Ibid., 328.

29. Roden, "Baseball," 519.

30. Ibid., 516.

31. Pyle, *New Generation*, 33, 36.

32. Ibid., 33.

33. Ronald Story, "Country of the Young," 122.

34. Pyle, *New Generation*, 37. Tokutomi, one needs to know, was not only a symbol for rebellious youth, but at only twenty-three years old when he penned *The Future of Japan*, a book that went through four printings, he, too, was a youth.

35. Harold Seymour, *Baseball: The People's Game* (New York: Oxford University Press, 1990), 169.

36. Roden, "Baseball," 520.

37. Robert F. Hackett, "The Meiji Leaders and Modernization: The Case of Yamagata Aritomo," in Marius B. Jansen, ed., *Changing Japanese Attitudes Towards Modernization* (Princeton, N.J.: Princeton University Press, 1965), 245.

38. Kenneth Pyle, *Making of Modern Japan*, 70.

39. Ryoichi Shibazaki, "Seattle and the Japanese–United States Baseball Connection, 1905–1926," master's thesis, University of Washington, 1981, 2.

40. Seymour, *Baseball*, 169.

41. On Inoue's ambivalence concerning Japan's ability to compete with the West, see Pyle, *New Generation*, 110.

42. Roden, "Baseball," 522–24.

43. Sylvester K. Stevens, *American Expansion in Hawaii: 1842–1898* (New York: Russell & Russell, 1968), 3.

44. Gavan Daws, *Shoal of Time: A History of the Hawaiian Islands* (Honolulu: University of Hawaii Press, 1968), 181.

45. Stevens, *American Expansion*, 282.

46. Ibid.

47. Ronald Takaki, *Strangers from a Different Shore: A History of Asian Americans* (New York: Penguin Books, 1989), 44.

48. Hilary Conroy, *The Japanese Frontier in Hawaii, 1868-1898* (Berkeley: University of California Press, 1953), 86.

49. Yukiko Kimura, *Issei: Japanese Immigrants in Hawaii* (Honolulu: University of Hawaii Press, 1988), 11.

50. Robert A. Wilson and Bill Hosokawa, *East to America: A History of the Japanese in the United States* (New York: William Morrow, 1980), 148.

51. Joel Stephen Franks, *Hawaiian Sports in the Twentieth Century* (Lewiston, N.Y.: Edwin Mellen Press, 2002), 20.

52. Joel S. Franks, *Asian Pacific Americans and Baseball* (Jefferson, N.C.: McFarland, 2008), 20.

53. Clifford Putney, *Muscular Christianity: Manhood and Sports in Protestant America, 1880-1920* (Cambridge, Mass.: Harvard University Press, 2001), 128.

54. Ibid., 132.

55. Franks, *Asian Pacific Americans*, 24.

56. Karleen C. Chinen, "Hawaii's AJA's Play Ball," in Brian Niija, ed., *More Than a Game: Sport in the Japanese American Community* (Los Angeles: Japanese American National Museum, 2000), 110.

57. Dennis M. Ogawa, *Kodomo no tame ni: For the Sake of the Children: The Japanese American Experience in Hawaii* (Honolulu: University of Hawaii Press, 1978), 139.

58. Ibid.

59. Kimura, *Issei*, 161.

60. Ibid., 171.

61. Joel Franks, *Crossing Sidelines, Crossing Cultures: Sport and Asian Pacific American Cultural Citizenship* (New York: University Press of America, 2000),53.

62. Chinen, "Hawaii's AJAs Play Ball," 110.

63. Ibid., 110.

64. Seymour, *Baseball*, 173. Chinese players affiliated with Hawaiian universities were exceedingly instrumental in furthering the islands' baseball reputation. They not only hosted clubs from Japan and the United States, but also took to the road. In 1913, for instance, Seymour revealed that a Chinese squad from Hawaii played in the United States "an amazing total of 144 games, winning 105, losing 38, and tieing 1."

65. Takaki, *Strangers*, 162. For context more directly related to plantation life and baseball, see Ronald Takaki, *Pau Hana: Plantation Life and Labor in Hawaii 1835-1920* (Honolulu: University of Hawaii Press, 1983), 103.

66. Ibid., 149-50.

67. Ibid., 162.

68. Michael M. Okihiro, *AJA Baseball in Hawaii: Ethnic Pride and Tradition* (Honolulu:

Hawaii Hochi, 1999), 11. For a comparison of baseball's role with the ethnic labor class and solidarity, one might also look at Jose M. Alamillo, *Making Lemonade Out Of Lemons: Mexican American Labor and Leisure in a California Town 1880-1960* (Urbana: University of Illinois Press, 2006).

69. Linda Tamura, *The Hood River Issei: An Oral History of Japanese Settlers in Oregon's Hood River Valley* (Urbana and Chicago: University of Illinois Press, 1993), 8.

70. Yuji Ichioka, *The Issei: The World of the First Generation Japanese Immigrants, 1885-1924* (New York: The Free Press, 1990), 3.

71. Tamura, *Hood River Issei*, 20.

72. Spickard, *Japanese Americans*, 10–11.

73. Ibid., 21.

Chapter 3. Transplanted Cherries

1. Kazuo Ito, *Issei: A History of Japanese Immigrants in North America* (Seattle: Japanese Community Service, 1973), 236.

2. *Seattle Post-Intelligencer,* May 23, 1910. Clipping in Frank Fukuda Collection. Special Collection Archives, Allen Library, University of Washington, Seattle.

3. Roger Daniels, *Concentration Camps: North America Japanese in the United States and Canada During World War II* (Malabar, Fla.: Robert E. Kreiger Publishing, 1989), 5.

4. Daniels, *Concentration Camps*, 2.

5. Roger Daniels, *Asian America: Chinese and Japanese in the United States since 1850* (Seattle: University of Washington Press, 1988), 35.

6. Ibid., 36.

7. Ibid., 58.

8. Interestingly, the Chinese found in the courts some respite from the discrimination, as a number of mandates failed to pass judicial muster. The case of *Yick Wo v. Hopkins* (1886), one that reached the United States Supreme Court and ended with a victory for Yick Wo, a San Francisco laundry owner, represented a crescendo for the Chinese. Kermit L. Hall, ed. *The Oxford Companion to The Supreme Court of the United States* (New York: Oxford University Press, 1992), 948–49.

9. Daniels, *Asian America*, 39.

10. Ronald Takaki, *Strangers From A Different Shore: A History of Asian Americans* (New York: Penguin Books, 1989), 40.

11. Dorothy Swaine Thomas, et al., *Japanese American Evacuation and Resettlement (JERS): The Salvage* (Berkeley: University of California Press, 1952), appendix.

12. Eileen Sunada Sarasohn, ed., *The Issei: Portrait of a Pioneer: An Oral History* (Palo Alto, Calif.: Pacific Books, Publishers, 1983), 25.

13. Thomas, *JERS*, appendix.

14. Stephen W. Kohl, ed., "An Early Account of Japanese Life in the Pacific Northwest: The Writings of Nagai Kafu," *Pacific Northwest Quarterly* 70, no. 1 (April 1979): 62.

15. Yuji Ichioka, *The Issei: The World of the First Generation Japanese Immigrants, 1885–1924* (New York: The Free Press, 1988), 157.

16. Daniels, *Asian America,* 130.

17. Ibid.

18. Shotaro Frank Miyamoto, *Social Solidarity among the Japanese in Seattle* (Seattle: University of Washington Press, 1939), 119.

19. Takaki, *Strangers from a Different Shore,* 195.

20. Aibara Collection, Yamato Colony at Livingston, CA, Box 41, Number 4, Special Collections Archives, California State University, Stanislaus, Turlock, California.

21. Chiura Obata, *Topaz Moon: Art of the Internment* (Berkeley: University of California Press, 2000), 3.

22. Ibid.

23. Susan Landauer's comments appear in *Obata's Yosemite: The Art and Letters of Chiura Obata from His Trip to the High Sierra in 1927* (Yosemite National Park, Calif.: Yosemite Association, 1993), 21.

24. Ibid.

25. Ibid.

26. Ibid.

27. According to Kerry Yo Nakagawa, the letters "KDC" had three different meanings: "K," for Kanagawa-ken, their prefecture; "D," for *Doshi,* a loose translation for "a bunch of guys"; and "C," meaning "Club." Kerry Yo Nakagawa, *Through a Diamond: 100 Years of Japanese American Baseball* (San Francisco: Rudi Publishing, 2001), 32. The use of team names drawn from cities or regions from where their organizers had migrated was not unusual. For instance, in the Mexican American barrio of East Los Angeles, in the 1920s among the most clubs was one named El Paso Shoe Store.

28. Nakagawa, *Through a Diamond,* 32.

29. Japanese American National Museum, "Diamonds in the Rough: Japanese Americans in Baseball," *Museum Magazine* (Spring 2000): 1, 8.

30. Frank Fukuda Collection, Box 1, Accession Number 128, Special Collections Archives, Allen Library, University of Washington, Seattle, Washington.

31. Ryoichi Shibazaki, "Seattle and the Japanese-United States Baseball Connection, 1905–1926," master's thesis, University of Washington, 1981, 74.

32. Frank Fukuda Collection, Box 1, Accession Number 128, Special Collections Archives, Allen Library, University of Washington, Seattle, WA; Samuel O. Regalado, "'Play Ball!' Baseball and Seattle's Japanese American Courier League, 1928–1941," *Pacific Northwest Quarterly* 87, no. 11 (Winter 1995–1996): 29–37.

33. Ibid., 79.

34. *Seattle Post-Intelligencer,* May 23, 1910. Clipping found in Frank Fukuda Collection.

35. *Seattle Post-Intelligencer,* no date. Clipping found in Frank Fukuda Collection.

36. Frank Fukuda Collection.

37. Ibid.

38. Kenji Kawaguchi interview with author. Seattle, Washington, June 15, 1993.

39. Robert A. Wilson and Bill Hosokawa, *East to America: A History of the Japanese in the United States* (New York: William Morrow, 1980), 45.

40. Oregon Editorial Association pamphlet, (1899), in Japanese in Oregon, File, Folder Number One. Oregon Historical Society Research Library, Portland, Oregon.

41. "Thrifty Japanese Live on $23 Per Year and Save Money," *The Oregonian* (Portland, Oregon), May 18, 1913. Clipping in Japanese in Oregon, File, Folder Number One. Oregon Historical Society Research Library.

42. Ibid.

43. Barbara Yasui, "The Nikkei in Oregon, 1834–1940," *Oregon Historical Quarterly*, 76, no. 3 (September 1975): 251.

44. *In this Great Land of Freedom: The Japanese Pioneers of Oregon* (Los Angeles: Japanese American National Museum, 1999), 18.

45. George Katagiri interview in the Japanese American Oral History Collection. Interview number 956. Oregon Historical Society, Portland.

46. *Nihonmachi: Portland's Japantown Remembered* (Portland, Oregon: Oregon Nikkei Legacy Center, 2002), 16.

47. Frank Fukuda Collection.

48. Paul R. Spickard, *Japanese Americans: The Formation and Transformations of an Ethnic Group* (New York: Twayne Publishers, 1996), 48.

49. Ibid.

50. Spickard, *Japanese Americans*, 49.

51. Ichioka, *The Issei*, 157.

52. Spickard, *Japanese Americans*, 51.

53. Ibid., 51.

54. *Los Angeles Rafu Shimpo*, July 18, 1926.

55. For more on xenophobia as it related to Asians in the United States during the 1920s, see Takaki, *Strangers from a Different Shore* and Daniels, *Asian America*. See also John Higham, *Strangers in the Land: Patterns in American Nativism, 1860-1925* (Piscataway, N.J.: Rutgers University Press, 2002).

56. Eiichiro Azuma, *Between Two Empires: Race, History, and Transnationalism in Japanese America* (New York: Oxford University Press, 2005), 112–13.

57. Ibid., 112–13.

58. Ibid.

59. Ibid., 123.

60. Ibid., 128–29.

61. Yuji Ichioka, et al., *Before Internment: Essays in Prewar Japanese American History* (Palo Alto, Calif.: Stanford University Press, 2006), 56.

62. Spickard, *Japanese Americans*, 32.

63. Ibid., 54.

64. Ibid., 58.

65. Shibazaki, "Seattle," 80.

66. Ibid.

67. Ibid., 81–82.

68. Ibid., 80.

69. Bill Staples Jr., *Kenichi Zenimura: Japanese American Baseball Pioneer* (Jefferson, N.C.: McFarland, 2011), 15.

70. Ibid., 22; Nakagawa, *Through a Diamond*, 85

71. Staples, *Kenichi Zenimura*, 22; Nakagawa, *Through a Diamond*, 85.

72. Andrew Rolle, *California: A History* (Wheeling, Ill.: Harlan Davidson, 2003), 192.

73. David Mas Masumoto, *Country Voices: The Oral History of a Japanese American Family Farm Community* (Del Rey, Calif.: Inaka Countryside Publications, 1987), 2.

74. "Kenichi Zenimura: The Dean of Japanese American Baseball," Nisei Baseball.com, http://www.niseibaseball.com/html%20articles/Nisei%20Legends/zenimura.htm (accessed March 15, 2006).

75. Nakagawa, *Through a Diamond*, 85; *Japanese American News*, May 29, 1929.

76. *Japanese American News*, May 18, 1929.

77. Nakagawa, *Through a Diamond*, 71–73, 85.

78. Ibid., 18–19.

79. Ralph M. Pearce, *From Asahis to Zebras: Japanese American Baseball in San Jose, California* (San Jose, Calif.: Japanese American Museum of San Jose, 2005), 20–21.

80. *Japanese American News*, July 4, 1926.

81. Nakagawa, *Through a Diamond*, 68.

82. Pearce, *From Asahi to Zebras*, 25.

83. Harvard Encyclopedia of American Ethnic Groups (Cambridge, Mass.: Harvard University Press,1980), 562.

84. Karleen C. Chinen, "Hawaii's AJAs Play Ball," in Brian Niiya, ed., *More Than a Game: Sport in the Japanese Community* (Los Angeles: Japanese American National Museum, 2000), 116.

85. Michael M. Okihiro, *AJA Baseball in Hawaii: Ethnic Pride and Tradition* (Honolulu: Hawaii Hochi, 1999) 13.

86. Ibid., 13–19.

87. Joel S. Franks, *Hawaiian Sports in the Twentieth Century* (Lewiston, N.Y.: Hawaiian Sports in the Twentieth Century, 2002), 70–71; Nakagawa, *Through A Diamond*, 53–54.

88. Staples, *Kenichi Zenimura*, 25.

89. Nakagawa, *Through A Diamond*, 63–64.

90. Chinen, "Hawaii's AJAs Play Ball," 112.

91. Samuel Hideo Yamashita, "The Aloha Team, 1942–1943," in Niiya, ed., *More Than a Game*, 164; Chinen, "Hawaii's AJAs Play Ball," 112.

92. Yamashita, "The Aloha Team, 1942–1943," 164.

93. Okihiro, *AJA Baseball in Hawaii*, 33.

94. Marshall Smelser, *The Life That Ruth Built: A Biography* (Lincoln: University of Nebraska Press, 1975), 461; Nakagawa, *Through A Diamond*, 461.

95. Daniels, *Asian America*, 156.

96. Ibid.

97. Ibid.

98. Linda Tamura, *The Hood River Issei: An Oral History of Japanese Settlers in Oregon's Hood River Valley* (Urbana and Chicago: University of Illinois Press, 1993), 43.

99. Spickard, *Japanese Americans*, 33.

Chapter 4. Baseball Is It!

1. Togo Tanaka, "History of Nisei Week," *Nisei Week Japanese Festival*, February 2009. Available at http://www.niseiweek.org/history.html (accessed February 4, 2009).

2. Yoichi Nagata, "The Pride of Lil' Tokio": The Los Angeles Nippons Baseball Club, 1926–1941," in Brian Niiya, ed., *More Than a Game: Sport in the Japanese American Community* (Los Angeles: Japanese American National Museum, 2000), 100.

3. Paul J. Zingg and Mark D. Medeiros, *Runs, Hits, and an Era: The Pacific Coast League, 1903-58* (Urbana: University of Illinois Press, 1994), 2.

4. Ibid.

5. Ibid., 15.

6. Ibid., 19

7. Roger Daniels, *Coming to America: A History of Immigration and Ethnicity in American Life* (New York: Harper Collins Publishers, 1991), 250.

8. Paul R. Spickard, *Japanese Americans: The Formation and Transformations of an Ethnic Group* (New York: Twayne Publishers, 1996), 170.

9. Spickard, *Japanese Americans*, 80.

10. Ibid., 73–75.

11. Ibid., 83; Samuel O. Regalado, "Sport and Community in California's Japanese American 'Yamato Colony,' 1930–1945," in *Journal of Sport History* 19, no. 2 (Summer 1992): 130–43; Kesa Noda, *Yamato Colony: 1906-1960: Livingston, California* (Livingston, Calif.: Livingston-Merced JACL Chapter, 1981), 99.

12. Ralph M. Pearce, *From Asahi to Zebras: Japanese American Baseball in San Jose* (San Jose, Calif.: Japanese American Museum of San Jose, 2005), 6.

13. Spickard, *Japanese Americans*, 48.

14. Tom Lewis, *Divided Highways: Building the Interstate Highways, Transforming American Life* (New York: Penguin Books, 1997), 23; John B. Rae, *The Road and the Car in American Life* (Cambridge, Mass.: MIT Press, 1971), 74.

15. Donald Roden, "Baseball and the Quest for National Dignity in Meiji Japan," *American Historical Review* 85 (June 1980): 513.

16. Wayne Maeda, *Changing Dreams and Treasured Memories: A Story of Japanese Americans in the Sacramento Region* (Sacramento, Calif.: Japanese American Citizens League, 2000), 149; for another example of baseball's connection between the Issei and Nisei, see Gail M. Nomura, "Beyond the Playing Field: The Significance of Pre-World War II Japanese American Baseball in the Yakima Valley," in Linda A. Revilla, ed., *Bearing Dreams, Shaping*

Visions: Asian Pacific American Perspectives (Pullman: Washington State University Press, 1993) and Regalado, "Sport and Community," 135–36.

17. Gary Ross Mormino, "The Playing Fields of St. Louis: Italian Immigrants and Sport, 1925–1941," *Journal of Sport History* 9 (Summer 1982): 5–16. For a broader perspective, see Steven A. Riess, *City Games: The Evolution of American Urban Society and the Rise of Sports* (Urban: University of Illinois Press, 1989), 103–7; among the most telling and poignant accounts which describe the relationship between the first-generation fathers and their sons over baseball is found in Peter Levine, *From Ellis Island to Ebbets Field: Sport and the American Jewish Experience* (New York: Oxford University Press, 1992), 91, 97–99.

18. There are several works that cover Latinos and baseball. For a more specified analysis of baseball's relationship to the Latin American community in the United States, see Roberto Gonzalez Echevarria, *The Pride of Havana: A History of Cuban Baseball* (New York: Oxford University Press, 1999) and Louis A. Perez, *On Becoming Cuban: Identity, Nationality, and Culture* (Chapel Hill: University of North Carolina Press, 2001). For the study of Latino professional baseball players and their impact on American Latinos, see Samuel O. Regalado, *Viva Baseball!: Latin Major Leaguers and their Special Hunger* (Urbana: University of Illinois Press, 1998).

19. David K. Yoo, *Growing Up Nisei: Race, Generation, and Culture among Japanese Americans of California, 1924–49* (Urbana: University of Illinois Press, 2000), 29.

20. Samuel O. Regalado, "'Play Ball!' Baseball and Seattle's Japanese-American Courier League, 1928–1941, *Pacific Northwest Quarterly* 87, no. 1 (Winter 1995–96): 29.

21. Harvey Kenji Tahara, "A Historical Study of the California Nisei 'A' Baseball Championship Tournaments From 1962 to 1973," master's thesis, Sacramento State College, 1967, 20–21.

22. Ibid., 21.

23. Bill Hosokawa, *Nisei: The Quiet Americans: The Story of a People* (New York: William Morrow, 1969), 164. Context, however, is necessary when reviewing Hosokawa's "sobering" comments. Wayne Maeda reveals that the noted journalist, a JACL leader, once stated that ". . . young Nisei . . . were more preoccupied with baseball and church socials than with their political obligations." Maeda, *Changing Dreams*, 149.

24. George Yoshio Matsumoto interview. Oral History Project, California State University, Sacramento.

25. Maeda, *Changing Dreams*, 150.

26. Roger Daniels, *Concentration Camps: North America: Japanese in the United States and Canada During World War II* (Malabar, Fla.: Robert E. Krieger, 1971), 25.

27. Noda, *Yamato Colony*, 87.

28. Ibid., 84–85.

29. Interview with Fred Kishi, May 18, 1991, Livingston, California.

30. Ibid.

31. Interview with Gilbert Tanji, July 24, 1991, Cressey, California.

32. Fred Kishi interview.

33. Ibid.

34. Interview with Robert Ohki, July 25, 1991, Livingston, California.

35. Regalado, "Sport and Community," 133.

36. Valerie Jean Matsumoto, "The Cortez Colony: Family, Farm and Community among Japanese Americans, 1919–1982," Ph.D. diss., Stanford University, 1986, 22–23.

37. Interview with Yuk Yatsuya, August 19, 1991, Turlock, California.

38. Yuk Yatsuya scrapbook. Turlock, California.

39. Interview with Yeichi Sakaguchi, August 19, 1991, Cortez, California.

40. Yatsuya interview.

41. Interview with Gilbert Tanji, July 24, 1991, Cressey, California.

42. Yatsuya interview.

43. Mack Yamaguchi scrapbook, Pasadena, California.

44. Sandy Lydon, *The Japanese in the Monterey Region: A Brief History* (Capitola, Calif.: Capitola Book Company, 1997), 47–48.

45. David T. Yamada, *The Japanese of the Monterey Peninsula: Their History and Legacy, 1895–1995* (David T. Yamada and Oral History Committee, MP/JACL, 1995), 186.

46. Ibid., 187.

47. *Monterey Peninsula Herald,* May 26, 1930.

48. Ibid., April 29, 1935.

49. Yamada, *Japanese of the Monterey Peninsula,* 187.

50. *Monterey Peninsula Herald,* August 17, 1936.

51. Ibid., October 6, 1941.

52. Robert E. Park, *The Immigrant Press and Its Control* (Westport, Conn.: Greenwood Press, 1922), 55.

53. David Yoo, "'Read All About It': Race, Generation and the Japanese American Ethnic Press, 1925–41," *Amerasia Journal* 19, no. 1, (1993): 72–73.

54. Katie Kaori Hayashi, *A History of the Rafu Shimpo: Japanese and Their Newspaper in Los Angeles* (Chuo-ku, Osaka, Japan: Union Press, 1997), 73.

55. Yoo, "Read All About It," 73–74.

56. Dorothy Ann Stroup, "The Role of the Japanese-American Press in Its Community," master's thesis, 1960, University of California, Berkeley.

57. Hayashi, *History of the Rafu Shimpo,* 69.

58. Stroup, "Role of the Japanese-American Press," 52.

59. Hayashi, *History of the Rafu Shimpo,* 72.

60. Daniels, *Concentration Camps,* 23.

61. Yoo, "Read All About It," 75.

62. Nagata, "Pride of Lil' Tokio," 100.

63. Ibid.

64. Peter Levine, *From Ellis Island,* 49.

65. *Los Angeles Rafu Shimpo,* May 9, 1927.

66. Ibid., May 16, 1927.

67. Spickard, *Japanese Americans,* 82.

68. Ibid., 83.

69. Ibid.

70. Lon Kurashige, "The Problem of Nisei Biculturalism," in Lon Kurashige and Alice Yang Murray, eds., *Major Problems in Asian American History* (Boston: Houghton-Mifflin, 2003), 280.

71. Lon Kurashige, *Japanese American Celebration and Conflict: A History of Ethnic Identity and Festival, 1934-1990* (Berkeley: University of California Press, 2002), 63.

72. Jere Takahashi, *Nisei, Sansei: Shifting Japanese Identities and Politics* (Philadelphia: Temple University Press, 1998), 56–57.

73. Daniels, *Concentration Camps*, 23.

74. Kathleen S. Yep, *Outside the Paint: When Basketball Ruled at the Chinese Playground* (Philadelphia: Temple University Press, 2009), 60.

75. Ibid., 59.

76. Nagata, "Pride of Lil' Tokio," 107.

77. Ibid., 108.

78. *Rafu Shimpo,* July 16, 1928.

79. Ibid., July 9, 1928.

80. Ibid., May 19, 1940, and May 24, 1940.

81. Ibid., July 11, 1927.

82. Nagata, "Pride of Lil Tokio," 104.

83. Ibid., 106.

84. Ibid.

85. Irving Howe, *World of Our Fathers: The Journey of the East European Jews to America and the Life They Found and Made* (New York: Simon and Schuster, 1976), 254.

86. George J. Sanchez, *Becoming Mexican American: Ethnicity, Culture and Identity in Chicano Los Angeles, 1900-1945* (New York: Oxford University Press, 1993), 263.

87. Yoo, *Growing Up Nisei, 32,*

88. Nagata, "Pride of Lil Tokio," 107.

89. Yoo, *Growing Up Nisei,* 27.

90. Nagata, "Pride of Lil Tokio," 104.

91. Ibid.

92. *Rafu Shimpo,* June 8, 1931.

93. Ibid.

94. Kerry Yo Nakagawa, *Through a Diamond: 100 Years of Japanese American Baseball* (San Francisco: Rudi Publishing, 2001), 85.

95. Ibid., July 4, 1926.

Chapter 5. The Courier League

1. Ryoichi Shibazaki, "Seattle and the Japanese-United States Baseball Connection, 1905–1926," master's thesis, University of Washington, 1981, 79; Samuel O. Regalado, "'Play Ball!' Baseball and Seattle's Japanese-American Courier League, 1928–1941," *Pacific Northwest Quarterly* 87, no. 1 (Winter 1995–96): 31.

2. *Japanese American Courier*, April 10, 1937.

3. Ibid., January 1, 1928.

4. S. Frank Miyamoto, *Social Solidarity among the Japanese in Seattle* (Seattle: University of Washington Press, 1939; rpt. 1984), 10.

5. Paul R. Spickard, *Japanese Americans: The Formation and Transformations of an Ethnic Group* (New York: Twayne Publishers, 1996), 24.

6. Roger Daniels, *Asian America: Chinese and Japanese in the United States since 1850* (Seattle: University of Washington Press, 1988), 115–16.

7. Yuji Ichioka, *The Issei: The World of the First Generation Japanese Immigrants, 1885-1924* (New York: The Free Press, 1988), 232.

8. Ibid.

9. Ibid., 233.

10. Ibid.

11. Yuji Ichioka, *The Issei*, 182–86.

12. Ibid., 184–85.

13. Ibid.

14. Ibid., 186.

15. Bill Hosokawa, *Nisei: The Quiet Americans* (New York: William Morrow, 1969), 181.

16. James Y. Sakamoto Papers. Available at http://www.lib.washington.edu/specialcoll/findaids/docs/papersrecords/SakamotoJames1609.xml (accessed March 15, 2005); Doug Blair, "The 1920 Anti-Japanese Crusade and Congressional Hearings," University of Washington Special Collections. http://depts.washington.edu/civilr/Japanese_restriction.htm (accessed March 20, 2006).

17. David. K Yoo, *Growing Up Nisei: Race, Generation, and Culture among Japanese Americans of California, 1924-49* (Urbana: University of Illinois Press, 2000), 32.

18. *Japanese-American Courier*, January 1, 1928; July 1, 1933.

19. Ibid., July 1, 1933.

20. Yuji Ichioka, "A Study in Dualism: James Yoshinori Sakamoto and the *Japanese American Courier, 1928-1942*," *Amerasia Journal* 13 (1986–87): 52.

21. Ibid., 80.

22. *Japanese American Courier*, January 1, 1928.

23. Ibid.

24. Courier League Constitution, N.D., Box 16, Sakamoto Papers.

25. S. Frank Miyamoto, *Social Solidarity*, xviii.

26. *Japanese American Courier*, January 1, 1928.

27. Ibid.

28. Ibid, April 10, 1937.

29. Ibid.

30. Ibid., January 1, 1928.

31. Interview with Kenji Kawagawa, Seattle, Washington, June 15, 1993.

32. Ibid.

33. Gail M. Nomura, "Beyond the Playing Field: The Significance of Pre-World War

II Japanese American Baseball in the Yakima Valley," in Linda A. Revilla, ed., *Bearing Dreams, Shaping Visions: Asian Pacific American Perspectives* (Pullman: Washington State University Press, 1993), 18.

34. *Japanese American Courier,* March 1, 1941.

35. Ibid., August 26, 1933.

36. Ibid., May 26, 1928.

37. Ibid., January 7, 1928.

38. Ibid., September 22, 1928.

39. Ibid., April 27, 1929.

40. Nomura, "Beyond the Playing Field," 20.

41. *Japanese American Courier,* July 7, 1934.

42. "'Oregon:' Population of Counties by Decennial Census: 1900–1990," Richard L. Forstall, compiler and editor, *Population Division, United States Bureau of Census,* Washington, D.C. Available at http://www.census.gov/population/cencounts/or190090.txt (accessed May 1, 2007); *U.S. Census Bureau, Department of Commerce, Fifteenth Census of the United States: 1930.* Volume 1, Population, Number and Distribution of Inhabitants (Washington D.C.: Government Printing Office, 1931), 1139, 1145–46, 1158–59. (accessed May 1, 2007).

43. Gordon Dodds, *Oregon: A History* (W.W. Norton, 1977), 138.

44. "Oshu Nippo," *The Oregon Encyclopedia.* Available at http://www.oregonencyclopedia .org/entry/view/oshu_nippo/ (accessed May 2, 2007).

45. George Katagiri, Cannon Kitayama, and Liz Nakazawa, *Nihonmachi: Portland's Japantown Remembered* (Portland: Oregon Nikkei Legacy Center, 2002), 25.

46. Barbara Yasui, "The Nikkei in Oregon, 1834–1940," *Oregon Historical Quarterly* 76, no. 3 (September 1975): 251.

47. Hiro Takeuchi interview. September 15, 2008, Portland, Oregon.

48. Ryoichi Shibazaki, "Seattle and the Japanese-United States Baseball Connection, 1905–1926," master's thesis, University of Washington, 1981, 67.

49. Deena K. Nakata, *The Gift: The Oregon Nikkei Story . . . Retold* (Portland, Ore.: Deena K. Nakata, 1995), 49.

50. Jerry Inouye interview. June 7, 1997. Portland, Oregon.

51. Kats Nakayama interview. July 31, 1996. Portland, Oregon.

52. Jerry Inouye interview.

53. Ibid.

54. John Murakami interview. July 31, 1996. Portland, Oregon.

55. Ibid.

56. Ibid.

57. Ibid.

58. Ibid.

59. Jerry Inouye interview.

60. Hiro Takeuchi interview. August 20, 1996. Portland, Oregon.

61. Ibid.

62. Tats Yada interview. June 7, 1997. Salem, Oregon.

63. Ibid.

64. Ibid.

65. Kay Kiyokawa interview. August 1, 1996. Dee, Oregon.

66. Homer Yasui interview. August 2, 1996. Portland, Oregon.

67. Kay Kiyokawa interview.

68. Ibid.

69. Homer Yasui interview.

70. Kay Kiyokawa interview.

71. John Murakami interview.

72. Jerry Inouye interview.

73. Kay Kiyokawa interview.

74. To further illuminate on Nisei women and athletics, see Samuel O. Regalado, "Incarcerated Sport: Nisei Women's Softball and Athletics during the Japanese American Internment Period," *Journal of Sport History* 27, no. 3 (Fall 2000): 431–44.

75. John Murakami interview.

76. Ibid.

77. Kay Kiyokawa interview.

78. Jerry Inoyue interview.

79. Hiro Takeuchi interview.

80. Tats Yada interview.

81. Kay Kiyokawa interview.

82. Homer Yasui interview.

83. Hiro Takeuchi interview.

84. Spickard, *Japanese Americans*, 80.

85. Yoo, *Growing Up Nisei*, 23.

86. Spickard, *Japanese Americans*, 80.

87. Ibid.

88. Roger Daniels, *Concentration Camps: North America Japanese in the United States and Canada During World War II* (Malabar, Fla.: Robert E. Kreiger), 23.

89. Spickard, *Japanese Americans*, 87.

90. Daniels, *Concentration Camps*, 23.

91. Yoo, *Growing Up Nisei*, 24.

92. At the California State Library in Sacramento, I examined each Monday, when Sunday box scores were printed, of each June and July between 1935 and 1941 to reach my conclusions. As a comparison, I found that Mexican American and Italian American clubs were listed from time to time. Even a club from the California State Prison at San Quentin made the box scores on occasion. Additionally, a reading of the *Los Angeles Times* was comparable to that found in the *San Francisco Chronicle*.

93. Bill Staples Jr., *Kenichi Zenimura: Japanese American Baseball Pioneer* (Jefferson, N.C.: McFarland, 2011), 109.

94. Ichioka, "A Study in Dualism," 71.

95. Tamura, *Hood River Issei,* 145.

96. Ibid.

Chapter 6. Barbed Wire Baseball

1. Mack Yamaguchi scrapbook.

2. Robert Ohki interview with author. July 25, 1991, Cressey, California.

3. Roger Daniels, *Concentration Camps: North America Japanese in the United States and Canada During World War II* (Malabar, Fla.: Robert E. Krieger, 1989), 38.

4. Audrie Girdner and Anne Loftis, *The Great Betrayal: The Evacuation of the Japanese-Americans During World War II* (London: Macmillan, 1969), 17.

5. Jeanne Wakatsuki Houston, *Farewell to Manzanar* (New York: Bantam Books, 1973), 5.

6. David K. Yoo, *Growing Up Nisei: Race, Generation, and Culture among Japanese Americans of California, 1924-49* (Urbana: University of Illinois Press, 2000), 126.

7. *Los Angeles Rafu Shimpo,* December 20, 1941.

8. Ibid.

9. Ibid., January 6, 1941.

10. Ibid.

11. Daniels, *Concentration Camps,* 76.

12. Ibid., 77.

13. Ibid.

14. Shizue Seigel, *In Good Conscience: Supporting Japanese Americans During the Internment* (San Mateo, Calif.: AACP, 2006), 2.

15. Yuji Ichioka, "A Study in Dualism: James Yoshinori Sakamoto and the Japanese American Courier, 1928-1942," *Amerasia* 13, no. 2 (1986-87): 70.

16. *Yasui v. United States* 320 U.S. 115 (1943); *Hirabayashi v. United States* 320 U.S. 81 (1943).

17. *Hirabayashi v. United States.*

18. Daniels, *Concentration Camps,* 75.

19. Bill Hosokawa, *Nisei: The Quiet Americans: The Story of a People* (New York: William Morrow, 1969), 248-49.

20. Daniels, *Concentration Camps,* 75.

21. Samuel O. Regalado, "Sport and Community in California's Japanese American 'Yamato Colony,' 1930-1945, *Journal of Sport History* 19, no. 2 (Summer 1992): 137.

22. Girdner and Loftis, *The Great Betrayal,* 157.

23. Yoo, *Growing Up Nisei,* 98.

24. Ibid., 98.

25. Hosokawa, *Nisei,* 333.

26. Daniels, *Concentration Camps,* 88-89.

27. Ibid., 88.

28. Seigel, *In Good Conscience*, 12.

29. Ibid.

30. Ibid., 82–85.

31. *Portland Oregonian*, May 10, 1942.

32. Ibid.

33. Regalado, "Sport and Community," 139.

34. Ibid.

35. *Portland Oregonian*, May 10, 1942.

36. *Pinedale Logger*, Pinedale Assembly Center, June 13, 1942.

37. On Fred Oshima, *El Joaquin*, Stockton Assembly Center, May 30, 1942; on Kenji Zenemura, *Fresno Center News*, May 30, 1942.

38. *Grapevine*, Fresno Assembly Center, July 4, 1942.

39. Ibid.

40. *Evacuazette*, Portland Assembly Center, June 9, 1942.

41. *El Joaquin*, Stockton Assembly Center, July 8 1942.

42. *The Mercedian*, Merced Assembly Center, August 7, 1942.

43. Ibid., August 14, 1942.

44. *Grapevine*, October 7, 1942.

45. Ibid.

46. Oral History Interviews with Karl R. Bendetsen, Harry S. Truman Library and Museum. Available at http://images.google.com/imgres?imgurl=http://www.trumanlibrary .org/oralhist/73–150.jpg&imgrefurl=http://www.trumanlibrary.org/oralhist/bendet .htm&usg=__InhgXywHqf51RHcLupWAA33Wrgw=&h=284&w=210&sz=12&hl= en&start=4&tbnid=z6F6omtk8s4t2M:&tbnh=114&tbnw=84&prev=/images%3Fq%3Dkarl %2Bbendetsen%26gbv%3D2%26hl%3Den%26sa%3DG (accessed September 5, 2008).

47. Daniels, *Concentration Camps*, 54.

48. Ibid., 102.

49. Ibid.

50. Ibid.

51. Dillon S. Myer, *Uprooted Americans: The Japanese Americans and the War Relocation Authority during World War II* (Tucson: University of Arizona Press, 1971), 6.

52. Daniels, *Concentration Camps*, 96.

53. Edward H. Spicer, "Anthropologists and the War Relocation Authority," *The Uses of Anthropology* 10 (1979): 222.

54. "Echoes in Silence: The Untold Stories of the Nisei Soldiers Who Served in World War II," Javacd.org-Poston. Available at http://www.javadc.org/poston.htm (accessed July 1, 2008).

55. "Manzanar," National Park Service archives. Available at http://www.nps.gov/ archive/manz/hrs/hrs11h.htm (accessed July 1, 2008); for more information about the Manzanar riots, one that included troops, gunfire, and casualties, see Daniels, *Concentration Camps*, 107–8.

56. H. Spicer, "Anthropologists," 223.

57. Ibid., 224.

58. Correspondence from Al Tsukamoto to John Provinse, September 30, 1943. War Relocation Authority (WRA) files. Box 414, Folder 4 (July 1942–February 1944). National Archives, Washington, D.C.

59. Correspondence from G. F. Castleberry to Edward B. Marks Jr., October 5, 1943, WRA files. Box 414, Folder 4 (July 1942–February 1944). National Archives, Washington, D.C.

60. Correspondence from Dillon Meyer to Congressman John M. Costello, undated. WRA files. Box 414, Folder 5 (March–December 1944). National Archives, Washington, D.C.; Woo, *Growing Up Nisei*, 108.

61. Correspondence from John H. Provinse to Edward B. Marks Jr. February 17, 1943. WRA files. Box 415, Reel 210.

62. Ibid.

63. Ibid.

64. Lauren Kessler, "Fettered Freedoms: The Journalism of World War II Japanese Internment Camps," *Journalism History* 15, no. 2–3 (Summer–Autumn 1988): 74.

65. Ibid., 73.

66. Arthur A. Hansen, "The Evacuation and Resettlement Study at the Gila River Relocation Center, 1942–1944," *Journal of the West* 38, no. 2 (April 1999): 48.

67. *Poston Chronicle*, June 16, 1942.

68. Letter from Edward B. Marks to John Provinse in WRA Field Documentation, Microfilm C0053, Granada Reel No. 46, October 27, 1942, National Archives, Washington, D.C.; Marks's impressions on "leadership" qualities appeared, based on an earlier memo, to be drawn by the vacuum of "caucasian" directorship of athletics. Letter from Marks to Provinse, WRA Field Documentation, October 15, 1942; *Granada Pioneer*, November 18, 1942; *Granada Pioneer*, November 21, 1942; *Granada Pioneer*, December 9, 1942.

69. *Rohwer Outpost*, November 14, 1942.

70. Ibid., November 18, 1942.

71. *Topaz Times Daily News*, April 15, 1943.

72. Ibid., April 8, 1943.

73. Ibid., May 8, 1943.

74. Ibid., May 29, 1943.

75. *Daily Tulean Dispatch*, May 4, 1943.

76. "The Recreation Recorder," Community Activities Division, WRA, Microfilm C0053, RG 210, April 14, 1943, National Archives, Washington, D.C.

77. Ibid.

78. Kerry Yo Nakagawa, *Through a Diamond: 100 Years of Japanese American Baseball* (San Francisco: Rudi Publishing, 2001), 85.

79. "Recreation," WRA Field Documentation, Microfilm C0053, Rohwer Reel No. 97, National Archives, Washington, D.C

80. Fred Kishi interview. Livingston, California. May 18, 1991.

81. "The Major Sports in Poston," WRA Community Analysis, Report No. 78, Microfilm M1342, RG 210, Roll No. 9, National Archives, Washington, D.C.

82. Gregory Lamb, "Backstory: The Players in the Shadows, June 29, 2006." Available at http://www.csmonitor.com/2006/0629/p20s01-alsp.html (accessed October 14, 2008).

83. David Davis, "A Field in the Desert that Felt like Home," *SI Vault* (November 16, 1998).

84. Nakagawa, *Through a Diamond*, 79.

85. Ibid.

86. *Topaz Times Daily News*, April 15, 1943, July 27, 1943.

87. Correspondence from Dillon Myer to Congressman John M. Costello, undated. WRA files. Box 414, Folder 5 (March–December 1944). National Archives, Washington, D.C.

88. Letter from Edward B. Marks Jr., Community Activities Adviser, to Mark A. McCloskey, Director of Relocation, Office of Defense, Health and Welfare Services. May 7, 1943. "Recreation," WRA Papers, RG 210, No. 67.030, Box 414, Folder 6, National Archives, Washington, D.C.

89. Letter from Charles F. Ernst, Project Director, Topaz Relocation Center, to Dillon S. Myer, July 20, 1943, regarding community athletics. WRA Papers, "Recreation," RG 210 67.010, Box 414, Folder 4. National Archives, Washington, D.C.

90. "Volunteers in Recreation," Report from A. G. Nielsen, Supervisor, Community Activities, Manzanar, CA on recreational activities. September 13, 1943. WRA Papers, 67.010. National Archives, Washington, D.C.

91. Memo from Gordon K. Chapman, Executive Secretary for the Protestant Commission for Japanese Service, to various churches. "Recreation," WRA Papers, RG 210, 67.030. National Archives, Washington, D.C.

92. Seigel, *In Good Conscience*, 159.

93. Fred Kischi interview. May 18, 1991, Livingston, California.

94. Kenji Kawaguchi interview. June 15, 1993. Seattle, Washington.

95. *Poston Chronicle*, February 5, 1944.

96. Community Analysis Reports, WRA Field Documentation, Microfilm M1342, RG 210, Minidoka Reel No. 66, May 27, 1943, National Archives, Washington, D.C.

97. Mack Yamaguchi interview. August 1, 1991. Pasadena, California.

98. Ibid.

99. *Granada Pioneer*, July 12, 1944.

100. Nakagawa, *Through a Diamond*, 82.

101. Community Analysis Reports, WRA Field Documentation, Microfilm M1342, RG 210, Minidoka Report No. 43, May 5, 1943, National Archives, Washington, D.C.

102. Ibid.

103. *Rohwer Outpost*, June 26, 1943.

104. Fred Kishi interview.

105. *Granada Pioneer*, August 2, 1944.

106. Ibid., August 30, 1944.

107. Ibid., September 13, 1944.

108. Nakagawa, *Through a Diamond*, 90.

109. *Topaz Times Daily News*, August 10, 1945.

110. Fred Kishi interview.

111. Daniels, *Concentration Camps*, 110.

112. Ibid.

113. *Rohwer Outpost*, June 12, 1943.

Chapter 7. Catching Up

1. A. J. Hayes, "A Major Minor League Accomplishment: Lenn Sakata Number 1 in California League," *Asian Week: The Voice of Asian America* (September 14, 2007). Available at http://www.asianweek.com/2007/09/14/a-major-minor-league-accomplishment -lenn-sakata-number-1-in-california-league-history/ (accessed January 20, 2009).

2. Ibid.

3. *Ex parte Endo*, 323 U.S. 283 (1944).

4. Roger Daniels, *Prisoners Without Trials: Japanese Americans in World War II* (New York: Hill & Wang, 1993), 86.

5. Ibid., 85–86.

6. Roger Daniels, *Concentration Camps: North America Japanese in the United States and Canada During World War II* (Malabar, Fla.: Robert E. Krieger, 1989), 159.

7. Linda Tamura, *The Hood River Issei: An Oral History of Japanese Settlers in Oregon's Hood River Valley* (Urbana: University of Illinois Press, 1993), 224.

8. Ibid.

9. Tamura, *Hood River Issei*, 224.

10. Ibid., 227.

11. Jerry Brewer, "Don Wakamatsu's grandparents' story puts new spin on life, baseball," *Seattle Times*, April 5, 2009. Available at http://seattletimes.nwsource.com/html/ mariners/2008986984_wakamatsu05.html (accessed March 30, 2009).

12. It should be noted that between the fall in 1944 and the spring 1946, camp closures varied. In some cases, such as in the Heart Mountain camp, Nisei baseball organizers did pull together a schedule of games from April through July. See Ralph M. Pearce, *From Asahi to Zebras: Japanese American Baseball in San Jose, California* (San Jose, Calif.: Japanese American Museum of San Jose, 2005), 83–85.

13. Louis Fiset, *Camp Harmony: Seattle's Japanese Americans and the Puyallup Assembly Center* (Urbana: University of Illinois Press, 2009), 144–45, 149.

14. *Hood River News*, February 2, 1945.

15. Kerry Yo Nakagawa, *Through A Diamond: 100 Years of Japanese American Baseball* (San Francisco: Rudi Publishing, 2001), 99.

16. Ibid.

17. "Kenichi Zenimura: The Dean of Japanese American Baseball," *Nisei Baseball*
.com, available at http://www.niseibaseball.com/html%20articles/Nisei%20Legends/
zenimura.htm (accessed March 15, 2006).

18. Nakagawa, *Through a Diamond*, 100.

19. *Nichi Bei Times*, June 11, 1946.

20. Ibid., July 1, 1947.

21. Joel S. Franks, *Asian Pacific Americans and Baseball: A History* (Jefferson, N.C.: Mc-
Farland, 2008), 63.

22. Letisia Marquez, "New book looks at photo used in World War II Japanese American resettlement effort," *UCLA Newsroom*, May 13, 2009. Available at http://newsroom
.ucla.edu/portal/ucla/ucla-professor-examines-institutional-89221.aspx (accessed January 10, 2010).

23. Greg Oliver and Steve Johnson, *The Pro Wrestling Hall of Fame: The Heels* (Toronto:
ECW Press, 2007), 373.

24. Brian Niiya, "More Than a Game: Sport in the Japanese American Community—
An Introduction," in Brian Niiya, ed., *More Than a Game: Sport in the Japanese American
Community* (Los Angeles: Japanese American National Museum, 2000), 53.

25. Ibid.

26. Oliver and Johnson, *Pro Wrestling Hall of Fame*, 373.

27. Niiya, ed., *More Than a Game*, 54.

28. Jules Tygiel, *Baseball's Great Experiment: Jackie Robinson and His Legacy* (New York:
Oxford University Press, 1983), i.

29. Nakagawa, *Through a Diamond*, 74

30. Ibid.

31. Daniels, *Concentration Camps*, 170.

32. The *Pacific Citizen* in its 1947 through 1948 issues rarely devoted more than a single,
brief paragraph on sports-related news.

33. *Nichi Bei Times*, July 1, 1950.

34. *Pacific Citizen*, July 15, 1950.

35. Pearce, *From Ashahi to Zebras*, 77–85.

36. Ibid., 89–92.

37. Ibid., 94–95.

38. *Pacific Citizen*, July 27, 1956.

39. The *Nichi Bei Times* in its July 1, 1962, issue announced no upcoming baseball schedule, as had been its practice in past years in preparation for the Fourth of July holiday.
In its July 3 issue, only a very brief announcement of the "State Nisei Junior Hardball"
game—a teenage baseball contest—appeared.

40. Robert K. Fitts, *Remembering Japanese Baseball: An Oral History of the Game* (Carbondale: Southern Illinois University Press, 2005), 1–3.

41. Robert K. Fitts, *Wally Yonamine: The Man Who Changed Japanese Baseball* (Lincoln:
University of Nebraska Press, 2008), 12.

42. Ibid., 13.

43. Karleen C. Chinen, "Hawaii's AJAs Play Ball," in Niija, ed., *More Than a Game*, 116.

44. Michael M. Orihito, *AJA Baseball in Hawaii: Ethnic Pride and Tradition* (Honolulu: Hawaii Hochi, 1999), 39–40.

45. Ibid., 114.

46. Ibid., 120.

47. Fitts, *Wally Yonomine*, 37.

48. Ibid., 74.

49. "Pearls: Wally Yonomine" promotional Web site. Available at http://www.janespearl .com/about2.html (accessed June 10, 2009).

50. Franks, *Asian Pacific Americans and Baseball*, 184.

51. Ibid., 184.

52. Bill Staples Jr., *Kenichi Zenimura, Japanese American Baseball Pioneer* (Jefferson, N.C.: McFarland, 2011), 99.

53. Ibid., 206.

54. Ibid.

55. Nakagawa, *Through a Diamond*, 122.

56. Andrew Rolle, *California: A History* (Wheeling, Ill.: Harlan Davidson, 2003), 321.

57. Paul R. Spickard, *Japanese Americans: The Formation and Transformations of an Ethnic Group* (New York: Twayne Publishers, 1996), 145.

58. Ibid.

59. Ironically, historian Paul Spickard points out that as Sansei and Yonsei fell into assimilation, so too did their crime rates when compared with mainstream society. Spickard, *Japanese Americans*, 164.

60. Spickard, *Japanese Americans*, 144.

61. Ibid.

62. Roger Daniels, *Prisoners Without Trials*, 107–8.

63. Helen Zia, *Asian American Dreams: The Emergence of an American People* (New York: Farrar, Straus and Giroux, 2001), 46.

64. Ibid., 47.

65. Franks, *Asian Pacific Americans and Baseball*, 174.

66. "45 Years Later, and Apology fro the U.S. Government," *A&S Perspectives* (Winter 2000). Available at http://www.artsci.washington.edu/news/Winter00/Hirabayashi .htm (accessed June 10, 2009).

67. Martha Minow, *Between Vengeance and Forgiveness: Facing History after Genocide and Mass Violence* (Boston: Beacon Press, 1999), 112–13. There are several important works on the topic of redress and reparations, including Peter Irons, *Justice at War: The Story of the Japanese American Internment Cases* (New York: Oxford University Press, 1983) and Roger Daniels, Sandra L. Taylor, and Harry H. K. Kitano, eds., *Japanese Americans: From Relocation to Redress* (Seattle: University of Washington, rev. ed., 1991).

68. Spickard, *Japanese Americans*, 156.

69. "Through a Diamond: Kerry Yo Nakagawa and the impact of baseball in his own

family," *Japanese American National Museum* (n.d.). Available at http://janmstore.com/ througdiamke.html (accessed June 15, 2009).

70. E-mail correspondence with Kerry Yo Nakagawa. October 9, 2011. Nakagawa was himself an athlete whose accomplishments included a swim from Alcatraz Island to San Francisco.

71. "Through a Diamond: Kerry Yo Nakagawa and the impact of baseball in his own family." Available at http://janmstore.com/througdiamke.html (accessed June 15, 2009).

72. E-mail correspondence with Kerry Yo Nakagawa. October 9, 2011.

73. Nakagawa, *Through a Diamond*, 134.

74. Ryan Kim, "S.F. Ballpark's Family Ties," *San Francisco Examiner*. Available at http:// articles.sfgate.com/1999–11–08/news/28590448_1 (accessed September 5, 2011).

75. Rebecca Chiyoko King, "'Eligible' to Be Japanese American: Multiraciality in Basketball Leagues and Beauty Pageants," in Linda Trinh Võ and Rick Bonus, eds. *Contemporary Asian American Communities: Intersections and Divergences* (Philadelphia: Temple University Press, 2002), 125.

76. Ibid., 130.

77. Rebecca Chiyoko King and Kimberly McClain DaCosta, "Changing Face, Changing Race: The Remaking of Race in the Japanese American and African American Communities," in Maria P. P. Root, ed., *The Multicultural Experience: Racial Borders as The New Frontiers* (Newbury Park, Calif.: Sage Publications, 1996), 236.

78. "Lenn Sakata," Baseball Reference.com. Available at http://www.baseball-reference .com/bullpen/Lenn_Sakata (accessed October 23, 2011).

79. Nakagawa, *Through a Diamond*, p. 124.

80. It should be noted that players who are "hapa," Hawaiians of mixed Asian or Pacific Island racial or ethnic heritage, such as Mike Lum and Shane Victorino, also hold big-league credentials. Plus, Dave Roberts of Okinawa, whose mother was Japanese, also enjoyed a productive career in the majors.

81. A. J. Hayes, "A Major Minor League Accomplishment: Lenn Sakata Number 1 in California League." Available at http://www.asianweek.com/2007/09/14/a-major -minor-league-accomplishment-lenn-sakata-number-1-in-california-league-history/ (accessed June 20, 2009).

82. *Seattle Times,* November 19, 2008.

83. Interview with Don Wakamatsu, Oakland, California, August 19, 2011.

84. Ibid.

85. "Mariners' manager wants to set example for other Asian-Americans in sports." Available at http://www.mercurynews.com/sports/ci_11613535 (accessed June 22, 2009).

86. Don Wakamatsu interview.

87. Interview with Kurt Suzuki in Oakland, California. August 19, 2011.

88. *Seattle Times,* November 20, 2008.

89. Ibid.

90. *News Tribune* (Tacoma, Washington), November 20, 2008.

91. Ibid.

92. Don Wakamatsu interview.

93. *New York Times*, February 2, 2009.

94. Don Wakamatsu interview.

95. *New York Times*, February 2, 2009.

96. *Seattle Times*, November 20, 2008.

97. *San Francisco Chronicle*, November 20, 2008.

98. Interview with Robert Taniguchi in Merced, California, August 20, 2009.

99. *Nichi Bei Times,* November 20–26, 2008 issue. On the Nisei Baseball Research Project see "NBRP Salutes Don Wakamatsu: First Asian-American Manager in MLB History," available at http://www.niseibaseball.com/news_don_wakamatsu_first_asian_american _manager_in_MLB_history.html (accessed June 22, 2009).

100. Brad Lefton, "Lenn Sakata doesn't expect to see more Japanese American managers anytime soon," *Seattle Times,* June 16, 2009.

101. Myles Valentin, "A Heckler's Apology to Hawaii's (Not Japan's) Kurt Suzuki," *Bleacher Report,* April 20, 2009. Available at http://bleacherreport.com/articles/159284-a-hecklers-apology-to-hawaiis-not-japans-kurt-suzuki. (accessed July 5, 2009).

102. *Nichi Bei Times,* April 9–15, 2009.

103. *Los Angeles Rafu Shimpo,* April 4, 2009.

104. Geoff Baker, "Don Wakamatsu benched Chone Figgins for failing to back up a throw, sparking dugout row; Jack Zduriencik to meet with both tomorrow," *Seattle Times,* July 23, 2010, available at http://seattletimes.nwsource.com/html/marinersblog/2012436420_don_wakamatsu_benched_chone_fi.html (accessed July 24, 2010).

105. "Wakamatsu Makes Gracious Exit," available at http://blog.seattlepi.com/baseball/archives/217582.asp (accessed August 10, 2010).

106. Don Wakamatsu interview.

107. Ibid.

108. Kurt Suzuki interview.

Bibliography

Books

Azuma, Eiichiro. *Between Two Empires: Race, History, and Transnationalism in Japanese America*. New York: Oxford University Press, 2005.

Beasley, W. G. *The Modern History of Japan*, Second Edition. New York: Praeger Publishers, 1974.

Burns, Edward M. *The American Idea of Mission: Concepts of National Purpose and Destiny*. New Brunswick, N.J.: Rutgers University Press, 1957.

Conroy, Hilary. *The Japanese Frontier in Hawaii, 1868-1898*. Berkeley: University of California Press, 1953.

Daniels, Roger. *Asian America: Chinese and Japanese in the United States since 1850*. Seattle, WA: The University of Washington Press, 1988.

——. *Concentration Camps: North America Japanese in the United States and Canada During World War II*. Malabar, Fla.: Robert E. Kreiger, 1989.

——. *Coming to America: A History of Immigration and Ethnicity in American Life*. New York: Harper Collins, 1991.

——. *Prisoners Without Trials: Japanese Americans in World War II*. New York: Hill & Wang, 1993.

Daniels, Roger, Sandra L. Taylor, and H.K. Kitano, ed. *Japanese Americans: From Relocation to Redress*. Seattle: University of Washington Press, rev. ed., 1991.

Daws, Gaven. *Shoal of Time: A History of the Hawaiian Islands*. Honolulu: University of Hawaii Press, 1968.

Duus, Peter. *Modern Japan*, 2nd Edition. Boston: Houghton Mifflin Harcourt, 1997.

Echevarria, Roberto Gonzalez. *The Pride of Havana: A History of Cuban Baseball*. New York: Oxford University Press, 1999.

Fitts, Robert K. *Remembering Japanese Baseball: An Oral History of the Game*. Carbondale: Southern Illinois University Press, 2005.

——. *Wally Yonamine: The Man Who Changed Japanese Baseball*. Lincoln: University of Nebraska Press, 2008.

Franks, Joel S. *Crossing Sidelines, Crossing Cultures: Sport and Asian Pacific American Cultural Citizenship*. New York: University Press of America, 2000.

——. *Hawaiian Sports in the Twentieth Century*. Lewiston, N.Y.: Edwin Mellen Press, 2002.

——. *Asian Pacific Americans and Baseball: A History*. Jefferson, N.C.: McFarland, 2008.

Gems, Gerald R. *The Athletic Crusade: Sport and American Cultural Imperialism*. Lincoln: University of Nebraska Press, 2006.

Girdner, Audrie, and Anne Loftis. *The Great Betrayal: The Evacuation of the Japanese-Americans During World War II*. London: Macmillan, 1969.

Gordon, Andrew. *A Modern History of Japan: From Tokugawa Time to the Present Day*. New York: Oxford University Press, 2008.

Hackett, Robert F. "The Meiji Leaders and Modernization: The Case of Yamagata Aritomo," in Marius B. Jansen, ed. *Changing Japanese Attitudes Towards Modernization*. Princeton, N.J.: Princeton University Press.

Hall, Kermit L., ed. *The Oxford Companion to The Supreme Court of the United States*. New York: Oxford University Press, 1992.

Harvard Encyclopedia of American Ethnic Groups. Cambridge, Mass.: Harvard University Press, 1980.

Hayashi, Katie Kaori. *A History of the Rafu Shimpo: Japanese and Their Newspaper in Los Angeles*. Chuo-ku, Osaka, Japan: Union Press, 1997.

Hopkins, C. Howard. *History of the YMCA in North America*. New York: Association Press, 1951.

Hosokawa, Bill. *Nisei: The Quiet Americans: The Story of a People*. New York: William Morrow, 1969.

Houston, Jeanne Wakatsuki. *Farewell to Manzanar*. New York: Bantam Books, 1973.

Howe, Irving. *World of Our Fathers: The Journey of the East European Jews to America and the Life They Found and Made*. New York: Simon and Schuster, 1976.

Ichioka, Yuji. *The Issei: The World of the First Generation Japanese Immigrants, 1885–1924*. New York: The Free Press, 1988.

In this Great Land of Freedom: The Japanese Pioneers of Oregon. Los Angeles: Japanese American National Museum, 1999.

Irons, Peter. *Justice at War: The Story of the Japanese American Internment Cases*. New York: Oxford University Press, 1983.

Ito, Kazuo. *Issei: A History of Japanese Immigrants in North America*. Seattle: Japanese Community Service, 1973.

Katagiri, George, Cannon Kitayama, and Liz Nakazawa. *Nihonmachi: Portland's Japantown Remembered*. Portland: Oregon Nikkei Legacy Center, 2002.

Kimura, Yukiko. *Issei: Japanese Immigrants in Hawaii*. Honolulu: University of Hawaii Press, 1988.

Kurashige, Lon. *Japanese American Celebration and Conflict: A History of Ethnic Identity and Festival, 1934–1990*. Berkeley: University of California Press, 2002.

Levine, Peter. *A. G. Spalding and the Rise of Baseball: The Promise of American Sport*. New York: Oxford University Press, 1985.

——. *Ellis Island to Ebbets Field: Sport and the American Jewish Experience*. New York: Oxford University Press, 1992.

Lewis, Tom. *Divided Highways: Building the Interstate Highways, Transforming American Life*. New York: Penguin Books, 1997.

Lyon, Sandy. *The Japanese in the Monterey Region: A Brief History*. Capitola, Calif.: Capitola Book Company, 1997.

Maeda, Wayne. *Changing Dreams and Treasured Memories: A Story of Japanese Americans in the Sacramento Region*. Sacramento, Calif.: Japanese American Citizens League, 2000.

Masumoto, David Mas. *Country Voices: The Oral History of a Japanese American Family Farm Community*. Del Rey, Calif.: Inaka Countryside Publications, 1987.

Meyer, Dillon S. *Uprooted Americans: The Japanese Americans and the War Relocation Authority during World War II*. Tucson: University of Arizona Press, 1971.

Minow, Martha. *Between Vengeance and Forgiveness: Facing History after Genocide and Mass Violence*. Boston: Beacon Press, 1999.

Miyamoto, Shotaro Frank. *Social Solidarity among the Japanese in Seattle*. Seattle: University of Washington Press, 1939.

Nakagawa, Kerry Yo. *Through a Diamond: 100 Years of Japanese American Baseball*. San Francisco: Rudi Publishing, 2001.

Nakata, Deena K. *The Gift: The Oregon Nikkei Story . . . Retold*. Portland, Ore.: Deena K. Nakata, 1995.

Niiya, Brian, ed., *More Than a Game: Sport in the Japanese American Community*. Los Angeles: Japanese American National Museum, 2000.

Noda, Kesa. *Yamato Colony: 1906–1960: Livingston, California*. Livingston, Calif.: Livingston-Merced JACL Chapter, 1981.

Obata, Chiura. *Obata's Yosemite: The Art and Letters of Chiura Obata from His trip to the High Sierra in 1927*. Yosemite National Park, Calif.: Yosemite Association, 1993.

——. *Topaz Moon: Art of the Internment*. Berkeley: University of California Press, 2000.

Ogawa, Dennis M. *Kodomo no tame ni: For the Sake of the Children: The Japanese American Experience in Hawaii*. Honolulu: University of Hawaii Press, 1978.

Okihiro, Michael M. *AJA Baseball in Hawaii: Ethnic Pride and Tradition*. Honolulu: Hawaii Hochi, 1999.

Oliver, Greg, and Steve Johnson. *The Pro Wrestling Hall of Fame: The Heels*. Toronto: ECW Press, 2007.

Park, Robert E. . *The Immigrant Press and Its Control*. Westport, Conn.: Greenwood Press, 1922.

Pearce, Ralph M. . *From Ashahi to Zebras: Japanese American Baseball in San Jose, California*. San Jose, Calif.: Japanese American Museum of San Jose, 2005.

Perez, Louis A. *On Becoming Cuban: Identity, Nationality, and Culture*. Chapel Hill: University of North Carolina Press, 2001.

Putney, Clifford. *Muscular Christianity: Manhood and Sports in Protestant America, 1880-1920*. Cambridge, Mass.: Harvard University Press, 2001.

Pyle, Kenneth B. *The Making of Modern Japan*. Toronto: D.C. Heath, 1996.

——. *The New Generation in Meiji Japan: Problems of Cultural Identity, 1885-1895*. Stanford, Calif.: Stanford University Press, 1969.

Rader, Benjamin G. *Baseball: A History of America's National Game*. Urbana: University of Illinois Press, 1992.

Rae, John B. . *The Road and the Car in American Life*. Cambridge, Mass.: MIT Press, 1971.

Regalado, Samuel O. *Viva Baseball!: Latin Major Leaguers and their Special Hunger*. Urbana: University of Illinois Press, 1998.

Riess, Steven A. *City Games: The Evolution of American Urban Society and the Rise of Sports*. Urbana: University of Illinois Press, 1989.

Rolle, Andrew. *California: A History*. Wheeling, Ill.: Harlan Davidson, 2003.

Sanchez, George J. *Becoming Mexican American: Ethnicity, Culture and Identity in Chicano Los Angeles, 1900-1945*. New York: Oxford University Press, 1993.

Sarasohn, Eileen Sunada, ed. *The Issei: Portrait of a Pioneer: An Oral History*. Palo Alto, Calif.: Pacific Books, 1983.

Seigel, Shizue. *In Good Conscience: Supporting Japanese Americans During the Internment*. San Mateo, Calif.: AACP, 2006.

Seymour, Harold. *Baseball: The People's Game*. New York: Oxford University Press, 1990.

Smelser, Marshall. *The Life That Ruth Built: A Biography*. Lincoln: University of Nebraska Press, 1975.

Spickard, Paul R. *Japanese Americans: The Formation and Transformations of an Ethnic Group*. New York: Twayne Publishers, 1996.

Staples, Bill, Jr. *Kenichi Zenimura: Japanese American Baseball Pioneer*. Jefferson, N.C.: McFarland, 2011.

Stevens, Sylvester K. *American Expansion in Hawaii: 1842-1898*. New York: Russell & Russell, 1968.

Takahashi, Jere. *Nisei, Sansei: Shifting Japanese Identities and Politics*. Philadelphia: Temple University Press, 1998.

Takati, Ronald. *Strangers from a Different Shore: A History of Asian Americans*. New York: Penguin Books, 1989.

Tamura, Linda. *The Hood River Issei: An Oral History of Japanese Settlers in Oregon's Hood River Valley*. Urbana: University of Illinois Press, 1993.

Bibliography

Thomas, Dorothy Swaine, et al. *Japanese American Evacuation and Resettlement (JERS): The Salvage*. Berkeley: University of California Press, 1952.

Tygiel, Jules. *Baseball's Great Experiment: Jackie Robinson and His Legacy*. New York: Oxford University Press, 1983.

Yamada, David T. *The Japanese of the Monterey Peninsula: Their History and Legacy, 1895-1995*. David T. Yamada and Oral History Committee, MP/JACL, 1995.

Yep, Kathleen S. *Outside the Paint: When Basketball Ruled at the Chinese Playground*. Philadelphia: Temple University Press, 2009.

Yoo, David K. *Growing Up Nisei: Race, Generation, and Culture among Japanese Americans of California, 1924-49*. Urbana: University of Illinois Press, 2000.

Zia, Helen. *Asian American Dreams: The Emergence of an American People*. New York: Farrar, Straus and Giroux, 2001.

Zingg, Paul J., and Mark D. Medeiros. *Runs, Hits, and an Era: The Pacific Coast League, 1903-58*. Urbana: University of Illinois Press, 1994.

Articles and Essays

Chinen, Karleen C. "Hawaii's AJA's Play Ball." In Brian Niija, ed., *More Than a Game: Sport in the Japanese American Community*. Los Angeles: Japanese American National Museum, 2000, 110.

Gelber, Steven M. "Working at Playing: The Culture of the Workplace and the Rise of Baseball." *Journal of Social History* 16 (June 1983): 3-22.

Hackett, Robert F. "The Meiji Leaders and Modernization: The Case of Yamagata Aritomo." In Marius B. Jansen, ed., *Changing Japanese Attitudes Towards Modernization*. Princeton, N.J.: Princeton University Press, 1965.

Hansen, Arthur A. "The Evacuation and Resettlement Study at the Gila River Relocation Center, 1942-1944." *Journal of the West* 38, no. 2 (April 1999): 48.

Ichioka, Yuji. "A Study in Dualism: James Yoshinori Sakamoto and the *Japanese American Courier*, 1928-1942." *Amerasia Journal* 13 (1986-87): 52.

Kessler, Lauren. "Fettered Freedoms: The Journalism of World War II Japanese Internment Camps." *Journalism History* 15, no. 2-3 (Summer-Autumn 1988): 74.

Kohl, Stephen W., ed. "An Early Account of Japanese Life in the Pacific Northwest: The Writings of Nagai Kafu." *Pacific Northwest Quarterly* 70, no. 1 (April 1979): 62.

Kurashige, Lon. "The Problem of Nisei Biculturalism." In Lon Kurashige and Alice Yang Murray, eds., *Major Problems in Asian American History*. Boston: Houghton Mifflin, 2003.

Mormino, Gary Ross. "The Playing Fields of St. Louis: Italian Immigrants and Sport, 1925-1941." *Journal of Sport History* 9 (Summer 1982): 5-16.

Nagata, Yoichi. "'The Pride of Lil' Tokio': The Los Angeles Nippons Baseball Club, 1926-1941." In Brian Niiya, ed., *More Than a Game: Sport in the Japanese American Community*. Los Angeles: Japanese American National Museum, 2000.

Niiya, Brian. "More Than a Game: Sport in the Japanese American Community—An Introduction." In Brian Niiya, ed., *More Than a Game: Sport in the Japanese American Community.* Los Angeles: Japanese American National Museum, 2000.

Nomura, Gail M. "Beyond the Playing Field: The Significance of Pre-World War II Japanese American Baseball in the Yakima Valley." In Linda A. Revilla, ed., *Bearing Dreams, Shaping Visions: Asian Pacific American Perspectives.* Pullman: Washington State University Press, 1993.

Regalado, Samuel O. "Sport and Community in California's Japanese American 'Yamato Colony,' 1930–1945." *Journal of Sport History* 19, no. 2 (Summer 1992): 130–43, 99.

——. "'Play Ball!' Baseball and Seattle's Japanese-American Courier League, 1928–1941." *Pacific Northwest Quarterly* 87, no. 1 (Winter 1995–96): 29.

——. "Incarcerated Sport: Nisei Women's Softball and Athletics during the Japanese American Internment Period." *Journal of Sport History* 27, no. 3 (Fall 2000): 431–44.

Roden, Donald. "Baseball and the Quest for National Dignity in Meiji Japan." *American Historical Review* 85 (June 1980): 513.

Spicer, Edward H. "Anthropologists and the War Relocation Authority." *The Uses of Anthropology* 11 (1979): 222.

Story, Ronald. "The Country of the Young: The Meaning of Baseball in Early American Culture." In David K. Wiggins, ed., *Sport in America: From Wicked Amusement to National Obsession.* Champaign, Ill.: Human Kinetics, 1995.

Wilson, Robert A., and Bill Hosokawa. *East to America: A History of the Japanese in the United States.* New York: William Morrow, 1980.

Yamashita, Samuel Hideo. "The Aloha Team, 1942–1943." In Brian Niiya, ed., *More Than a Game: Sport in the Japanese American Community.* Los Angeles: Japanese American National Museum, 2000.

Yasui, Barbara. "The Nikkei in Oregon, 1834–1940." *Oregon Historical Quarterly* 76, no. 3 (September 1975): 251.

Yoo, David K. "'Read All About It': Race, Generation and the Japanese American Ethnic Press, 1925–41." *Amerasia Journal* 19, no. 1 (1993): 72–73.

Newspapers

Daily Tulean Dispatch (Tule Lake, California, Assembly Center)
Fresno Center News (Fresno, California, Assembly Center)
El Joaquin (Stockton, California, Assembly Center)
Evacuazette (Portland, Oregon, Assembly Center)
Granada Pioneer (Amache, Colorado, Relocation Center)
Grapevine (Fresno, California, Assembly Center)
Hood River News (Hood River, Oregon)
Japanese American Courier (Seattle, Washington)
Japanese American News (San Francisco)

Los Angeles Japanese Daily News
The Mercedian (Merced, California, Assembly Center)
Monterey Peninsula Herald (Monterey, California)
New York Times
News Tribune (Tacoma, Washington)
Nichi Bei Times (San Francisco)
Pacific Citizen (San Francisco)
Pinedale Logger (Pinedale, California, Assembly Center)
Portland Oregonian
Poston Chronicle (Poston, Arizona, Relocation Center)
Rafu Shimpo (Los Angeles)
Rohwer Outpost (Rohwer, Arkansas, Relocation Center)
San Francisco Chronicle
Seattle Post-Intelligencer
Seattle Times
Topaz Times Daily News (Topaz, Idaho, Relocation Center)

Dissertations and Theses

Matsumoto, Valerie Jean. "The Cortez Colony: Family, Farm and Community among Japanese Americans, 1919–1982." Ph.D. diss., Stanford University, 1986.
Shibazaki, Ryoichi. "Seattle and the Japanese-United States Baseball Connection, 1905–1926." Master's thesis, University of Washington, 1981.
Stroup, Dorothy Ann. "The Role of the Japanese-American Press in Its Community." Master's thesis, 1960, University of California, Berkeley.
Tahara, Harvey Kenji. "A Historical Study of the California Nisei 'A' Baseball Championship Tournaments From 1962 to 1973." Master's thesis, Sacramento State College, 1967.

Archival Sources

Aibara Collection, "Yamato Colony at Livingston, CA," Box 41, Number 4, Special Collections Archives, California State University, Stanislaus, Turlock, California.
Frank Fukuda Collection. Special Collection Archives, Allen Library, University of Washington, Seattle, Washington.
George Katagiri interview in the Japanese American Oral History Collection. Interview number 956. Oregon Historical Society, Portland, Oregon.
George Yoshio Matsumoto interview. Oral History Project, California State University, Sacramento.
James Y. Sakamoto Papers, Special Collection Archives, Allen Library, University of Washington, Seattle, Washington.Oral History Project, "Japanese Americans: Nisei," California State University, Sacramento.

Mack Yamaguchi scrapbook, Pasadena, California.

"Oregon Editorial Association" pamphlet, (1899), in "Japanese in Oregon," File, Folder Number One.

Oregon Historical Society Research Library, Portland, Oregon.

"Thrifty Japanese Live on $23 Per Year and Save Money," *The Oregonian* (Portland, Oregon), May 18, 1913. Clipping in "Japanese in Oregon," File, Folder Number One. Oregon Historical Society Research Library.

Yuk Yatsuya scrapbook. Turlock, California.

NATIONAL ARCHIVES, WASHINGTON, D.C.

Community Analysis Reports, WRA Field Documentation, Microfilm M1342, RG 210, Minidoka Report No. 43, May 5, 1943, National Archives, Washington, D.C

Community Analysis Reports, WRA Field Documentation, Microfilm M1342, RG 210, Minidoka Reel No. 66, May 27, 1943, National Archives, Washington, D.C.

Correspondence from G. F. Castleberry to Edward B. Marks, October 5, 1943, WRA files. Box 414, Folder 4 (July 1942–February 1944). National Archives, Washington, D.C.

Correspondence from Dillon Myer to Congressman John M. Costello, undated. WRA files. Box 414, Folder 5 (March–December 1944). National Archives, Washington, D.C.

Correspondence from John H. Provinse to Edward B. Marks, February 17, 1943. WRA files. Box 415, Reel 210. National Archives, Washington, D.C.

Correspondence from Al Tskamoto to John Provinse, September 30, 1943. War Relocation Authority (WRA) files. Box 414, Folder 4 (July 1942–February 1944). National Archives, Washington, D.C.

Letter from Charles F. Ernst, Project Director, Topaz Relocation Center to Dillon S. Meyer. July 20, 1943, regarding community athletics. WRA Papers, "Recreation," RG 210 67.010, Box 414, Folder 4. National Archives, Washington, D.C.

Letter from Edward B. Marks, Community Activities Adviser, to Mark A. McCloskey, Director of Relocation, Office of Defense, Health and Welfare Services. May 7, 1943. "Recreation," WRA Papers, RG 210, No. 67.030, Box 414, Folder 6, National Archives, Washington, D.C.

Letter from Edward B. Marks to John Provinse in WRA Field Documentation, Microfilm C0053, Granada Reel No. 46, October 27, 1942, National Archives, Washington, D.C.

Letter from Marks to Provinse, WRA Field Documentation, October 15, 1942;

"The Major Sports in Poston," WRA Community Analysis, Report No. 78, Microfilm M1342, RG 210, Roll No. 9, National Archives, Washington, D.C.

Memo from Gordon K. Chapman, Executive Secretary for the Protestant Commission for Japanese Service to various churches. "Recreation," WRA Papers, RG 210, 67.030. National Archives, Washington, D.C.

"Recreation," WRA Field Documentation, Microfilm C0053, Rohwer Reel No. 97, National Archives, Washington, D.C

"The Recreation Recorder," Community Activities Division, WRA, Microfilm C0053, RG 210, April 14, 1943, National Archives, Washington, D.C.

"Volunteers in Recreation," Report from A. G. Nielsen, Supervisor, Community Activities, Manzanar, CA on recreational activities. September 13, 1943. WRA Papers, 67.010. National Archives, Washington, D.C.

Interviews

Jerry Inouye interview. June 7, 1997, Portland, Oregon.
Kenji Kawaguchi interview. June 15, 1993, Seattle, Washington.
Fred Kishi interview. May 18, 1991, Livingston, California.
Kay Kiyokawa interview. August 1, 1996, Dee, Oregon.
John Murakami interview. July 31, 1996, Portland, Oregon.
Kats Nakayama interview. July 31, 1996, Portland, Oregon.
Robert Ohki interview. July 25, 1991, Livingston, California.
Yeichi Sakaguchi interview. August 19, 1991, Cortez, California.
Kurt Suzuki interview. August 19, 2011, Oakland, California.
Hiro Takeuchi interview. September 15, 2008, Portland, Oregon.
Robert Taniguchi interview. August 20, 2009, Merced, CA.
Gilbert Tanji interview. July 24, 1991, Cressey, California.
Don Wakamatsu interview. August 19, 2011, Oakland, California.
Tats Yada interview. June 7, 1997, Salem, Oregon.
Mack Yamaguchi interview. August 1, 1991, Pasadena, California.
Homer Yasui interview. August 2, 1996, Portland, Oregon.
Yuk Yatsuya interview. August 19, 1991, Turlock, California.

Court Cases

Ex parte Endo, 323 U.S. 283 (1944).
Yasui v. United States, 320 U.S. 115 (1943).
Hirabayashi v. United States, 320 U.S. 81 (1943).

Internet Sources

Baker, Geoff. "Don Wakamatsu benched Chone Figgins for failing to back up a throw, sparking dugout row; Jack Zduriencik to meet with both tomorrow." *Seattle Times*, July 23, 2010. Available at http://seattletimes.nwsource.com/html/marinersblog/2012436420_don_wakamatsu_benched_chone_fi.html (accessed July 24, 2010).

Blair, Doug. "The 1920 Anti-Japanese Crusade and Congressional Hearings," University of Washington Special Collections. Available at http://depts.washington.edu/civilr/Japanese_restriction.htm (accessed March 20, 2006).

Brewer, Jerry. "Don Wakamatsu's grandparents' story puts new spin on life, baseball," *Seattle Times,* April 5, 2009, Available at http://seattletimes.nwsource.com/html/mariners/2008986984_wakamatsu05.html (accessed March 30, 2009).

"Echoes in Silence: The Untold Stories of the Nisei Soldiers Who Served in World War II," *Javacd.org-Poston.* Available at http://www.javadc.org/poston.htm (accessed July 1, 2008).

"45 Years Later, an Apology from the U.S. Government," *A & S Perspectives* (Winter 2000). Available at http://www.artsci.washington.edu/news/Winter00/Hirabayashi.htm (accessed June 10, 2009).

"Guide to the James Y. Sakamoto Papers, 1928–1955," University of Washington Library Special Collections. Available at http://www.lib.washington.edu/specialcoll/findaids/docs/papersrecords/SakamotoJames1609.xml; http://depts.washington.edu/civilr/Japanese_restriction.htm (accessed March 20, 2006)

Hayes, A. J. "A Major Minor League Accomplishment: Lenn Sakata Number 1 California League History." *Asian Week: The Voice of Asia America,* September 14, 2007. Available at http://www.asianweek.com/2007/09/14/a-major-minor-league-accomplishment-lenn-sakata-number-1-in-california-league-history/ (accessed June 20, 2009).

"Hiraoka Hiroshi," Baseball Reference.com. Available at http://pressherald.mainetoday.com/story.php?id=106835&ac=PHspt. http://www.baseball-reference.com/bullpen/Hiraoka_Hiroshi (accessed January 15, 2009).

"History of Kendo." *All Japan Kendo Federation.* Available at http://www.kendo-fik.org/english-page/english-page2/brief-history-of-kendo.htm (accessed September 18, 2011).

James Y. Sakamoto Papers. Available at http://www.lib.washington.edu/specialcoll/findaids/docs/papersrecords/SakamotoJames1609.xml (accessed March 15, 2005).

Johnston, Mariam. "Gorham Man's Gift to Japan: A National Pastime; Horace Wilson Took His Japanese Students Out to Play in 1872 and Planted a Love of Baseball." *Portland Press Herald,* May 20, 2007. Available at http://pressherald.mainetoday.com/story.php?id=106835&ac=PHspt (accessed January 15, 2009).

Katagiri, George. "*Oshu Nippo,*" *Oregon Encyclopedia,* Oregon History and Culture, 2008–2010, Portland State University. Available at http://www.oregonencyclopedia.org/entry/view/oshu_nippo/ (accessed May 2, 2007).

"Kenichi Zenimura: The Dean of Japanese American Baseball." Available at http://www.niseibaseball.com/html%20articles/Nisei%20Legends/zenimura.htm (accessed March 15, 2006).

Kim, Ryan. "S.F. Ballpark's Family Ties." *San Francisco Examiner.* Available at http://articles.sfgate.com/1999-11-08/news/28590448_1 (accessed September 5, 2011).

"Kurt Suzuki praises Don Wakamatsu's hiring." *San Jose Mercury News* (November 20, 2008), Available at http://w.w.w.mercurynews.com/sports/ci_11613535 (accessed June 22, 2009).

Lamb, Gregory Lamb. "Backstory: The players in the shadows." *Christian Science Monitor,* June 29, 2006. Available at http://www.csmonitor.com/2006/0629/p20s01-alsp.html (accessed October 14, 2008).

"Lenn Sakata," *Baseball Reference.com.* Available at http://www.baseball-reference.com/bullpen/Lenn_Sakata (accessed October 23, 2011).

"'Manzanar': Historic Resources Study/Special History Study." *National Park Service,* January 1, 2002. Available at http://www.nps.gov/archive/manz/hrs/hrs11h.htm (accessed July 1, 2008).

"Manzanar," National Park Service archives. Available at http://www.nps.gov/archive/manz/hrs/hrs11h.htm (accessed July 1, 2008).

Marquez, Letisia. "New book looks at photos used in World War II Japanese American resettlement efforts." UCLA Newsroom (May 13, 2009). Available at http://newsroom.ucla.edu/portal/ucla/ucla-professor-examines-institutional-89221.aspx (accessed January 10, 2010).

Nakagawa, Kerry Yo. "Through a Diamond: Kerry Yo Nakagawa and the impact of baseball in his own family." *Japanese American National Museum.* Available at http://janmstore.com/througdiamke.html (accessed June 15, 2009).

"NBRP Salutes Don Wakamatsu: First Asian-American Manager in MLB History," *Nisei Baseball Research Project,* Available at http://www.niseibaseball.com/news_don_wakamatsu_first_asian_american_manager_in_MLB_history.html (accessed June 22, 2009).

Niiya, Brian, ed. "Poston, Arizona." *Japanese American National Museum,* 1997. Available at http://www.javadc.org/poston.htm (accessed July 1, 2008).

"Oral History Interviews with Karl R. Bendetsen." Harry S. Truman Library & Museum. Available at http://images.google.com/imgres?imgurl=http://www.trumanlibrary.org/oralhist/73-150.jpg&imgrefurl=http://www.trumanlibrary.org/oralhist/bendet.htm&usg=__InhgXywHqf51RHcLupWAA33Wrgw=&h=284&w=210&sz=12&hl=en&start=4&tbnid=z6F6omtk8s4t2M:&tbnh=114&tbnw=84&prev=/images%3Fq%3Dkarl%2Bbendetsen%26gbv%3D2%26hl%3Den%26sa%3DG (accessed July 5, 2008).

"'Oregon': Population of Counties by Decennial Census: 1900–1990." Richard L. Forstall, complier and editor. *Population Division, United States Bureau of the Census,* Washington, D.C. 20233. Available at http://www.census.gov/population/cencounts/or190090.txt (accessed May 1, 2007).

"Oshu Nippo," *The Oregon Encyclopedia.* Available at http://www.oregonencyclopedia.org/entry/view/oshu_nippo/ (accessed May 2, 2007).

"Pearls: Wally Yonamine," promotional Web site. Available at http://www.janespearl.com/about2.html (accessed June 10, 2009).

Tanaka, Togo. "The History of Nisei Week." *Nisei Week Foundation.* Available at http://www.niseiweek.org/about/history.php (accessed February 4, 2009).

"Through a Diamond: Kerry Yo Nakagawa and the impact of baseball in his own family." Available at http://janmstore.com/througdiamke.html (accessed June 15, 2009).

U.S. Census Bureau, Department of Commerce, *Fifteenth Census of the United States: 1930*. Volume 1, Population, Number and Distribution of Inhabitants. Washington. D.C.: Government Printing Office, 1931,. Available at http://www.census.gov/population/cencounts/or190090.txt (accessed May 1, 2007).

Valentin, Myles. "A Heckler's Apology to Hawaii's (Not Japan's) Kurt Suzuki," *Bleacher Report*, April 20, 2009. Available at http://bleacherreport.com/articles/159284-a-hecklers-apology-to-hawaiis-not-japans-kurt-suzuki (accessed July 5, 2009).

"Wakamatsu Makes Gracious Exit." Available at http://blog.seattlepi.com/baseball/archives/217582.asp (accessed August 10, 2010).

Yonmine, Wally and Jane. "Two Countries, Two Sports (Wally Yonamine)." Available at http://www.janespearl.com/about2.html (accessed August 10, 2009).

Index

Samuel O. Regalado is a professor of history at California State University, Stanislaus, and the author of *Viva Baseball! Latin Major Leaguers and Their Special Hunger.*

The University of Illinois Press
is a founding member of the
Association of American University Presses.

———————————————————————

Designed by Jim Proefrock
Composed in 11/14 Kinesis
with Kompact display
at the University of Illinois Press
Manufactured by Thomson-Shore, Inc.

University of Illinois Press
1325 South Oak Street
Champaign, IL 61820-6903
www.press.uillinois.edu